Modern Office Technology and Practice

Modern Office Technology and Practice

Joan Gallagher and Siobhán Coghlan

Gill & Macmillan

Gill & Macmillan Ltd

Goldenbridge

Dublin 8

with associated companies throughout the world

© Joan Gallagher and Siobhán Coghlan 1997

0 7171 2514 9

Design by Identikit

Print origination in Ireland by Carole Lynch

Printed in Ireland by ColourBooks Ltd, Dublin

Contents

Preface

The objective of Modern Office Technology and Practice is to explain in detail the workings of an office, the impact of technology on the office, and the services available to a business from the banks, the Post Office and Telecom Éireann.

The text is written from both a practical and educational point of view. The student is educated to deal with activities that are common to both large and small offices. The essential secretarial skills such as planning and organising work, using the telephone, reception duties, processing business documents, handling money and dealing with the post are comprehensively covered in a step-by-step approach. Since almost all offices have been touched by the electronic age, an appropriate mix of technology and application is also presented. The student is introduced to computer hardware, software and networks and their applications such as increasing productivity at work, electronic communication and accessing information sources.

Modern Office Technology and Practice was written to meet the requirements of the NCVA Level II Office Practice syllabus and the NCEA Office Information Systems syllabus. It is also a suitable text for the RSA Level II Secretarial Procedures syllabus, Pitman Level II Office Practice syllabus and City & Guilds Information Technology and Business syllabus. Furthermore, it can be used as a supplementary text for any office practice or office technology examination.

All the chapters have a common structure designed to facilitate comprehension, self-study and retention. They include a) 'learning outcomes', which are brief statements of the major topics covered and which act as a preview to the chapter; b) an introduction, which is a brief description of the topic in question to emphasise why it is important; c) illustrations and photographs to clarify the ideas presented; d) a summary, which provides a concise review of the chapter and is directly related to the learning outcomes; and e) questions, which are in line with the examination format, such as multiple choice and short questions. Practical assignments are included with the chapters where relevant.

We wish to thank the following: John Hegarty, Marie Collins and Siobhán Kissane, for their encouragement and support, the information they provided, and their assistance with the reviews. We also extend a special thanks to our colleagues at Dun Laoghaire Senior College and Tralee RTC, who provided the facilities and continuous support.

Acknowledgments

For permission to reproduce material, grateful acknowledgment is made to the following:

- Apple Computers
- Cable & Wireless
- Canon (UK) Ltd
- M.J. Flood (Ireland) Ltd
- O'Sullivan Graphics
- An Post
- Sygma Wireless Communications Ltd (Motorola Distributors)
- Telecom Éireann
- Zefa Pictures

Photo Research: Anne-Marie Ehrlich

1. The Business and the Office

After studying this chapter you should be able to:
- ◆ Distinguish between the public and the private sector in Ireland
- ◆ Explain the different types of private businesses common in Ireland
- ◆ Prepare a simple organisation chart for a small business
- ◆ List the functions of typical departments within the organisation
- ◆ Describe the functions of the office in relation to information
- ◆ Use information sources to extract general information

Introduction

To understand the role of the office within the context of an organisation, it is necessary to examine the types of organisations that exist. An organisation exists where people and resources combine to achieve some objective. Objectives will differ according to the type of organisation. For example, the objective of a voluntary organisation may be to provide a social service to the community, while the main objective of a private enterprise, ie, a **business,** is to make a profit.

Types of Organisations

Three main types of organisations exist in Ireland.

Voluntary Organisations

Voluntary organisations are non-profit making organisations that depend on State funding and/or voluntary contributions to survive. This type of organisation is run largely by volunteers and the main objective is to provide aid, support or some social service to the community. Examples of voluntary organisations are charities, (Goal and Concern) and non-profit making sporting societies (local GAA and rugby clubs). Charities are generally exempt from paying tax on donations received.

Public Sector Organisations

The main objective of public sector organisations such as the Health Boards is to provide cost-effective services to the community rather than to make a profit. While the general public is charged for the use of the services, these organisations are heavily subsidised by the Government. They are managed by civil servants and are accountable to the Government.

Private Sector Organisations

Private sector organisations are privately owned business enterprises. A business is an organisation that is set up to produce or distribute a product or service. The primary objective of a business must be to make a profit. Without profits or some spending power, the business will not survive in a competitive market. Business objectives will vary from time to time depending on circumstances. For example, in the first year of trading, the main objective may be to **break even**, (ie, to cover expenses, not make a profit or a loss). If the business is successful, maintaining market share or developing new products may become important objectives.

Forms of Business

The four most common forms of private business enterprises in Ireland are:

1 Sole trader
2 Partnerships
3 Co-operatives
4 Limited companies
   a) Private limited company (Ltd)
   b) Public limited company (Plc)

Sole Trader

Sole trader is a term used to describe a business wholly owned by one person. The owner takes responsibility for all the activities of the business such as selling, purchasing, marketing, hiring staff, preparing the accounts and distributing products or services. Typical examples are: small retail outlets, local grocery shops and farms.

FEATURES OF A SOLE TRADER

- Sole owner of the business. S/he has choice of operating total control.
- Generally small in nature with a small number of staff employed.
- Has **unlimited liability.** This means that while the owner controls all aspects of the business and reaps all the profits, s/he is also personally liable for any debts that the business may incur. Therefore if the business goes bankrupt, the sole trader may sacrifice personal assets to pay creditors.
- The sole trader can offset business losses against personal income.
- The business ceases to exist on the death of the sole trader.

The sole trader must register:

a) with the Registrar of Business Names by sending a completed form and appropriate fee to the Register of Business Names, Dublin Castle.
b) with the Revenue Commissioners for tax purposes. The sole trader pays income tax on profits and appropriate taxes (eg, PRSI) if s/he is an employer.

c) for Value Added Tax (VAT), if the turnover of the business exceeds £40,000 on goods or £20,000 on services.

Partnerships

A **partnership** exists where two or more people (normally to a maximum of 20) come together and contribute either finance and/or expertise to a business. Accountants, solicitors and doctors commonly practise under the partnership structure.

FEATURES OF PARTNERSHIPS

◆ When forming a partnership, it is usual to draw up a Deed of Partnership. This is an agreement between the partners that specifies the duties and responsibilities of each partner. As the partners may contribute to the business in varying ratios, the Deed of Partnership also specifies the extent of liability of each partner and how profits and losses are to be distributed.

◆ The partnership contract can restrict the liability of some partners to the debts of the partnership. However, a partnership must have at least one partner with unlimited liability.

◆ It may be easier to access credit facilities where more than one person is responsible for repayments.

◆ Partners, like sole traders, are charged income tax on profits.

◆ A new partnership must be formed on the death or resignation of a partner.

Co-operatives

A co-operative is formed with seven or more members. The ethos of the co-operative is to gain better buying and selling terms than the members would receive if they were trading as individuals. Co-operatives in Ireland are mainly agriculturally based, eg, Waterford Co-operative and Kerry Co-operative. Recently tourist groups have also been operating as co-operatives.

EXAMPLE

The co-operative purchases fertilisers in bulk from a manufacturer. The co-operative member, ie, farmer, in turn will purchase some fertiliser from the co-operative and will use this raw material to improve his/her milk yield. The milk is sold back to the co-operative which will process it further (eg, make butter) and will sell the finished product to the market.

In this case, the farmer producing the milk may not have had the machinery necessary for processing the product further, nor the necessary skills to package, market and sell the finished product on the market.

FEATURES OF A CO-OPERATIVE
- A co-operative consists of seven or more members.
- A co-operative must register with the Registrar of Friendly Societies, Dublin Castle, and can also register as a limited company to avail of limited liability.
- Members invest in the co-operative by purchasing shares and appoint managers to run the co-operative on their behalf.
- There is a maximum limit on the amount invested by each member.
- Members are entitled to vote regardless of the amount of shares held, ie, if one member has 1,000 shares and another has 500, each will be entitled to one vote.
- Surplus funds are issued to the members in direct proportion to the amount purchased by the members from the co-operative during the trading year.

Limited Companies

Most Irish companies are formed as limited companies. The owners of the company are the **shareholders** who purchase shares in the company. A limited company has a legal status (separate entity) distinct from the owners. This means that the liability of the shareholders is limited to the amount invested, ie, if the company is declared bankrupt, the shareholders only lose the amount invested. The shareholders elect a Board of Directors or a Managing Director to manage the company on their behalf.

When forming a limited company, the following documentation must be sent with the appropriate fee to the Registrar of Companies:
1. *Memorandum of Association*: This gives details regarding the nature of the business, who is involved in the company, and the amount of shares that will be issued.
2. *Articles of Association*: a document detailing the internal rules of the company, eg, how meetings are convened, the rules governing transfer of shares, the rules governing election procedures, etc.
3. A declaration stating the amount of money received from shares that are paid to date.

FEATURES OF A LIMITED COMPANY
- The limited company is legally recognised as a separate entity.
- Liability of the shareholders is limited to the amount invested.
- The company is managed by a Board of Directors or by a Managing Director.
- Detailed documentation is required to register as a limited company.
- A limited company is taxed at corporation tax levels, unlike partnerships and sole traders.
- A minimum of two shareholders is required. There is a maximum limit of 50 for a private limited company, with no upper limit of shareholders in a public limited company.

◆ Detailed financial accounts must be available for shareholders, auditors, creditors and potential investors.

A limited company can be formed as a public limited company or as a private limited company.

a) A **public limited company (Plc)** is a company that is quoted on the stock exchange. This means that the company can raise finance by selling shares to the general public. Depending on the type of shares purchased, the shareholder may be entitled to a share of profits, known as a **dividend** and may be entitled to vote at the Annual General Meeting (AGM) of the company.

Public limited companies are obliged to prepare detailed accounts such as Profit & Loss Accounts, Balance Sheets, Auditors' Reports and Directors' Reports, for shareholders, auditors and other interested parties (eg, potential investors in the company and creditors).

Examples of Irish Plcs include the commercial banks, Kerry Group Plc and Waterford Wedgewood Plc.

b) A **private limited company (Ltd)** is similar in legal standing to a Plc, but membership cannot exceed 50 shareholders and there are strict regulations regarding the buying and selling of the company's shares.

Comparisons of Business Forms					
Business Form	No of Owners	Owned By	Managed by	Liability	Tax
Sole trader	1	Owner	Owner	Unlimited	Income
Partnership	2–20	Partners	Senior partners	Unlimited	Income
Co-operative	7 +	Members	Manager	Limited	Corporation
Private Ltd	2–50	Shareholders	Directors	Limited	Corporation
Plc	2+	Shareholders	Directors	Limited	Corporation

The decision to form a business as a sole trader, partnership, co-operative or company depends on:

a) the number of people involved.
b) the nature of the business and level of risk attached.
c) the resources necessary to the business.

Sources of funds available to a business include private funds, loans from financial institutions and Government grants.

Grants are available from a variety of agencies, for example, IDA, Forbairt and Shannon Development, to help start up a business, train staff and purchase equipment. Grants are also available for the business to develop, for example, grant aid for research and development of new products.

Organising the Business

When the business is formed, the resources must be organised so that the objectives can be achieved. Organising means how the business is structured so that work can take place effectively. Once the structure is in place, rules and procedures for carrying out tasks can be developed and responsibility for the performance of these tasks can be allocated to individuals or groups within the business. The structure of a business can be depicted on an **organisation chart**.

Organisation Chart

An organisation chart is a diagram outlining the work relationships between people and tasks and is generally used in a large business. It shows:

a) formal lines of communication, ie, who reports to whom

b) the framework of the business, ie, departments

c) levels of management (known as the 'chain of command')

d) the **span of control**, ie, the number of people a supervisor or department head is responsible for

It does not show:

a) the duties associated with the positions shown on the chart

b) informal relationships between staff

The diagram below depicts a simple organisation chart for a public limited manufacturing company, showing 6 levels of management, in a hierarchical structure, ie, the general workers report to the supervisor, the supervisor reports to the department manager, etc.

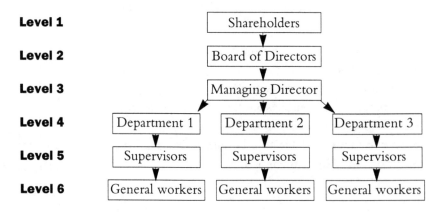

Business Functions

In a small business, all the business activities may be carried out by one person or a small number of people. For example, a sole trader will order supplies, produce, market and sell the goods, negotiate finance with the banks and recruit staff.

As a business grows, both in physical size and complexity, it may be necessary to divide business activities into departments according to their function, such as:

- Production
- Marketing & Sales
- Accounts/Finance
- Personnel
- Administration Office

These functions may be further divided as shown in the organisation chart below.

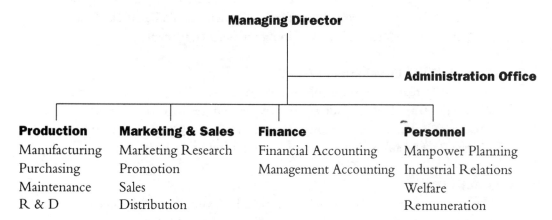

Managing Director

Administration Office

Production	Marketing & Sales	Finance	Personnel
Manufacturing	Marketing Research	Financial Accounting	Manpower Planning
Purchasing	Promotion	Management Accounting	Industrial Relations
Maintenance	Sales		Welfare
R & D	Distribution		Remuneration

Production Activities

The function of the Production Department is to manufacture goods and services as required by the customer. The Production Manager is concerned with the complete manufacturing process, which includes purchasing quality materials, maintaining premises, machinery and equipment, and developing new products or procedures for carrying out the production process.

Manufacturing

The Production Manager must ensure that the production process is operating at an optimum level. This involves devising a schedule to minimise disruptions to the production process.

The planning and scheduling process can be aided by computer applications such as CAM (Computer-Aided Manufacture) and MRP (Materials Requirements Planning). CAM controls production machinery and MRP facilitates materials planning and machinery scheduling.

At all times, the quality of inputs (eg, raw materials) to the production process and the resulting outputs (eg, finished goods) must be monitored.

Purchasing

A Purchasing Officer may be appointed within the Production Department to negotiate with suppliers for the best available terms such as prices, credit terms, discounts and delivery service. S/he ensures the quality of the materials purchased, establishes a system for ordering and is responsible for stock control.

Maintenance

The maintenance team should ensure that machinery and equipment are regularly maintained to avoid breakdowns in the production process. Breakdowns can cost the business in terms of production time lost in fulfiling orders and paying employees for non-productive work. Recent safety at work legislation requires every business to provide a safe place of work. Therefore, equipment should be checked regularly and a reporting procedure implemented to report faulty equipment.

Research and Development (R&D)

The R&D team is responsible for researching, designing, testing prototypes (models) of products and devising new procedures to carry out the production more efficiently. Computer programs such as CAD (Computer-aided Design) can aid the R&D team in designing new products and procedures.

Marketing Activities

The function of the Marketing Department is to satisfy consumer needs by selling a quality product at an appropriate price. This is achieved by identifying:
1. What the **product** is.
2. What **price** to sell the product at.
3. Where to sell the product, ie, in what **place.**
4. How to **promote** the product.

The above activities are often expressed in marketing terms as obtaining the correct **marketing mix**. The marketing mix refers to all aspects of the **4 Ps** (Product, Price, Place and Promotion). To obtain the correct marketing mix, the Marketing Department must engage in market research to identify what the consumer requires.

Market Research

Market research is a process of gathering and analysing information to identify who the customer is, what products or services are required by the customer and how best the Marketing Department can meet the requirements of the market.

Promotion

Promotion involves bringing the products/services to the attention of the customer. The promotion campaign can consist of:

(i) *advertising:* aimed at a wide audience through the media (ie, television, papers, journals, magazines and the Internet).

(ii) *sales promotions:* such as samples, in-store demonstrations, price cuts and competition offers. This form of promotion is best suited to retail products such as food items, cosmetics and general household items.

(iii) *publicity:* is concerned with obtaining 'good press' reports from the media. A business may gain publicity by supporting local or national events, eg, donating money to charity or sponsoring sporting events.

(iv) *personal selling:* suitable for selling products that require demonstration (eg, industrial products) or one-to-one products or services (eg, insurance).

Sales

The marketing team must sell products. Apart from the product itself, the level and quality of service offered to a customer can often be a distinct selling advantage.

The sales team regularly supplies invaluable information to the marketing research team directly from the customer so that competitive advantages can be gained.

Distribution

Large export businesses will have a separate shipping department responsible for getting the product to the final destination. However, in a small business, the Marketing Department is responsible for deciding what **channel of distribution** is most suitable to get the product to the market. Once the type of sales outlet is decided upon, the marketing team can organise warehousing (storing) the products and co-ordinating transport for effective delivery to the market.

The three main channels of distribution are:

Manufacturer ⟶ Consumer
Typical businesses that use this channel produce tailor-made (customised) products, eg, specially commissioned furniture, paintings, etc.

Manufacturer ⟶ Retailer ⟶ Consumer
Typical businesses that use this channel are producers of perishable items, or where the manufacturer needs an agent or broker to distribute goods on their behalf. For example, a dairy sells milk to the retail outlet where the consumer will purchase it, car manufacturers will sell to an agent (garages) for sale to the customer.

Manufacturer ⟶ Wholesaler ⟶ Retailer ⟶ Consumer

Typical businesses that use this channel are manufacturers of large volume, non-perishable consumer goods such as detergents, drink and household items.

Personnel Activities

The Personnel Department in the business is not directly linked to the manufacturing of products. It provides a service to all the departments within the business by developing overall employment policies and maintaining employee records. This department is responsible for staffing planning, industrial relations, employee welfare and remuneration policies.

Manpower Planning

Manpower planning is an on-going process to ensure that the business has employees who are skilled to perform the tasks necessary for the survival of the company. The planning process involves:

(i) *recruitment, selection and training:* A combination of selection processes such as aptitude tests and interviews may be used when **recruiting** staff. When staff are **selected,** an **induction course** should be arranged so that new employees can become familiar with company policies, their duties and responsibilities. **Training** will be provided for staff when new procedures are implemented.

(ii) *management development:* It is important that the business has a management development policy to ensure the management structure is not weakened. Training for potential managers should include courses on: Time Management, Communication and Stress Management.

(iii) *performance appraisal:* Performance appraisals should be carried out on a regular basis to obtain feedback from employees on their work. The information received is used to improve methods of performing the task.

(iv) *terminations (redundancies and retirement):* The Personnel Department negotiates with management and unions in the event of redundancies. The business may devise its own redundancy package but it must adhere to the minimum legal requirements. Conditions of retirement are detailed in the employee's contract of employment.

Industrial Relations

The Personnel Department will devise **grievance procedures** for employees, should they have a complaint at work, and will facilitate at consultations between management, unions, employees and the various adjudication bodies (eg, Appeals Tribunal).

Welfare

Personnel is responsible for providing employee services, eg, first aid or nurse on call, canteen, washing and changing facilities, etc. They may also co-ordinate a social club to improve informal relations in the workplace.

Every business is now legally obliged to provide a safe place of work. The Personnel Department is instrumental in ensuring health and safety procedures are in place.

Remuneration

This involves devising pay structures and job evaluations so that employees are paid fairly.

(i) *pay structures:* To increase job satisfaction at work, most businesses will endeavour to create a career ladder for their employees. Pay structures should be in line with employees' duties and responsibilities. The pay structure should be clearly defined and regularly reviewed.

(ii) *job evaluations:* An evaluation of the job is carried out to assess the level of skill and ability necessary for the job. Job evaluations are used to devise job descriptions when recruiting staff and in devising pay structures.

Financial Activities

The function of the accountant in a small business is to ensure that proper procedures are in place for recording all accounting activities, such as debtors control, creditors control, banking, wages, etc. All businesses are required to produce accounts. In a large business there will be both Financial and Management Accountants.

Financial Accounting

The Financial Accountant is responsible for recording past accounting activities. S/he prepares the yearly final accounts, and throughout the trading year will produce monthly or quarterly reports (interim reports) stating the current trading situation. This information is used by management for decision making purposes. For example, if the first quarterly report shows that sales are falling in a particular foreign market, management may decide to invest more in advertising, employ a local agent to distribute the product or discontinue the product.

Management Accounting

The Management Accountant is responsible for analysing costs and prepares budgets to control procedures and eliminate inefficiency in the business.

The Administration Centre – The Office

The administration centre or the **office** is responsible for handling information that flows to and from the business. The location and size of the office is determined by the nature and size of the business.

A large business will have offices attached to each department. Clerical assistants will carry out work specific to that department, for example, the clerical assistants in the Marketing Department may be responsible for preparing sales presentations, processing sales orders and calculating travel expenses for sales representatives. However, it is common practice for a large business to have a **centralised office** to deal with the activities that are common to all departments.

Some of the support services that may be centralised are shown below.

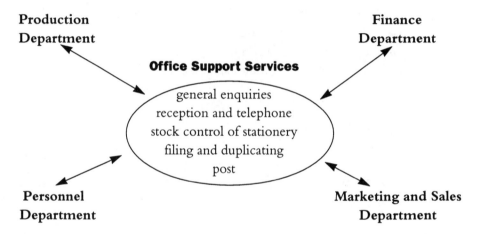

Production Department

Finance Department

Office Support Services

general enquiries
reception and telephone
stock control of stationery
filing and duplicating
post

Personnel Department

Marketing and Sales Department

Benefits of a Centralised Office

- ◆ Easier to control and supervise centralised functions
- ◆ Business documents and procedures such as ordering stationery and filing are standardised for every department
- ◆ Cost savings in terms of equipment purchased, eg, photocopier, fax machine, filing and postal equipment
- ◆ Improved efficiencies as the centralised activities are carried out by expert staff
- ◆ General security and protection of information is enhanced

Functions of the Office

The functions of the office can be broadly classified as follows:

a) Receiving information

b) Sorting information

c) Processing information

d) Communicating information
e) Recording and storing information
f) Protecting information

RECEIVING INFORMATION

Information is received in the office through written, oral or electronic means, eg, through the post, over the telephone or via e-mail or fax. Typically, the office deals with information which is received from:

Sources	Examples
The business	company reports, internal memoranda, minutes of meetings, final accounts and other internal business documents
Customers	enquiries, requesting quotations, submitting orders, issuing payments and making a complaint
Suppliers	receiving invoices, statements, promotional literature, catalogues
Government	Revenue Commissioners, Central Statistics Office, Employee Welfare agencies
Banks/Financial Institutions	statements, interest rates, currency rates, stock valuations

When the information is received by the office, it may be recorded before being processed or communicated to a third party. For example, information received by telephone is recorded on a telephone message pad and then communicated to the appropriate person. Similarly, a remittance (money) received through the post will be recorded in a remittance book before being passed to the Accounts Department for processing.

SORTING INFORMATION

When the office receives information, it is sorted to establish whether the information requires further processing or whether that information is complete and ready for distribution to a third party.

The secretary may need to prioritise work as it comes into the office. Urgent information should be processed immediately. Information that is not useful may be discarded.

PROCESSING INFORMATION

Generally information received through the office requires some further processing before it can be used effectively. For example, additional information such as product codes or prices may be required on an order received from a customer, or an up-to-date price list must be obtained from a supplier before the business can order supplies.

The information received may require a different layout before being distributed to a third party. For example, it may be more meaningful to display a list of figures in chart form. This type of processing can be carried out using computer application packages, eg, word processing, spreadsheets and graphics.

COMMUNICATING INFORMATION

The office must impart the processed information to the recipient in the most effective way for clear understanding. There are four basic ways to communicate:

(i)   *Orally:* face-to-face meetings or by telephone. While this method of communication is immediate, the information may become distorted. Facts, such as figures or times, may be misheard or incorrectly transcribed from an oral conversation. There is no evidence of what actually was said unless the message is recorded.

(ii) *In written form:* letters, reports, memos and minutes of meetings. This method of communication takes a little longer to prepare and send to the recipient, but the sender of the message has time to read and ensure its accuracy. It should be clear and concise so that the recipient can understand the message. The written message also serves as a record of the communication.

(iii) *Electronically:* fax and e-mail. Technological developments have improved the speed of sending written messages which can be sent to the receiver almost as quickly as a telephone conversation and replies can be returned immediately.

(iv) *Visually:* bar charts, pie charts, histograms and other graphical displays are used to present information in a 'reader-friendly' format. This is particularly useful where lists of figures or comparisons are being made.

RECORDING AND STORING INFORMATION

When information is processed, it is stored for future reference using a manual or computerised filing system. As well as setting up a procedure for recording information, the office is responsible for maintaining that system. Information regarding individuals that is held on computers must be maintained according to the Data Protection Act 1988.

PROTECTING INFORMATION

The Office Manager should ensure that confidential information is safely stored. Access to computer data can be restricted using passwords. The Data Protection Act 1988 outlines strict duties for those who collect and maintain personal data on computer files. Manual filing cabinets should be locked and keys restricted to authorised personnel. Confidential information should not be disclosed without prior authorisation.

General Sources of Reference in the Office

Most offices deal with a variety of general business enquiries during the working day. The office personnel should have a series of references books from which to obtain accurate and up-to-date information. The following section lists typical reference sources that should be available in the office. The list is not exhaustive as the references required will depend on the nature of the business.

DICTIONARY AND THESAURUS

A dictionary is used to check the meaning and spelling of words and a thesaurus is used to find different words with the same meaning (synonyms), eg, 'busy' can be interchanged with 'occupied', 'engaged' or 'employed'. Modern word processing packages have an in-built spell-check and thesaurus facility.

ACCOMMODATION REFERENCES

Office personnel who prepare travel arrangements should have information on accommodation available and places of interest in the surrounding area. Up-to-date information is available from Bord Fáilte or the local Tourist Office.

TIMETABLES

Timetables are necessary to check times of buses, trains, aeroplanes and sea ferries for employees travelling on behalf of the business. Timetables of buses and trains can be obtained from the local Bus Éireann and Iarnrod Éireann stations respectively. Iarnrod Éireann operates a talking timetable facility and the telephone numbers for specific routes are listed in the telephone directory. When the number is dialled, a recorded message gives the times of departures and arrivals for that route. Some travel timetables can also be viewed on 'Aertel', RTE's Teletext service.

ROAD MAPS

Road maps are necessary in any office where employees travel as part of the business. Maps of local areas, national and international routes may be obtained from the AA (Automobile Association) or any book shop.

Most road maps have a scale to calculate the distance from point A to point B. For example, if the scale reads 1 inch = 1 mile, then 3 inches = 3 miles. Some maps have a mileage chart which gives details of distance in kilometres and miles. A mileage chart can be used to calculate travel expenses and the duration of the journey.

INTERNAL TELEPHONE DIRECTORY

The receptionist will maintain a list of all employees telephone extension numbers and an internal telephone directory for commonly used external telephone numbers.

TELEPHONE DIRECTORY AND *GOLDEN PAGES*

Every office and household that subscribes to Telecom Éireann receives a Telephone Directory and *Golden Pages* for their telephone area. The Telephone Directory is used to source telephone numbers, addresses, national and international dialling codes. The numbers are listed in alphabetical order according to the name of the telephone account holder.

The *Golden Pages* is a directory of services available in 7 versions. One directory is available for each of the telephone zones , ie, 01, 02, 03, 04, 05, 06, and 07–09.

The *Golden Pages* directory is organised alphabetically under products and services and gives the telephone number and address of businesses or individuals offering products or services. For example, if a customer does not know of anyone who supplies a particular product or service, they can refer to the *Golden Pages* for names, addresses and telephone numbers of a number of suppliers. This is particularly useful where a business requires a number of quotations from suppliers. Some businesses advertise their products or services on a larger scale within the *Golden Pages*. They may buy full-page or half-page advertising that gives specific details of their product range.

There are two ways to search the *Golden Pages* for information:
a) Search by Classification
All the pages in the *Golden Pages* directory are headed with the classification of products or services located on that page. This method of searching is useful when the user knows what the product or service is classified under. For example, to locate a stationery supplier, the user searches for the classification 'stationery' and locates the name, address and telephone number of a number of suppliers.

b) Fast Finding Index
If the user is unsure of the classification, then the fast finding index at the back of the *Golden Pages* should be used. All classifications are listed here in alphabetical order with cross-references and page numbers.

The *Golden Pages* is a very useful source of reference. Besides listing services and products, telephone numbers and addresses, it also contains useful local information such as a map of the city centre and a mileage chart.

LOCAL BUSINESS COMMUNITY DIRECTORY

Some cities and towns prepare a local directory of services and facilities within the local business community.

KOMPASS

Manufacturing companies should have a copy of *Kompass*, a national directory of manufacturing businesses in Ireland. This directory gives a brief description of the types of goods manufactured and a list of the directors involved in the business.

STUBB'S GAZETTE

This Irish journal gives details of those businesses that have been legally declared bankrupt. This magazine is relevant to those who are owed money from businesses named in *Stubb's Gazette*, as they may wish to be included on the creditors list.

THE POST GUIDE

The *Post Guide* (available from the Post Office) gives current details of postage costs both national and international.

COMPUTER MANUALS

Computer operators should be familiar with the computer manual and refer to the manual if they are unable to operate the system. It is a good idea to place the supplier's telephone number inside the manual.

INDUSTRY MAGAZINES

Industry magazines, newsletters and reports may be left with the secretary for circulation among employees. The variety of magazines available in the office will depend on the nature and budget of the business.

Summary

This chapter outlines the types of business common in Ireland and how they are formed. Sole traders own and control their business, but the main disadvantage is that they have unlimited liability. Partnerships also are unlimited (generally) in their liability for the debts of the business. A business that wishes to reduce the risk of losing personal funds may form a limited company. Limited companies are governed by the Memorandum of Association and the Articles of Association, and can be public or private, depending on the number of shareholders. A co-operative can register as a limited company and thus obtain limited liability.

Once the business is formed, the resources are organised to achieve the objectives. The size and nature of the business will determine the number of departments. Typical departments include: Production, Marketing, Finance and Personnel. In a small business the office may be the only administration centre for the entire business, dealing with all clerical activities, such as enquiries, processing business documents, correspondence, dispatching post, petty cash, etc.

As the business grows, each department may have their own office to process information particular to that department. For example, the Production Department may have clerical staff to control the movement of incoming and outgoing stocks, the Marketing Department will have clerical staff to process sales information and the Personnel Department will have clerical staff to maintain employee records. In this situation, there may be a central office to provide common services such as word processing, filing, duplicating, reception and general enquiries for the other departments.

The office plays a central role in co-ordinating the information necessary for business activities. The office is responsible for receiving, sorting, processing, recording and storing, distributing and protecting information. The office receives information from the business itself and from outside sources such as customers, suppliers and competitors. There should also be several sources of general information available in the office.

Questions

1. The directors of a limited company are usually appointed by:
   a) the Managing Director
   b) the workforce
   c) the shareholders
   d) the Registrar of Companies
   e) the workers and shareholders

2. An example of a public sector organisation is:
   a) GOAL
   b) Precision Engineering Ltd
   c) Concern
   d) the Southern Health Board
   e) Jones' Drapery and Daughters

3. An example of a public limited company is:
   a) Barry's Newsagents
   b) Waterford Crystal Plc
   c) GOAL
   d) Shaw's & Sons Ltd
   e) the Department of Education

4. An organisation chart shows:
   a) the office layout
   b) the formal relationships between different departments
   c) filing procedures
   d) employee responsibilities
   e) informal relationships in the company

5. An important activity in the Production Department is:
   a) maintenance of equipment
   b) costing and preparing budgets
   c) promoting products
   d) industrial relations
   e) administration

6. If you were asked to visit a firm in order to attend for interview you would probably be asked to report to:
   a) the Personnel Department
   b) the Finance Department
   c) the Managing Director
   d) the Production Department
   e) the Marketing Department

7. Information is received by the office from various sources. Which of the following is an example of information received from an internal source?
   a) quotation from customers
   b) statements from suppliers
   c) minutes of a meeting
   d) interest rate fluctuations from the bank
   e) population statistics from the Central Statistics Office

8. What source of reference would you use to discover if a company is bankrupt?
   a) *Kompass*
   b) *Stubb's Gazette*
   c) CSO
   d) Local Business Community Directory
   e) Thesarus

Short Questions

1. List four types of business common in Ireland.
2. Why would a business form as a company rather than as a partnership?
3. Distinguish between a public limited company and a private limited company.
4. Give four features of a sole trader.
5. List the advantages and the disadvantages of an organisation chart.

6. Identify the levels of authority usually found in a large manufacturing company.

7. List four activities of the Personnel Department.

8. The Marketing Department activities are based on the four Ps. What are the four Ps?

9. The office is at the centre of all business activities. Describe five functions of the office.

10. In a busy office, staff often have to look for information which it is not really necessary to commit to memory. List four reference books which would serve this purpose and briefly describe the type of information to be found in each.

11. Where would you find the following information?
    a) locally available courier services
    b) times and duration of a flight
    c) the distance by road from Monaghan to Dingle
    d) the current rate of exchange between IR£ and French Francs (NCVA 1994)

Assignments

1. Draw an organisation chart for the following people: Sales Manager, Managing Director, Production Manager, Board of Directors, shareholders and Financial Controller.

2. Using information from a local small to medium-sized firm (up to 50 employees) establish the various departments and key positions in the firm. Draw up an organisation chart showing the lines of authority within the company and write a description of the work carried out by each department within the company.

3. The office receives information through written, oral and electronic means. Write a brief note on each.

4. The marketing team is launching a new product, an audiotaping machine and has asked your advice in promoting the product. What promotion techniques would you recommend and why?

5. A new junior assistant is being appointed in the Personnel Department. Describe the functions and activities of the Personnel Department that s/he may be involved in.

6. Look up a thesaurus and find synonyms for the following words: interview, stock, business, duplicate and department. Devise three sentences for each of the words showing different ways of using the synonyms.

7. Look up the current *Golden Pages* directory and find:
    a) The telephone number of the talking timetable for trains going from Dublin to Rosslare. If the boat sails for Le Havre at 15.00 hours, what train should you take to be in Rosslare at least one hour before sailing?

b) You wish to install electronic locks on your office doors and need more than one price quotation for the Financial Controller. Search the *Golden Pages* for the names, addresses and telephone number of two locksmiths/ security companies in your area.

8. Using a map, discover the shortest routes for the following journeys. Estimate approximate distance in kilometres and miles. List any large towns en route.
   a) Cork to Waterford
   b) Athlone to Dublin
   c) Belfast to Donegal
   d) Galway to Limerick
   e) Wexford to Mayo

2. Office Design, Equipment and Safety

After studying this chapter you should be able to:

♦ Distinguish between the various types in office design
♦ List the considerations to take into account when planning an office layout
♦ Describe the equipment typical in an office
♦ Explain the duties of the employer and employee under the Safety, Health & Welfare Act
♦ Describe how security can be maintained in the office

Introduction

The design of an office will largely depend on the space allocated by the business to the office. Office layout refers to how the office is organised in terms of the number of workstations and the equipment used in the office.

Motivation theories suggest that the physical environment in the workplace has a significant effect on employee morale and productivity. It is important that the office is designed so that the maximum work can be completed safely with minimum disruption. An unhealthy physical environment can cause unnecessary stress, fatigue and strain on employees and result in poor productivity.

In many cases the Office Manager will be constrained by the amount of space allocated to the office and by financial constraints which will affect the eventual design selected.

Office Design

There are three common types of office design.

Open-plan Office

In open-plan offices there are no obvious divisions or partitions between working areas. Managers and staff work in one area and usually share resources such as printers, a photocopier and a fax machine. The workstations are normally organised so that the work **flows** from station to station in a logical manner.

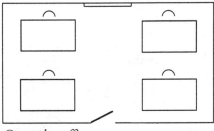

Open-plan office

The open-plan office is suited to a business that handles a large volume of general (non-sensitive) information, for example, a travel agent.

Advantages of an open-plan office:
- Space is optimised as there are no partitions dividing work areas.
- Economies of scale are obtained with the shared use of electricity, heating and facilities such as telephones, printers, photocopier and the fax machine.
- Easier to maintain and decorate.
- Communication improves between managers and staff.
- Facilitates the supervision of staff.

Disadvantages of an open-plan office:
- There is a lack of privacy when dealing with clients.
- Continuous movement can distract and reduce efficiency.
- Management may become too involved in routine matters and serious issues may be left unattended.
- It is difficult to implement and maintain security procedures.

The Corridor/Closed Door Style

Some offices still operate a corridor style, where a small number of staff are segregated into separate private offices. Usually the manager will have a private office and a small number of office staff may share an office.

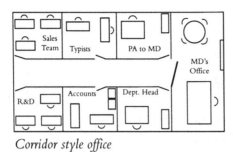

Corridor style office

This style of office design is suited to a business that handles highly sensitive information. For example, banks will have private offices for advising customers on loans, solicitors will have private offices where confidential issues can be discussed with the client.

Advantages of a corridor-style office:

♦ A high level of privacy is achieved.
♦ Managers can continue with urgent work without unnecessary interruptions and distractions.
♦ Easier to physically protect information (eg, access can be restricted by locking doors).

Disadvantages of a corridor-style office:

♦ General communication between managers and staff is more difficult.
♦ The rate of processing information may be reduced as it may be more difficult to consult with the manager.
♦ Office space can be under-utilised with permanent walls dividing the offices.
♦ The business will not benefit from economies of scale.
♦ Supervision of office staff is more difficult to control.

Landscaped Office

This is generally the preferred style. The open-plan office is re-designed by moveable screens that can reduce or enlarge the workstation area. The landscaped office can consist of semi-permanent partitions or else a modular approach can be used. A modular approach uses furniture (ie, desks and chairs) to create work areas and can be easily rearranged.

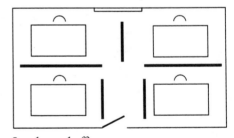

Landscaped office

Landscaped offices are suited to a business that deals with a large volume of work, but also requires some privacy for group work.

Advantages of landscaped offices:

◆ Benefits from economies of scale.
◆ Some privacy can be attained within the large office.
◆ Easy access to other office staff and resources.

Disadvantages of landscaped offices:

◆ Constant movement and rearranging of temporary partitions may cause distractions.
◆ Total privacy is not attained.

Planning Office Layout

A change in office layout or a move to a new office needs to be carefully planned to avoid or reduce any resistance from office staff. When planning the physical layout of the office area the Office Manager should consider:

1. *Space:* What space is available for the office? How should it be utilised? How many staff?
2. *Work flow:* What kind of work? Quantity? How frequent? Confidential?
3. *Equipment:* Are specialised areas required? Where should equipment be located for easy access and minimum disruption?
4. *Safety legislation:* Are procedures in place for implementing and maintaining a safe and secure office?

SPACE

In an existing building, the Office Manager may have little control over the total area allocated to the office, but s/he should ensure that space is utilised efficiently within the office.

The office workers should have adequate space for their work areas to perform work effectively. In planning the office layout, the number of staff working in the office and the amount of equipment must be considered before space can be allocated to each workstation. A workstation consists of a desk, chair, drawers, shelves, computer and perhaps a telephone extension. The manager should also consider whether it is likely that the number of office workers will expand in the future. If so, additional space will be required.

WORK FLOW

In planning the office, the volume, frequency and confidentiality of work that flows through the office should be taken into account. Sensitive information may be dealt with in a more secure location, eg, in a private office. General information may be handled in an open-plan office.

Offices and workstations should be arranged to facilitate a smooth flow of work. A work study analysis may be carried out by the Office Manager to determine a straight-line flow of work that will minimise interruptions in the work flow, ie, reduce the movement of staff to other offices and facilities.

EQUIPMENT

Depending on the volume of work flowing through the office, it may be necessary to cater for centralised equipment areas, such as an area for dispatching post, a central filing area or a printing and photocopying area. These services are often centralised in one room to minimise disruptions of the normal flow of work in the main office.

Shared equipment, eg, computers, printers and telephones could be clustered in locations within the office, where movement is minimised. For example, in an open-plan office of 30 people, clusters of computers may be located at two or three points in the room to avoid staff in the top area moving to the end to access a machine.

LEGISLATION

Office layouts must conform to current legislation that caters for the health, welfare and safety of employees.

Office Equipment

A typical modern office may have the following equipment:
workstations
computers and peripherals (see Chapter 7)
telephone system (see Chapter 10)
fax machine (see Chapter 10)
filing cabinets (see Chapter 9)
franking machine and postal equipment (see Chapter 4)
photocopier
binders, guillotines and laminating equipment
calculators
desktop equipment

PHOTOCOPIER

A photocopier is a reproduction machine used to make copies of written or printed material. Modern photocopiers range in size from desktop to freestanding machines.

Features of a Photocopier

There are many models of photocopier on the market, each with a range of high-powered facilities. Sophisticated models will have some or all of the following features:

Photocopier

- *Number selector:* This facility allows you to set and photocopy the number of copies required automatically.
- *Copy paper:* Accommodates a variety of paper types: bond paper (good quality paper), plain paper, photocopiable overhead transparencies and mailing labels.
- *Copying speed:* Generally from 3 copies to 15 copies per minute.
- *Paper size:* A range of paper sizes may be catered for, eg, A6 to A3, and the correct paper size may be selected automatically.
- *Automatic sorting:* This feature is useful for copying multi-page documents. The document is placed on the feeder and the last page is photocopied first. The sort facility will print the required number of copies of the last page and place them into individual collating compartments (output trays). Then the second-last page is photocopied and placed on top of the last page in each of the collating compartments. This process is repeated until the document is copied. Some machines have a stapling facility.
- *Automatic grouping:* This feature allows individual documents to be photocopied and stacked in groups. For example, 20 copies of each page will be held in separate collating compartments.
- *ARDF (automatic reverse document feeder):* A facility usually located on the lid of the photocopier, which allows the user to stack a number of pages which are automatically fed through the photocopier. This feature eliminates the need to lift the cover of the photocopier each time a page is to be copied.
- *Duplex feature:* Produces photocopies on both sides of the page automatically. The pages are first photocopied on one side and held in the machine. When the cycle is finished, the pages are automatically taken from inside the machine and photocopied on the other side.
- *Enlarging facility:* Documents can be increased from 100% to 200% in one per cent increments. For example, a small diagram on an A4 page can be increased to fill the page or an A4 page can be increased to an A3 page.

◆ *Reducing facility:* Documents can be reduced from 100% to 50% in one per cent increments. For example, a magazine article which is slightly wider than A4 can be reduced to A4.

◆ *A two single copy feature:* For example, a magazine when opened is approximately A3 in size. This feature will automatically photocopy an A3 page into *two separate* A4 pages. This saves the time involved in moving the magazine by hand.

◆ *Auto exposure:* This facility analyses the page to be photocopied and selects the proper image density, ie, how dark or bright the copy should be.

◆ *Margin shift:* The margins of the original can be adjusted by up to 15 mm (less than ½") to allow for binding or punching holes.

◆ *Interrupt mode:* An interrupt temporarily stops a job in progress to allow somebody else to use the photocopier. The interrupted job resumes from where it was stopped.

◆ *Diagnostic display:* A control panel which indicates problems with the machine, ie, paper jam, no paper, etc.

◆ *Code facility:* Codes can be allocated to individuals or departments to monitor and control copying costs. To use the photocopier, a user enters their code on the keypad and the number of copiers made is recorded against their code.

Using the Photocopier

1. Remove any staples.
2. Align the page according to the correct paper size displayed on the platen (glass screen) and close the lid of the photocopier.
3. Select the correct settings for the machine before starting, ie:
   - the size of paper required, such as A4.
   - check that the correct 'cassette paper holder' is inserted.
   - the density of the copy, which is generally set half way between bright and dark. However, if photocopying from dark coloured paper, select a brighter setting.
   - required function, ie, sort, group, two single copy features etc.
4. When using the special settings, ie, enlarging, a test copy should be photocopied and checked.
5. Set the number of copies required.
6. Press the start button.

Purchasing a Photocopier

Consider the following factors:

1. *Budget allocated:* This will limit the purchaser's choice of models.
2. *Costs:* The purchase price must be analysed. Is servicing and delivery included? What are the typical running costs? Is training required for operators?

3. *Requirements:* What functions are required? How frequently is the machine used? What is the volume of work? How often are special features used?
4. *Size:* Will the machine take up too much space in the office?
5. *Noise:* Will the machine be noisy and interrupt work?
6. *Durability:* Will the machine need to be maintained regularly?

Care of the Photocopier

1. Do not photocopy stapled documents as the staples will scratch the glass surface.
2. Do not photocopy paper which has wet Tippex, as the Tippex will stick to the glass surface.
3. Do not use damp paper when photocopying, as it will get jammed in the machine.
4. Do not photocopy with the lid of the photocopier opened. It can damage your eyes and it also causes more toner to be attracted to the paper. This excess use of toner will cause the machine to break down.
5. When photocopying onto transparencies, check that they are the photocopiable type. Write-on transparencies will melt in the machine, causing damage.
6. If paper jams in the machine notify the appropriate person. If you are required to fix the machine yourself, take note of the error code displayed and refer to the user's manual.

The Photocopying Process

When the paper is placed on the glass surface known as the **platen**, and the start button is pressed, the following happens:

– Where the image is dark, there is an electrostatic charge.
– Toner (powdered ink) is attracted to the charged 'dark' area, forming an image of the page.
– The copy paper is passed through the machine, and the particles of toner which form the image are attracted to the paper.
– The copy paper is then passed through heated rollers which fixes the image permanently on the page.

BINDING EQUIPMENT

Binders are used to hold individual pages together in booklet form which is a more permanent method of securing pages than stapling or using paper clips.

Spiral Binder

1. A binder which punches holes in a number of pages by means of a lever which is operated manually or electrically.
2. When all the pages are punched, a 'spiral' is inserted on the spikes of the machine and opened with the lever.

3. The punched paper is then placed into the opened 'spiral', working from the back of the document to the front.

4. When all the pages are inserted, the 'spiral' is closed with the lever and the bound booklet is removed.

Thermal Binder

A thermal binder works by melting the wax on the inside spine of special 'thermal covers'.

1. The pages to be bound are placed in a 'thermal cover'.

2. The spine of the 'thermal cover' is placed upright into the heated thermal binder.

3. The wax on the spine melts, causing the pages to stick to the spine.

4. The booklet is allowed to cool before opening.

Velobinder

1. A binder which punches holes in a number of pages.

2. When all the pages are punched, they are inserted into the velobinder strips.

3. The velobinder strips consists of two parts: one part consists of prongs which hold the punched paper and the other part is a clamp

Velobinder

which holds the pages together. A document bound with a velobinder can be easily re-opened and re-closed to insert or remove pages. The booklet, however, does not open out flat as with spiral binding.

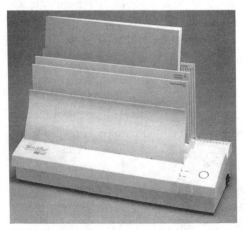

Thermal binders

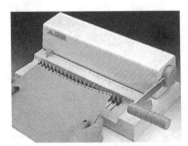

Spiral binder and combs

CALCULATING EQUIPMENT

Calculators are essential in every office to perform arithmetic functions. There are three main types of calculators: handheld, desktop display units and desktop printers (also known as an adding machine or a totting machine). The choice of calculator depends on the volume and type of work to be accomplished.

With a handheld calculator, the keys and display unit are small, whereas they are much bigger with a desktop display unit. The desktop printer provides a printout of the numbers entered,

Calculators — desktop display and printers

allowing data entry to be checked; it can also be used as a receipt.

GUILLOTINE

A guillotine is used to cut paper, cards and acetates to the correct size evenly. It consists of a flat table area, generally pre-printed with paper sizes, a safety guard to the right, behind which is the blade for cutting the paper.

To cut paper
1. The blade is moved upright by a handle.
2. The pages to be cut are positioned on the paper size required, the excess going under the blade.
3. The pages are held firmly by a movable clamp which is locked into position.
4. The blade is pushed down by its handle cutting the paper.

Guillotine

LAMINATORS

A laminator machine places a transparent plastic, durable cover over paper and cards. It is used to protect documents, ID cards, certificates, charts, photographs, etc from wear and tear, dirt, grease and moisture. A laminated document can be wiped clean. There are two types of laminating machines: a pouch laminator and a roll laminator.

Pouch laminator

A pouch laminator machine is suitable where usage is not constant, due to the cost of the pouches. The document is placed in the correct size pouch and inserted into the machine. The machine uses heat to bond the plastic pouch to both sides of the document. The item to be laminated should be at least 3mm smaller than the pouch to give a protective border.

Roll laminator

Roll laminator machines are more expensive but are very economical for frequent long runs. The document is inserted into the machine and a roll of transparent film is used to laminate the document. The finished product may have to be trimmed at the edges.

Laminator with an assortment of pouches

LABEL MAKER

A desktop machine used to make self-adhesive labels for shelves, folders, letter trays, etc. The models vary and may consist of a small keyboard similar to an electronic diary or a rotary wheel where the wheel is turned to select each letter.

Label maker

DESKTOP EQUIPMENT

The following items of equipment may be placed on desks:

Letter trays: Also known as in and out trays for holding incoming and outgoing correspondence.

Tape dispenser: To hold and cut Sellotape.

Desk organisers: To hold sundries such as pens, pencils, rubbers, pencil parer, paper clips, Post-its (note paper), highlighters, treasury tags (string with metal at both end to hold punched documents together), etc.

Bookends: To hold books upright on desk.

Copyholder: To hold pages at eye level while entering data.

Puncher: To punch holes in paper to place into ring binder folders.

Stapler: To hold pages together with a metal fastener (staple). More secure than paper clips, but not as secure as a binder.

Book-ends   *Copyholder*   *Desk organisers*

Safety and Security in the Office

Since Ireland joined the EU, a number of directives from the EU have been implemented to improve the levels of safety and welfare at work. When designing the office and planning the layout, the Office Manager must consider the legal requirements as laid down by the *Safety, Health and Welfare at Work Act 1989 (and General Regulations 1993)*, and the *Safety in Industry Act 1980*.

The HSA (Health & Safety Authority) estimates that over 500,000 working days are lost due to accidents and ill-health every year. Thus, it is in both employers' and employees' interests to ensure that safe practices are carried out in a safe environment.

Safety, Health and Welfare at Work Act 1989

The fundamental aim of the Safety, Health and Welfare at Work Act 1989 is to provide a safe place of work for both employers and employees.

The Act places general duties and responsibilities on employers and employees to prevent accidents and to increase the safety levels at work. Manufacturers, designers and suppliers of materials also have a duty under the Act to ensure that the goods and materials produced will not interfere with the welfare of those using them.

HEALTH & SAFETY AUTHORITY (HSA)

Since the introduction of the Safety, Health and Welfare at Work Act of 1989, the HSA is responsible for enforcing occupational safety in the workplace. The HSA establishes health and safety regulations and 'codes of practice' at work. While the HSA is an advisory body, employers who fail to comply with these regulations may be fined or imprisoned. Safety inspectors are appointed by the HSA and regularly inspect premises to ensure safety standards are implemented and maintained.

THE SAFETY REPRESENTATIVE

All businesses must have at least one safety representative elected by the employees.

The safety representative will be responsible for negotiating with management on behalf of the employees on issues regarding employee welfare. S/he can inspect the workplace (with management's permission) to identify dangerous elements at work and to ensure that safety measures are being adhered to. Management must supply information and training to allow the safety representative to carry out his/her duties.

Large businesses will operate Joint Safety Committees with a number of employees and managers together taking responsibility for ensuring safety standards are being met and maintained.

CONSULTATION

The Act provides for consultation between employers and employees to increase safety at work. The arrangements for consultation should be detailed in the safety statement.

EMPLOYER'S DUTIES

The main duties of the employer are as follows:

1. **To provide a safe place of work** for employers, employees and casual visitors to the workplace. This may be attained by designing the layout of the workplace to reduce the risk of accidents and ill-health at work. Warning notices of dangerous areas and all exists should be clearly marked and identified.

2. **To ensure reasonably safe plant and equipment.** This can be achieved by regular maintenance of machinery and providing the necessary equipment and protective clothing for employees in an effort to control or eliminate accidents.

3. **To ensure reasonably safe systems of work.** The employer should organise systems of work to promote safety and should review and update safety measures on a regular basis.

4. **To ensure reasonably safety-conscious (competent) staff.** Management should provide appropriate training and instructions for all employees to enable them to carry out their work safely. Safety should be promoted in the workplace at all times.

5. **To provide a Safety Statement**.

6. **To consult** with employees in the preparation and application of the Safety Statement.

EMPLOYEE'S DUTIES

The Act places a legal obligation on employees to:

1. **Take reasonable care** to perform duties safely so that the health, safety and welfare of other employees is not affected.
2. **Co-operate with employers** in matters of safety to avoid causing injury to themselves or to others at work.
3. **Use any protective clothing or safety guards provided** to ensure their own safety and the safety of others.
4. **Report any hazardous or unsafe conditions** to the Safety Office or Supervisor, eg, faulty machinery, dangerous cables, loose sockets, etc.

THE SAFETY STATEMENT

The Safety Statement is a document that specifies how health and safety can be secured within the workplace. The Safety Statement can be prepared by:

a) the employer in conjunction with the safety representative, or
b) an outside consultant hired by the employer to prepare the statement.

A complete Safety Statement must:

a) specify how standards of safety can be obtained.
b) specify the resources available from the employer to implement and maintain safety measures.
c) suggest precautions necessary to prevent accidents in the workplace.
d) identify the safety representatives or members of the safety committee and give details of their responsibilities in the area of safety.
e) specify the co-operation expected from the employees in implementing and maintaining safety standards.
f) arrange how consultation on safety issues between employer and employee should take place.
g) specify how to report accidents.

Purpose of the Safety Statement:

1. Identifying and assessing the risk of potential dangers in the workplace

To prepare the Safety Statement, a **safety audit** is carried out on the premises to identify anything that may harm employers, employees or casual callers to the business. Equipment and procedures at work, noise levels, dust levels, lighting, heating and all other physical elements are examined.

A **risk assessment audit** is carried out on identified danger areas. This involves critically examining the level of risk attached to the hazard, and the action to be taken to eliminate or reduce the risk of injury to the workforce. Risks can be categorised into three groups:

High risk: An accident that results in fatal or serious injury to personnel.
Medium risk: Where an accident results in loss of 3 or more working days.
Low risk: Refers to minor incidents such as bruising or slight cuts where medical attention is necessary.

Hazard Identification, Risk Assessment and Control Measures				
Premises: Carmody Products Ltd				
Section: Administration				
Assessor: Cait McInerney				
Date of Assessment: September 20, 1996				
Date to rectify by: November 1 1996				
Hazard Identification	**Risk Assessment**	**Control Measures**	**Manager Responsible**
Printer Cables	H = high M = medium L = low M	Insulate cables and run underground	Ms Crowley

Risk assessment audit sheet

2. Identifying measures to prevent accidents

Though it is impossible to eliminate accidents totally from the workplace, precautions can be taken to reduce the risk of accidents occurring. Common reasons for accidents include: slippery floors, frayed carpets, loose cables, cluttered work areas, faulty electrical areas, faulty equipment, lack of training, poor procedures for carrying out work and lack of supervision of unskilled employees.

The Office Manager can prevent accidents from occurring at work by:
♦ providing training and supervision when new staff are operating equipment.
♦ providing training for emergency situations (eg, fire or explosions).
♦ maintaining equipment regularly.
♦ clearly defining safe procedures for carrying out tasks (eg, turning off printer before changing toner, carrying heavy loads etc).
♦ providing protective clothing and safety guards for hazardous equipment.
Clearly this list is not exhaustive, as every workplace will differ in the work that is performed.

The Safety in Industry Act 1980

This Act states that office workers should be provided with standard facilities as follows:
♦ The office should be warm and have sufficient lighting and ventilation.
♦ The decor should be conducive to work.

- Partitions between work areas should be sound-proof. Particular attention should be given to the type of flooring (eg, non-slip, noise-absorbent).
- The work environment should be pleasant and clean. Floors should be cleaned regularly and waste should be removed daily.
- There should be adequate working space for each workstation.

The Safety, Health and Welfare at Work (General Application) Regulations 1993

This outlines general regulations for the office worker with regard to the physical working environment and also outlines the categories of accidents which must be reported to the HSA.

Regulations for the physical working environment:
a) Chairs should be placed at a comfortable level to avoid back strain.
b) Keyboards should slope downwards to avoid **repetitive strain injury** (RSI is a common complaint amongst computer operators).
c) VDU (visual display unit) should have a non-reflective screen or should be positioned to eliminate light reflection.
d) Adequate space for storage of stationery, rubbish bins and other consumables should be provided.
e) Equipment should be maintained regularly.
f) Cables should be cased and laid properly to avoid employees cutting themselves or tripping over them.

Accidents which must be reported to HSA:
a) an accident that results in the death of an employee;
b) an injury where the employee is out of work for more than 3 days;
c) where a casual caller to the workplace is injured and receives medical attention.
The report is made by the employer or supervisor completing Form IR1.

Security in the Office

As the office handles information that may be sensitive to the business and/or to individual personnel, it is imperative that strict controls are implemented and maintained to protect the flow of information. It is also necessary to implement controls to secure the physical assets in the office, ie, the equipment and personal belongings of staff.

Procedures to **protect physical assets** in the office:
1. Access to the building by intruders may be prevented by TV cameras, security alarms, security guards or guard dogs.
2. The receptionist will act as a screening device to people entering the building during the working day.

3. Employee ID cards can be distributed in large organisations. These cards contain a magnetic strip to allow access to the building and also aid in the identification of the employee.
4. Visitors may be required to sign a visitor's book when entering and leaving the building.
5. A keypad entry board can be used to restrict entry to private areas.
6. Lockers or safe areas should be provided for staff personal belongings.

Procedures to **protect information** in the office:
1. Information that is confidential should be locked in filing cabinets or held on a computer with Password protection implemented.
2. Keys to filing cabinets should be allocated with care.
3. Strict controls over codes and passwords should operate. Codes and passwords should be changed regularly to prevent 'hackers' (code breakers) entering the system.

Summary

The design and layout of the office can have a significant effect on the productivity and morale of office staff. The Office Manager is responsible for ensuring that the type of office design, the layout of workstations and equipment are organised to allow a smooth flow of work through the office. The Office Manager may be constrained in his/her ideal office design by space and financial restrictions, but as far as possible, s/he should ensure that the office is designed to facilitate work flow and pleasant work relations amongst office staff.

Three styles of office design were discussed. Open-plan attains economies of scale but at the cost of lack of privacy. Corridor or closed office style, provides a greater level of privacy, but communications and supervision of office staff are made more difficult. The landscaped approach is a popular office design, where moveable partitions can be placed to block off separate 'offices'.

When planning the office layout, the space allocated, type and volume of work, equipment, and health and safety legislation should be considered. Some equipment may be centralised in one location outside the main office, eg photocopiers, large printers, etc, while other equipment may be shared among a number of staff within the main office, eg, computers, telephones. The location of equipment should allow for easy access and minimum movement of staff.

Office equipment discussed in this chapter were photocopiers, binding equipment, calculating equipment, laminators, guillotines and label makers. Sundry equipment such as in/out trays, desk organisers, bookends, copyholders and paper punchers are usually found on a typical office desk.

The Office Manager is responsible for ensuring that the office is a safe place to work in. Safety procedures as required by the Safety, Health and Welfare Act 1989 should be implemented in the office. The business must produce a Safety Statement and appoint a safety representative who will identify potential hazards and ensure that safety measures are being implemented. Office staff have a duty to report any potential dangers in the office and must co-operate with the safety regulations at work. Security procedures should be implemented to control access to the office. This can be achieved by using a visitor logbook and badges at reception, keypad entry facilities at the office door or security cameras. The information within the office can be protected by establishing controls over keys to filing cabinets and changing passwords to prevent access to files stored on computers.

Questions

Multiple Choice Questions

1. The office design most suited to a solicitor's office is:
   a) open-plan
   b) corridor style
   c) open-plan or corridor style
   d) landscaped office
   e) open-plan or landscaped office

2. A disadvantage of an open-plan office is:
   a) it benefits from economies of scale
   b) supervision is easier
   c) space is optimised
   d) privacy is very limited
   e) it is easier to maintain

3. Another name for a corridor style office is:
   a) landscaped office
   b) open-plan office
   c) centralised office
   d) closed door office
   e) modular office

4. An ARDF facility is found on a:
   a) laminator
   b) guillotine
   c) photocopier
   d) label maker
   e) velobinder

5. A thermal binder works by:
   a) punching holes in the pages and inserting the pages in a comb binder
   b) placing the pages inside a special cover and heating
   c) inserting the pages in the binder and pressing a button to bind the pages
   d) punching holes in the pages and inserting the pages in a laminator
   e) binding the pages with treasury tags

6. A laminator is used:
   a) to cut paper to the correct size evenly
   b) to make self-adhesive labels
   c) to bind documents
   d) to highlight information on a document
   e) to protect documents from wear and tear

7. Automatic grouping is a feature of a:
   a) calculator
   b) spiral binder
   c) laminator
   d) photocopier
   e) label maker

8. You can prevent people changing data on identification cards (ID cards) by using a:
   a) thermal binder
   b) label maker
   c) password
   d) laminator
   e) copy holder

9. Which one of the following items is most suited to holding punched paper temporarily:
   a) treasury tags
   b) staples
   c) paper clips
   d) elastic bands
   e) puncher

Short Questions

1. List four factors to consider when designing office layout.
2. Identify the equipment typical of a workstation in an office.
3. Identify four factors an Office Manager should consider when organising workstations for office staff.

4. What are the advantages and disadvantages of a) open-plan offices b) corridor-style offices and c) landscaped offices?

5. Outline the procedure to follow when using a photocopier to produce 10 copies of a three-page document.

6. Identify three types of binders and describe how they work.

7. Distinguish between a standard and scientific calculator.

8. List four items suitable for laminating.

9. Identify five items usually found on an office desk.

10. What would you do to try and ensure that your premises and staff were as safe as possible from fire hazards?

11. What is a Safety Statement?

12. State four duties of employees under the Health and Safety at Work Act.

(NCVA 1994)

13. State four duties of employers under the Health and Safety at Work Act.

(NCVA 1995)

14. List four features that a large systems copier has which are not available on a small desktop copier.   NCVA 1996)

Assignments

1. The Office Manager has been informed that the office staff are moving to a new building. S/he wishes to ensure that the best possible layout is achieved and has asked for suggestions from office staff to help design an appropriate layout. What factors should be considered in planning the layout of the office?

2. You are working in a modern office with 10 other office staff. Draw a sketch of the 'ideal' office, showing individual workstations and other modern office equipment. Make and state any assumptions you wish.

3. The office has been broken into for the second time in two months. The petty cash box was empty and nothing else was stolen. However, the office deals with highly sensitive information. Write a report to the Office Manager recommending how to make the office more secure.

4. The Safety, Health and Welfare at Work Act 1989 has made people more aware of safety levels at work. Look around the classroom (or your home) and identify 10 potential hazards, assess the risk level of injury and recommend how you could make the environment safer.

3. Office Personnel and Employment Legislation

After studying this chapter you should be able to:

- Identify the general duties of the Office Manager, Secretary, Receptionist and Accounts Clerk
- Maintain an appointments diary
- Prepare a check list for a business meeting abroad
- Calculate travel expenses
- Write up a petty cash book
- Perform wage calculations
- Identify items contained in a contract of employment
- Explain the procedure taken if an employee has been unfairly dismissed
- Outline the main conditions attached to taking maternity leave

Introduction

The location, size and activities carried out by an office depends on the size of the business. In a small business, the location of the office depends on whether the public deal directly or indirectly with the office. For example, in a business that sells finished products such as groceries, clothes or hardware, the office will be situated away from the main entrance as no reception area is required. However, where the business sells a service, for example, a travel agency, dentist's surgery or auctioneering firm, the public will deal directly with the office. The office, in this situation, will be located at the main entrance to the building.

Depending on the size of the business, the duties of the office staff will vary. In a large business each department will have its own office to perform activities specific to that department. A centralised office is used for common activities such as filing, word processing, photocopying, handling the post, etc. In a medium-sized business, (ie, less than 50 employees), there may be one central office with skilled personnel such as secretaries, receptionists and accounts clerks employed to carry out the office activities. An Office Manger is responsible for co-ordinating the clerical activities.

In a small business, for example, a small hardware shop, the office may consist of one person who carries out all the clerical functions, such as ordering stocks, dealing with items returned, preparing lodgements, dealing with correspondence, organising payments to suppliers and handling general enquiries.

The Office Personnel

The diagram below indicates the tasks carried out by office personnel typical of a small to medium-sized business.

Office Manager			
Secretaries	**Receptionists**	**Accounts Clerk**	**Office Junior**
Correspondence Appointments Arranging travel General administration	Switchboard Visitors General administration	Petty cash Wages Banking Debtors control Creditors control	Post in/post out Photocopying Filing General administration

Office Manager

It is the duty of the Office Manager to ensure that effective clerical systems are in place and adhered to. The Office Manager will:

◆ Design the layout of the office

◆ Implement management policies by defining duties and allocating tasks and responsibilities to office staff

◆ Devise and maintain efficient procedures for processing information, eg, routing business documents from initial order to final payment stage

◆ Assist in developing information technology (IT) systems to enhance the quality and speed of information processing

◆ Plan and supervise office activities

◆ Identify staffing requirements

◆ Develop security procedures to protect information and the physical assets

◆ Maintain office equipment

As modern offices are computerised, the Office Manager will generally have a good working knowledge of computer hardware and software. The Office Manager will assist in the development of computerised information systems to improve the quality and speed of processing information. A computer technician may service the computing needs of the business.

PERSONAL SECRETARY/PERSONAL ASSISTANT (PA)

A personal assistant to a senior executive in the business is responsible for the day-to-day organising of events that take place in the executive's working day. The personal assistant becomes a specialist in his/her area; for example, the PA to the Marketing Manager may be responsible for preparing sales presentations and processing orders from the sales representatives. The personal assistant deals with confidential correspondence, arranges the executive's appointment schedule, prepares travel itineraries, and often has to deal with visitors on behalf of the executive and supervise junior staff.

JUNIOR OFFICE ASSISTANT

Most offices will employ a junior assistant. In a small office, this person will be trained in carrying out general office tasks, such as word processing, handling the post, operating the telephone switchboard, filing, photocopying and other general administration duties.

GENERAL SECRETARY

The modern secretary should be competent in the use of computer applications and modern office equipment. The size and nature of the business will determine the skills required. With the speed of technological developments, the role of the secretary has changed from that of a decade ago. For example, the modern secretary will have a good working knowledge of a word processing package, and other computer packages such as spreadsheets, databases and payroll packages.

In a small business, the secretary is often the first point of contact that visitors make with the business. Therefore, it is important that the secretary gives a good impression and is professional in his/her dealings with visitors.

The secretary should be:

◆ pleasant, courteous and well groomed
◆ skilled in oral and written communication
◆ efficient and professional at all times
◆ tactful and discreet, especially when dealing with complaints
◆ willing to assist and show initiative in times of crisis

Some of the duties regularly carried out by general secretaries are:

1. Dealing with correspondence
2. Planning and organising work
3. Arranging appointments
4. Arranging travel
5. Preparing for meetings and conferences

DEALING WITH CORRESPONDENCE

Correspondence generally refers to information received by the business through the post, telephone, e-mail and fax machine. The secretary will distribute the correspondence to the appropriate personnel and reply to correspondence as requested. The secretary must maintain a record of all important correspondence for future reference. The filing system used may be manual or computerised.

Some managers require the secretary to be skilled in taking dictation by using shorthand. However, it is now more common for the manager to use a dictaphone to record correspondence. The secretary listens to the audio-tapes and types the correspondence at a later stage. Audio-transcription requires the secretary to be skilled in both written and oral communication.

Advantages of audio-transcription:
a) The manager can dictate the tapes without the secretary being present.
b) The secretary can arrange the priority of tapes.
c) The secretary can replay the tapes to ensure accuracy.

Disadvantages of audio-transcription:
a) Confidential tapes may get into the wrong hands if proper security procedures are not maintained.
b) The secretary may have difficulty understanding the information on the tape and the manager may not be available when s/he is processing the tape.

PLANNING AND ORGANISING WORK

As the secretary's normal working day involves the preparation of work for a future date both for her/himself and others, it is vital that plans are made. Generally the secretary will plan in the short term, ie, on a day-to-day basis, but s/he will also make arrangements for dates in the future, for example, organising meetings, booking appointments, arranging travel or planning conferences.

However, even the best made plans can go wrong in a dynamic office environment. Emergencies occur and new priority work may arrive in the office, deadlines may change but the routine work must also get finished. The secretary must therefore be organised to deal with these situations as efficiently as possible. S/he must **plan,** but must also be **flexible** to rearrange plans if necessary.

To help plan the work, the secretary may use some of the following:
An Appointments Diary
An appointments diary is used to record details of appointments or meetings for some date in the future. A manual or electronic diary may be used.
'Things to do' Checklist
A 'Things to do' checklist is drawn up by the secretary to list work that needs to be completed that day.
Calendar
A calendar is essential for the secretary to identify days, dates and months when planning for future events, such as staff holidays, arranging travel, meetings, conferences, etc.

Concertina Folder

A concertina folder consists of a succession of pockets which open out. Each pocket can be labelled with a date for each day of the month. It is a temporary filing system; information is filed in the appropriate pocket and retrieved on the appropriate date. This procedure, known as a 'follow-up system' is an essential part of a filing system.

Diaries

There are two basic forms of diary on the market. The secretary may use:

(i) Manual Diary

When selecting a manual diary, the secretary should select a hard cover book with appropriate space to record the information. For routine appointments, eg, arranging appointments for a doctor's surgery, a one-page per day appointments diary may be sufficient, with times specified and space allocated to allow the secretary to write the details when accepting appointments.

APPOINTMENTS

MONDAY   *JANUARY 12*

	Patient	Telephone no	Doctor
0900	Mrs Joan Doyle	45394	Dr Byrne
	Mr Tom Dawson	39641	Dr O'Sullivan
1000			
1100	Miss Nora Gaffney	53684	Dr Byrne
1200			
1300			
1400	Mr Tadgh Coakley	49865	Dr O'Sullivan
1500	Mr Paul Cooney	49655	Dr Byrne
1600	Miss Patricia Doherty	82101	Dr Byrne

A one-page appointment diary for doctor's surgery

(ii) Electronic Diary (PIMs)

For more complex appointments, for example, arranging internal meetings and conferences for a large number of people, the secretary may operate an electronic diary system, also known as a personnel information manager (PIM).

A PIM is a computerised version of a comprehensive manual diary, ie, filofax, with appropriate index tabs. By selecting the correct index tab, the secretary can access a diary, address book, internal telephone directory, calendar, alarm clock, world time clock, calculator etc. Examples of PIMs on the market include: Corel Planner and Commence 3.

Features of the Electronic Diary:

◆ Diary is already structured to store information

◆ Easy to search for information using fast search and indexing facilities

◆ Layout of the diary can be customised to suit particular requirements

◆ The secretary can insert reminders to highlight priority tasks

◆ Appointments can be moved to a different date/time at the press of a button

◆ Hard copy of information, eg, itineraries, can be printed

◆ The PIM can be integrated with other software packages and reports can be produced (eg travel expense report)

◆ A mileage chart may be included

◆ When linked up to a modem (see chapter 10), the PIM can dial a telephone number from the address card

◆ If the PIMs are networked the secretary can link up to other PIMs to check for a free day or time slot to convene a meeting

◆ Multiple users can access the diary to book a conference room or appointment time

How to Plan

1. Record all known deadlines in a daily, weekly or monthly diary. The secretary may plan to complete the task before the deadline, to allow for changes in the work load that may take priority.

2. Estimate the time required to complete each task recorded in the diary.

3. The secretary should consult with his/her manager each day (if possible) to arrange the 'Things to do' checklist. Entries on this checklist will include unfinished tasks that must be completed, routine tasks and the new entries taken from the diary and/or concertina folder for that day.

4. The activities on the 'Things to do' checklist should be prioritised, ie, placed in order of importance. For example:

   ◆ urgent work that must be completed immediately

   ◆ routine activities that must be done, eg, dealing with correspondence, outgoing post

   ◆ work that will soon become a priority unless completed

   ◆ routine activities that are less important and can be completed at some later stage

5. As new work comes in, the order of the items on the 'Things to do' checklist may change as the new work may take priority.

6. When activities are completed, they are ticked off the checklist.

7. Activities not completed today will be:

   ◆ placed on the 'Things to do' checklist for the following day if a high priority task, or

   ◆ placed in the follow-up system and dealt with at a later date.

Maintaining a Diary

Whether a manual diary or an electronic diary is used, it is essential that the secretary establish 'house-keeping' rules for maintaining the diary. The secretary should:

◆ keep one main diary, where all entries are made. This avoids double-booking.

◆ consult with the manager on a regular basis to discuss activities. Usually the secretary will meet every morning with the manager, or may set aside time during the day.

◆ limit access to the diary. The secretary must take charge of the diary.

◆ always be informed if appointments are made by other people; for example, while s/he is on their lunch-break, an assistant may take appointments, or the manager may make an oral appointment and forget to inform the secretary.

◆ keep the diary in a safe place, usually on the secretary's desk, from which it must not be removed.

ARRANGING APPOINTMENTS

In general, incoming appointments are arranged by telephone or the secretary may receive a written request for an appointment by post or fax. The secretary should keep the appointment diary at hand, to check free times and dates. The nature of the business will determine the appointment details taken by the secretary. If the nature of the appointment is **in-house,** ie, a visitor is coming to the business premises, the secretary should:

◆ write the visitor's name and who s/he wishes to see in the appointment diary in the appropriate date, day and time slot.

◆ enter the telephone number of the client in case there is a need to cancel the appointment or an earlier appointment can be arranged.

◆ repeat details such as the date, day and time to the caller to ensure accuracy.

In a business where a person must meet clients **outside the premises,** eg, doctors on house calls or insurance representatives, auctioneers etc, the secretary should, as well as the above, record the address of the meeting point and when arranging the appointment time allow time for travel to the meeting point.

The secretary may use the appointment diary to prepare a daily itinerary for the manager on the move.

Daily Itinerary
MR JOE CLARKE – TUESDAY, 28 JANUARY 1997

1000 hrs:	Meeting with General Manager
1100 hrs:	Visit to site and meeting with site foreman
1400 hrs:	Viewing with Mrs Nolan, 36 Willow Park
1500 hrs:	Meeting with John O'Brien at O'Brien Builders, 16 The Mall
1630 hrs:	Return to office

In some cases, a general appointments diary may not be sufficient to record all the details. The secretary may design a form to facilitate the recording of non-standard information. For example, the Enquiry Form (displayed below) details the information required by the booking office of a coach business.

The secretary uses the booking form to take the details and transcribes the basic details from the booking form to the appointments diary for the date when the coach is required.

ENQUIRY FORM – COACH HIRE

Day and date of hire: . ...

Destination: ....

Pick-up points: ....

Pick-up time ....

Return time to garage:..

Number of passengers (coach size): ....

Luggage capacity:...

Special requests (microphone, disability facilities, etc):................................

Price (if quoted):..

Contact name: ....

Booked by:..

ARRANGING TRAVEL

An important duty of the secretary may be to arrange business travel. The secretary must identify:

◆ the destination
◆ the date and time of departure
◆ the date and time of return
◆ the duration and purpose of the visit
◆ the accommodation preferences (hotel, guesthouse)
◆ the preferred mode of transport, (eg, air, rail, bus, sea or car)

If the person is travelling by aeroplane, then it is likely that the business has already established a working relationship with a reputable travel agent. If no arrangement exists, the secretary should consult with more than one travel agency to ensure the best value is obtained, in terms of both finance and quality of service.

The secretary may need to arrange for transport to and from the point of arrival (ie, airport, seaport or train station). S/he may need to hire a car, arrange a taxi, or obtain train/bus timetables for the person travelling.

Booking Accommodation

When the type of accommodation required is identified (eg, hotel or guest house, single or double room, *en suite*, fax facilities, etc) the secretary should research a variety of accommodation establishments in the appropriate approved tourist guidebooks. The travel agency may recommend approved hotels or guest houses or the secretary can contact Bord Fáilte or the local tourist office.

Once accommodation has been identified, the secretary should:
- telephone or fax the accommodation establishment to find a room that suits the requirements of the traveller. If the accommodation is satisfactory a provisional booking will be made.
- request details of the booking to be faxed or posted, before confirming.
- check the details when received to ensure that the dates and room type correspond to the initial booking requirements.
- ring or fax to confirm the booking and request written confirmation.
- ring the accommodation a day or two before the person departs to ensure that the accommodation details are in order and remind the receptionist of any special requests.

Preparing an Itinerary

If the person travelling has a series of appointments to attend, an itinerary is prepared. An itinerary is a brief schedule of the day's activities typed as a one-page document or post card.

All correspondence, confirmation of bookings and the final itinerary should be retained in a travel file and kept by the secretary at the office for reference. Copies of booking details should be given to the person travelling in order to rectify any problems they may encounter on their trip.

TRAVEL ITINERARY

MR JAMES RYAN – Trip to England November 13 – 14 1996

Mon 13 November	
0830 hrs	Depart house for Dublin Airport – check in at 0930 hrs.
1000 hrs	Depart Dublin Airport for Manchester – Flight No IE 113.
1130 hrs	Arrive Manchester – Meet Ms Jane Carty at Terminal 2, Gate No 11. Leave airport for Hilton Hotel, Stoke-on-Trent.
1400 hrs	Collected by Ms Carty at hotel to go to Wedgewood plant to meet senior executives. Tour of plant.
1600 hrs	Presentation to Senior Executives – Strategic Planning.

Tues 14 November	
0900 hrs	Depart hotel by car to manufacturing plant – tour.
1100 hrs	Meet production managers – Demonstrations of new techniques.
1400 hrs	Depart factory for Manchester Airport – check in 1600 hrs
1700 hrs	Depart Manchester Airport for Dublin.

Travelling Abroad

Prior to departure the secretary should:

- ensure passports and visas are valid
- order traveller's cheques, Eurocheques (and Eurocard) and a business credit card if necessary
- arrange medical vaccinations if required for country of travel and enclose a list of vaccines that have been taken in the travel kit
- arrange for an international driving licence and insurance cover if the traveller intends driving
- prepare a checklist and tick off each item as it is completed and packed into the travel kit

☐	Passport
☐	Tickets
☐	Visa
☐	Eurocheques/traveller's cheques★
☐	Credit cards
☐	Material and resources for presentation
☐	Itinerary
☐	Names, telephone numbers and addresses of appointments
☐	Vaccination certificate and medicines
☐	International driving licence
☐	Copy of booking details

★a copy of cheque numbers should be retained at the home office

Calculating Travel Expenses

Travel expenses are paid by the business to employees who travel on behalf of the business. The business will pay for the employee's meals, accommodation and costs of travel while they are away from home.

Some businesses will give employees expenses before they travel, while other businesses will reimburse employees on their return. To claim travel expenses, the employee completes a Travel Expense Form and usually attaches receipts.

When processing the claim form, the secretary must ensure that details are correct (ie, dates, number of days away, distance travelled) and that the claim form is signed by someone in authority, usually a department senior.

Mileage charts can be found in the *Golden Pages*, some road maps or electronic diaries. An Electronic Diary will also calculate the cost of travel if appropriate rates are entered. As some mileage charts may record distances in terms of kilometres, it may be necessary to convert from kilometres to miles or vice versa.

EXAMPLE 1

1 mile = 1.6093 kilometres

1 kilometre = 0.6214 miles

Therefore, rounding the answer to the nearest decimal:

2 miles = 3.2 km (1.6093 km x 2)

20 miles = 32.1 km (1.6093 km x 20)

2 kilometres = 1.2 miles (0.6214 miles x 2)

20 kilometres = 12.4 miles (0.6214 miles x 20)

EXAMPLE 2

Employees are paid 57p per mile for business travel. The expense form for Mr O'Donnell shows he travelled from Tralee in Kerry to Cork city and returned that evening. Calculate how much should be paid to Mr O'Donnell for miles travelled. (Use mileage chart below.)

1. Check the mileage chart and locate Cork and Tralee on the grid.
2. The intersection point of Cork and Tralee is the amount of miles travelled. Tralee to Cork is 73 miles (or 117 km).
3. Mr O'Donnell travelled a return trip, so 73 miles by 2 = 146 miles travelled. He should receive 57p for 146 miles travelled = £83.22.

EXAMPLE 3

Mr O'Connor must drive from Tralee to Limerick tomorrow and will return tomorrow night. How many kilometres does he travel? The travel rate in the company is 25p per kilometre. How much is he owed?

1. The distance from Tralee to Limerick is 63 miles. Mr O'Connor will travel a total of 126 miles return trip.
2. If 1 mile = 1.6093 km, then 126 miles = 202.77 km (126 x 1.6093 km).
3. Mr O'Connor should receive 25p for 202.77 km travelled = £50.69.

Mileage and Kilometre Chart

```
          Athlone Ballina Belfast Carlow Clonmel Cork Derry Donegal Dublin Dundalk Ennis Galway Kilkenny Killarney Limerick Mallow Mullingar Portlaoise Sligo Tipperary Tralee Waterford Wexford Wicklow

Athlone      -    85m  136m  70m   87m  136m  144m 112m  79m   88m  69m  56m   72m  141m   73m  111m   29m    44m   72m   87m  137m  102m  114m  106m
Ballina    136k    -   167m 155m  170m  184m  123m  76m 154m  143m 108m  74m  157m  192m  124m  162m  102m   129m   36m  153m  190m  187m  199m  184m
Belfast    218k  267k   -   156m  205m  262m   74m 116m 103m   51m 205m 187m  174m  277m  209m  250m  110m   152m  130m  216m  275m  204m  187m  133m
Carlow     112k  248k  250k   -    56m  116m  184m 177m  51m  104m 115m 117m   24m  146m   86m  104m   62m    23m  113m   71m  157m   47m   48m   54m
Clonmel    140k  272k  328k  90k    -    60m  225m 199m 102m  154m  72m 115m   31m   91m   49m   49m  100m    62m  159m   24m  107m   30m   68m  111m
Cork       218k  294k  419k 186k   96k    -   271m 245m 159m  211m  83m 128m   91m   53m   63m   22m  146m   108m  205m   53m   73m   77m  115m  156m
Derry      230k  197k  118k 294k  360k  434k    -   47m 147m   99m 207m 173m  201m  285m  217m  255m  130m   172m   87m  224m  283m  231m  231m  177m
Donegal    180k  122k  186k 283k  318k  392k   75k   -  141m  102m 168m 126m  184m  253m  185m  223m  108m   151m   40m  194m  249m  209m  225m  171m
Dublin     126k  246k  165k  82k  163k  354k  235k 226k   -    52m 147m 135m   71m  189m  127m  147m   54m    52m  135m  111m  190m  101m   84m   32m
Dundalk    141k  229k   82k 166k  246k  338k  158k 163k  83k    -  157m 145m  123m  229m  156m  199m   59m    96m  105m  161m  216m  153m  136m   82m
Ennis      110k  173k  328k 184k  115k  133k  331k 269k 235k  251k   -   42m   92m   91m   23m   61m   98m    94m  128m   47m   89m  102m  140m  172m
Galway      90k  118k  299k 187k  184k  205k  277k 202k 216k  232k  67k   -   107m  128m   65m   98m   85m    89m   86m   89m  126m  145m  157m  162m
Kilkenny   115k  251k  278k  38k   50k  146k  322k 294k 114k  197k 147k 171k    -   122m   69m   80m   73m    30m  144m   47m  132m   30m   50m   80m
Killarney  226k  307k  443k 234k  146k   85k  456k 405k 302k  456k 205k 195k  171k    -    68m   42m  163m   139m   83m   20m  121m  159m  202m
Limerick   117k  198k  334k 138k   78k  101k  347k 296k 203k  250k  37k 104k  110k  109k    -    41m   93m    70m  145m   24m   63m   79m  117m  149m
Mallow     178k  259k  400k 166k   78k   35k  408k 357k  98k  157k 128k  67k   66k    -   134m   42m  163m   139m   83m   20m  121m  159m  160m
Mullingar   46k  163k  176k  99k  160k  234k  208k 173k  86k   94k 157k 136k  117k  261k  149k  214k    -    42m   85m   95m  159m  100m  112m   88m
Portlaoise  70k  206k  243k  37k   99k  173k  275k 242k  83k  150k 142k  48k  222k  112k  154k   67k    -   116m   59m  133m   60m   70m   71m
Sligo      115k   58k  208k 181k  254k  328k  139k  64k 216k  168k 205k 138k  230k  341k  232k  293k  136k   186k    -   154m  211m  174m  186m  165m
Tipperary  139k  245k  346k 114k   38k   85k  358k 310k 178k  258k  75k 142k   75k  133k   38k   66k  152k    94k  246k    -    83m   54m   92m  125m
Tralee     119k  204k  440k 251k  171k  117k  453k 398k 304k  346k 142k 202k  211k   32k  101k   82k  254k   213k  338k  133k    -   130m  179m  212m
Waterford  163k  299k  326k  75k   48k  123k  370k 334k 162k  232k  48k 194k  126k  126k  160k   96k  278k   160k  278k  208k    -    38m   88m
Wexford    182k  318k  299k  77k  109k  184k  370k 360k 134k  202k 224k 251k   80k  254k  187k  187k  179k   112k  298k  147k  286k   61k    -    54m
Wicklow    170k  294k  213k  86k  178k  250k  288k 274k  51k  131k 275k 259k  128k  323k  238k  256k  141k   114k  264k  200k  339k  141k   86k    -
```

Mileage chart (taken from the Golden Pages)

PREPARING FOR MEETINGS AND CONFERENCES

In many cases, the secretary will be expected to organise a conference or meeting on behalf of the business. The following checklist should be used for both occasions:

- Find out exact dates of the conference and book an appropriate hotel or conference centre. Keep in mind the size of the room, layout of the room, audiovisual facilities and refreshments.
- Prepare invitations.
- Obtain literature on the local area for delegates, eg, lists of accommodation, tourist maps and other local information. This information may be enclosed with the invitation.
- Prepare a checklist to confirm the number of delegates attending.
- Book accommodation for guests if required.
- Prepare essential paper work for members of the conference (ie, speaker's notes, reports etc).

♦ Prepare name/title badges for delegates.

♦ Arrange social programme for guest speakers.

♦ Arrange for a representative to meet guests at the airport, railway or bus station.

♦ Be on hand for any queries that may occur for the duration of the conference.

♦ Draw up post-conference details: evaluate the organisation of the conference for future reference, particularly accommodation, food and the conference room.

The Receptionist

Large businesses will employ a receptionist to deal with the duties outlined below. The reception desk is usually located at the point of entry to the business.

The reception desk should ideally be placed facing the door, so that visitors are seen when entering the building. However, the reception desk should be some distance away from the waiting area, so that work can continue while visitors are waiting, but the receptionist should be able to view visitors at all times. The reception desk should not be left unattended.

As the receptionist is often the first point of contact with the business, a smart personal appearance and good interpersonal and communication skills are essential qualities of the receptionist.

Often the receptionist will help out with clerical work such as filing and dealing with correspondence during quiet periods. In small offices where there is no junior office assistant, the receptionist may also be responsible for incoming and outgoing post.

The main duties of the receptionist are as follows:

1. Maintaining the reception area
2. Receiving visitors
3. Security and reception
4. Operating the switchboard
5. Dealing with complaints

MAINTAINING THE RECEPTION AREA

The reception area should be kept clean and free from untidy magazines, dirty ashtrays and empty coffee cups. The receptionist will water plants, clear ashtrays (most reception areas have a no smoking policy in keeping with recent legislation) and arrange reading material. Comfortable seating should be provided for the visitor. If it is policy to offer refreshments, these should be kept close at hand.

The receptionist should keep on hand:

♦ telephone message pad

♦ appointments book

♦ visitor log book and visitor badges

◆ telephone and fax directories, internal telephone lists and emergency numbers (eg, doctor, guards, fire brigade, etc)
◆ stationery
◆ calendar
◆ first aid kit

RECEIVING VISITORS

The receptionist should always be pleasant and greet incoming visitors with a smile. The receptionist should not be too familiar with visitors and should greet the expected visitor formally: eg, 'Good Morning, Mr O'Connor.'

If the receptionist is busy with a telephone call or another visitor, s/he should acknowledge any visitor approaching the desk and invite them to sit down while they are waiting.

The following procedure may be used when dealing with expected visitors:
◆ Greet visitor pleasantly and check their name, their business name and who they wish to see with the details recorded in the appointments diary.
◆ Request the visitor to sign the visitor log book. (This is a security precaution in case of an emergency, so that the receptionist will have a record of who is in the building.)
◆ Distribute a visitor badge, if necessary.
◆ Inform the person concerned that the visitor has arrived. As the receptionist should not leave the desk unattended, this is usually done by telephoning the extension number of the person concerned.
◆ Depending on company policy, direct the visitor to the appropriate office or call an office junior to accompany the visitor to the desired location.

Even though appointments are made in advance, emergency situations may occur that cause delays or even prevent the meeting from taking place. The receptionist should be discreet when dealing with this situation. The receptionist should:
◆ apologise for the delay and inform the visitor of the approximate delay.
◆ offer to make another appointment, if the visitor is unable to wait.
◆ if the visitor decides to wait, invite the visitor to sit down and offer some reading material and refreshments if appropriate.
◆ after the estimated time of waiting, remind the person that the visitor is still waiting.
◆ when the visitor can be received, direct the visitor to the appropriate office or call an office junior to do so.

Often the receptionist will encounter visitors to the business who do not have an appointment. These visitors may be:

◆ important clients who happen to be in the area
◆ sales representatives 'cold calling' in the hope of obtaining new business
◆ a customer with an urgent message or problem
◆ a personal emergency

Whatever the reason for the visit, the receptionist must use his/her initiative and assess the urgency of the caller. Sometimes the manager may not wish to meet unexpected visitors. The experienced receptionist will judge whether or not s/he can deal with the visitor. The receptionist should be polite at all times and should:

◆ greet the visitor and obtain his/her name, name of organisation and nature of the business. The visitor may have a business card which can be filed for future reference.
◆ if s/he cannot deal with the enquiry, invite the visitor to sit in the waiting area, while s/he checks to see if the person requested is free to meet with the visitor.
◆ if the person required is unavailable to meet the visitor, offer to make a preliminary appointment with the visitor for another day. Details of the visitor's call should be given to the person concerned as soon as possible.
◆ in an emergency situation, inform the person concerned of the visitor immediately, even if s/he must interrupt a meeting to do so.

SECURITY AND RECEPTION

As the receptionist is the first point of contact with the company, it is his/her duty to screen visitors. Visitors should not be left unattended and should not be allowed to wander through the premises.

If the receptionist receives crank calls or threats over the telephone or through the post s/he should alert security and the manager immediately.

The reception desk should not be left unattended. The receptionist may enhance security by:

◆ maintaining a visitor log book to identify visitors in the premises.
◆ distributing visitor badges, if necessary.
◆ ensuring the visitor log book is signed out when the visitor leaves.
◆ retrieving the visitor's badge from the visitor before departure.
◆ ensuring all confidential documents and audio-tapes are kept safe.
◆ ensuring computer screens at reception cannot be viewed by unauthorised personnel.
◆ restricting access to electronic diaries and computers by using passwords.
◆ ensuring filing cabinets are locked and keys are stored safely.

Power LTD Main Street, Wexford						
Name	**Company**	**Date of arrival**	**Time of arrival**	**Referred to**	**Signed**	**Time of departure**
G Larkin	Glen Ltd	June 10	1000 hrs	L Kiernan	K Shea	1200 hrs
L Flynn	Carbury Products	Jun 10	1500 hrs	A O'Connor	K Shea	1510 hrs
G Deegan	ACT Ltd	June 12	1550 hrs	V Shanahan	K Shea	1640 hrs

Visitor log book

OPERATING THE SWITCHBOARD

When dealing with enquiries over the telephone, the receptionist must always sound pleasant, friendly and efficient. The receptionist should have a clear speaking voice and should speak slowly, particularly when dealing with foreign callers.

Busy telephone switchboards often have a recorded message that instructs the caller to dial straight through to an extension number, if that number is known. This relieves the pressure of incoming calls and allows the receptionist to deal with other calls more efficiently. The caller can contact the person concerned directly or leave a message on the answering machine.

Handling Incoming Calls

◆ Keep a pen and telephone message pad close at hand to the telephone.
◆ Answer the telephone as soon as possible (eg, on the second ring).
◆ Greet the caller pleasantly and identify the business by name, eg, 'Good morning, Power Products Ltd, how may I help you?'
◆ Obtain the caller's name, business name and who they wish to speak to. Sometimes the receptionist will make further enquiries as to the nature of the enquiry as she may be able to deal with the issue herself.
◆ Ask the caller to 'hold' and dial that person's extension number. Inform the person concerned of the caller's name and the telephone line number.
◆ If the person concerned cannot take the call, return to the caller and inform him/her that the person is unavailable at present and offer to take a message.
◆ If the person concerned is on another telephone call, the receptionist may ask the caller if they wish to 'hold'.
With modern switchboards the receptionist can see what extension lines are busy and when an extension line becomes free. She can then put through a caller who is on 'hold'. The 'call waiting' facility is also used to alert a person on a telephone call that another caller is waiting.

- If the caller is waiting longer than expected, the receptionist should return to the caller and offer to take a message.
- The message is recorded on a telephone pad. Write down the caller's name, organisation, telephone number, date and time of call and details of the message. Repeat details to caller, if necessary, to ensure accuracy.
- Distribute the message to the person concerned as soon as possible.

Telephone Message Pad

Date: _____   For: _____   From: _____

Tel no.: _____   Please call back: ☐

Returned your call: ☐   Will call again: ☐

Message: _____

_____

Taken by: _____   Time: _____

EXAMPLE 1

Receptionist: Good morning, Walsh Bros. Ltd, how may I help you?

Caller: Hi, I want to speak to Mr James Walsh please.

Receptionist: Who shall I say is calling?

Caller: Oh, this is Barry O'Brien.

Receptionist: Mr O'Brien – from?

Caller: Oh – from Highway Wholesalers.

Receptionist: Just one moment, Mr O'Brien, I'll check if he is available. *(The receptionist checks the switchboard and sees that Mr Walsh is on another call.)* I'm sorry, but Mr Walsh is on another call. May I help you?

Caller: I'm ringing in connection with my account from last month.

Receptionist: Ms Ryan also deals with accounts, would you like to speak to her?

Caller: Yes, thank you, I need to get this problem sorted out immediately. *(The receptionist should inform Ms Ryan of the caller's name and nature of his business.)*

Receptionist: I'm putting you through to Ms Ryan now.

In a small office, where the secretary acts as the receptionist, s/he will be familiar with the daily routine of employees within the office and will be familiar with their business from dealing with correspondence.

EXAMPLE 2

Secretary: Good morning, Fitzgerald Insurances – Margaret speaking.

Caller: Hi, I wish to speak with Mary Drohan please.

Secretary: Just a moment please, who shall I say is calling.?

Caller: This is Mrs Cooney.

(The secretary checks to see if the person required is available and returns to the caller.)

I'm sorry, Mrs Cooney, but Mary is with a client, would you like to hold?

Caller: No thanks.

Secretary: Can I take a message?

Caller: Yes, I'm calling to see if my motor policy is ready yet.

Secretary: I believe that that policy is ready, but may I take your telephone number, and Mary will call you back when she is free?

Caller: OK, the number is 35475 and I'll be here for another 20 minutes.

Secretary: That is (writing down) Mrs Cooney at 35475. I'll give Mary the message, and if she can't contact you this evening, she will telephone you tomorrow morning.

Caller: Thank you.

Note that in this example, the name and telephone number of the caller are repeated to ensure that the secretary heard the details correctly.

Outgoing Calls

Before making a telephone call, the receptionist should:

◆ Locate the telephone number from the telephone directory or other source, ie, letter head or Telecom Éireann operator.

◆ plan the telephone call, identify whom you wish to speak to, the department and/or extension number, content of the call.

◆ keep files and correspondence nearby for easy reference.

Making Telephone Calls within Ireland

Ireland is divided into a number of telephone zones which are represented by an area code, eg, the area code for the Dublin area is 01. The area codes are listed in the telephone directory. To make a local telephone call (ie, dialling within the same area code), the number to dial is simply the local number.

Calls outside the local area are known as STD calls (Subscriber Trunk Dialling). To dial from one area code to another, eg, to make a telephone call from Cork to Waterford, the area code for Waterford is dialled first, followed by the local number.

EXAMPLE

Joan is on her way from Waterford to Cork Airport. When she gets to Cork city, she discovers that she has forgotten her passport and needs to telephone home for it to be sent by courier. Her local number in Waterford is 382111. To dial from Cork, Joan dials the area code for Waterford, followed by the local number: (051) 382111.

Making International Calls from Ireland

When making an international telephone call from Ireland, an **access code** and a **country code** are required. The access code is necessary to enable the caller to **dial out** of Ireland. The access code from Ireland to all other countries is 00. The country code is the code necessary to **dial into** another country. The country code will differ for every country.

To make a direct international telephone call, (ie, without using the telephone operator) dial the number in the following order:

> **access** code
>
> **country** code
>
> **area** code
>
> **local** number (dial 1198 for Telecom Éireann International Enquiries)

If the area code begins with **zero**, the caller should omit the first zero from the area code when making an international call.

EXAMPLE

You wish to make a telephone call to Liverpool from Ireland. Dial:

the access code – (00)

the British country code – (44)

the area code for Liverpool – (0151)

the local number.

The number to dial is: 00 44 151 + the local number (omitting the zero from the area code).

EXAMPLE

You are requested by your boss to contact a supplier in Great Britain. She has given you the number of the company, which is based in Manchester. The local number is 4410700 but when you dial this number you discover that the number is incomplete. What do you do?

From the Telephone Directory locate:

the access code – (00)

the country code for Great Britain – (44)

the area code for Manchester – (0161)

To dial from Ireland, drop the first zero in the area code.

The number you should dial is 00 44 161 4410700.

Making International Calls to Ireland

When making an international telephone call to Ireland, the procedure is similar. The access code remains the same, **00**. The country code for Ireland is **353**. For example, if dialling from France to Cork, the procedure is:

Access Code – (00)

Country Code for Ireland – (353)

Area code for Cork – (021)

Local number

The number to dial will be 00 353 21 + local number (omitting first zero from area code).

Telephone Charges

The telephone directory lists charges for telephone calls at three different rates:

Standard Rate:	From 8am to 6pm, Monday to Friday.
Reduced Rate:	From 6pm to 8am, Monday to Friday, all day on Saturday, Sunday and Public Holidays.
Weekend Trunk Rate:	From midnight on Friday to midnight on Sunday and all day on Public Holidays. The charge is *not* dependent on distance within Ireland and the unit charge is for each 10 minutes.

	Dialled Direct			Operator Assisted			
Local	Standard rate: 11.5p for up to 3 minutes Reduced rate: 11.5p for up to 15 mins			Standard and Reduced rates: 72p for first 3 minutes and 11.5p per subsequent 3 minutes			
Trunk	Standard	Reduced	Weekend	Standard Rate		Reduced Rate	
	Amount of time per 11.5p unit			first 3 mins	each minute after	first 3 mins	each minute after
A Rate up to 56 km	66.7 sec	100 sec	10 minutes	£1.00	13p	86p	8.5p
B Rate over 56 km	31.7 sec	47.6 sec	10 minutes	£1.40	27p	£1.11	17p

---

EXAMPLE

How much will a call from Waterford to Cork (>56 km) for 3 minutes made on Tuesday at 10.00am cost?

The call is charged at the 'B', Trunk Standard rate of 11.5p per 31.7 seconds. The call is of 180 seconds duration. Every 31.7 seconds costs 11.5p, therefore the cost of the call is 180/31.7 multiplied by 11.5p = 65.29p

---

DEALING WITH COMPLAINTS

The receptionist will often have to deal with complaints over the telephone. In situations like this, the receptionist must retain his composure and be polite at all times to the caller. Even though the nature of the complaint will differ from business to business, a general procedure to deal with complaints is to:

◆ listen attentively to the caller and avoid unnecessary interruptions
◆ carefully record details of the complaint
◆ neither agree nor disagree with the complaint
◆ offer assistance

If the receptionist cannot deal with the problem herself, she should refer the problem to an appropriate employee.

Accounts Clerk

In a small office, the secretary and office junior may operate accounting-type activities such as maintaining the petty cash book, carry out banking activities such as lodging and withdrawing money, reconciling the business's bank balance with that balance stated on the bank statement (ie, preparing a bank reconciliation statement) and preparing wages. In a larger office, an accounts clerk may be employed to carry out the above activities.

PETTY CASH

A petty cash box is maintained in the office for purchasing or reimbursing employees for sundry items such as bus fares, emergency stationery supplies, lunches, stamps and refreshments. As these transactions are of such small amounts it is impractical to write a cheque. (The charge to the business may be more than the actual cost of the sundry item!)

A **voucher system** is maintained to keep control over the petty cash transactions. When cash is requested from petty cash, a voucher is completed stating the date, amount of cash and purchase details. Both the recipient of the cash and the person issuing the cash sign the voucher.

The voucher system controls the amount of money in the petty cash box, and vouchers are used to write up the **petty cash book.**

PETTY CASH VOUCHER	
Voucher no 34 **Date** Aug. 7 '96	
Details	**Amount**
	£ P
Stamps	2 54
Signed by *Carol Ryan*	_____
Authorized by *Jack O'Reilly*	£2 54

Imprest System

Petty cash generally operates on an imprest system where an imprest (ie, a float) is received at the beginning of the petty cash period, usually weekly. The float is restored to the original amount of the imprest at the end of the period.

The procedure is:

a) An initial amount of cash is received from the Accounts Department for the petty cash float. The float is the opening balance on the petty cash book.

b) When there is a request for money from petty cash, a petty cash voucher is completed giving details of the amount, item purchased and date of expenditure. It is signed by both the recipient of the money and the person operating the petty cash.

c) The vouchers are used to write up the petty cash book at the end of the petty cash period.

d) The petty cash book is totted and balanced at the end of the petty cash period. More cash is requested to restore the imprest to the original amount for the next period.

EXAMPLE

The imprest at the beginning of the petty cash period is £50. During the week, three vouchers were signed for:

stamps (£2.54)

stationery (£4.62)

cleaning agents (£6.38).

The total spent for the week was £13.54, leaving a balance of £36.46. £13.54 is required to restore the imprest to £50.

The Petty Cash Book

The petty cash book analyses each petty cash transaction. This analysis is displayed on the right-hand side of the petty cash book. The left-hand side of the book records the money received. The balance on the petty cash book is the original amount of imprest minus the total of the petty cash vouchers. This balance should match the amount of cash remaining in the petty cash box. The petty cash book for the above example is written up as follows:

PETTY CASH BOOK

Received	Date	Details	Voucher no	Total payment	Post	Stationery	Travel	Sundries
50.00	Aug 1	Bank						
	Aug 1	Stamps	34	2.54	2.54			
	Aug 2	Stationery	35	4.62		4.62		
	Aug 4	Cleaning	36	6.38			6.38	
		Cash		£13.54	£2.54	£4.62	£6.38	
	Aug 5	Balance c/d		£36.46				
£50.00				£50.00				
£36.46		Balance b/f						
£13.54	Aug 8	Bank						

The sum £13.54 represents the amount of money received to restore the imprest to £50 for the next period.

WAGES AND SALARIES

A common duty of the accounts clerk is to prepare wages and salaries for all the employees. Some large businesses may outsource this task to a computer bureau. A computer bureau is a business that operates a variety of computerised services on behalf of other businesses. A business will avail of the bureau services where the expertise or technology is not available within the business or if an emergency arises, ie, the technology breaks down!

Rate of Pay

Wages are earned by employees on a hourly basis. Generally the employee will receive **wages** for hours worked at the end of every week. Employees who are paid a **salary** receive a fixed amount of money on a fortnightly or monthly basis. Employees' wages can be determined on:

a basic hourly rate: employees who work a standard week (39 hours) are paid a basic rate per hour. The total amount paid is known as the basic wage. Any hours worked above the standard week are paid at overtime rates.

a piece rate: employees are not paid a basic wage, but according to the quantity of output produced.

a basic wage plus commission: employees are paid a basic wage and can earn more depending on their performance, eg, sales representatives are often awarded commission on the volume of sales over a specific target.

overtime: this refers to extra hours worked above the standard week. These hours are paid at a rate higher than the basic rate. Businesses will generally have a range of overtime rates, for shift work, bank holidays and Sundays. Typical overtime rates are time and a half, double time and triple time.

EXAMPLE

If the employee's basic hourly rate is £7, one hour of overtime is worth:

at time and a half: £7 x 1.50 = £10.50

at double time: £7 x 2 = £14

at triple time: £7 x 3 = £21

Calculation of Wages

Before looking at how wages are calculated, it is important to understand the following terms.

Gross Pay

Gross pay consists of the total income earned by the employee *before* any deductions are made. If the employee is paid according to hours worked, the gross pay is calculated by multiplying the total hours worked by the rate per hour.

EXAMPLE 1

Tom worked a total of 38 hours at £5.50 per hour last week.

His gross wage last week was 38 hours by £5.50 = £209.

EXAMPLE 2

John worked a total of 38 hours at £5.50 and 3 hours' overtime paid at time and a half. His gross wage is:

38 hours by £5.50 = 209.00
3 hours by £8.25 = <u> 24.75</u>
£233.75

Superannuation Contributions (SAC)

Many employees contribute to a pension fund at work. This is known as a superannuation contribution (SAC). Approved pension fund contributions are not subject to tax, therefore the contribution is deducted from gross wages *before* the tax rates are applied.

Tax Free Allowances (TFA)

An employee is allowed to earn a certain amount without paying tax on it. This amount is known as a tax free allowance (TFA).

Obtaining a TFA

a) If an employee has just started work, s/he must complete **Form 12A** (obtainable from the Tax Office) giving details of income, personal circumstances (ie, single, married, age, disabilities, etc) and certain expenditure such as VHI subscriptions and mortgage interest paid. The tax office uses the information received to calculate the amount of income the employee can earn **before** paying tax and the rate of tax to be applied on the balance of income. A certificate of tax free allowance (TFA) will be issued both the employee and the employer.

b) Where an employee is changing jobs s/he will give the new employer a **P45** which states the TFA of the employee. A P45 is given to employees on termination of their employment.

An employer needs a TFA for each employee in order to calculate tax. However, it is the employee's duty to get the TFA. If an employer does not have a TFA for an employee, s/he will deduct tax at the **emergency rates** as obliged by law. With emergency rates, the employee will pay more tax than is necessary, and will remain on emergency tax until s/he supplies the employer with a TFA. Any overpayment of tax is refunded.

Taxable Income

The amount of income that an employee is taxed on is known as taxable income. It is calculated as follows:

Gross Pay − Superannuation Contribution − TFA = Taxable Income

EXAMPLE 3

Jim has a weekly gross income of £250. He pays £10.00 into an approved pension fund.

His TFA certificate states he has a TFA of £70.00 per week.

How much of Jim's income is subject to tax?

Gross pay	250.00
Less SAC	10.00
	240.00
Less TFA	70.00
Taxable income	£170.00

Jim will be taxed on £170.00 of his income.

Tax Rate

The employee's taxable income is subject to tax according to which Tax Table the employee is on.

There are two categories of Tax Tables: one for single individuals and another for married individuals. Within a category, the Tax Table that applies depends on the employee's level of income.

Single Individual		Married Individual	
Table A	26%	Table R	26%
Table B	48%	Table S	48%

Net Pay

Net pay consists of gross pay minus all deductions. It is the employee's take-home pay.

EXAMPLE 3 CONTINUED, SHOWING TAX CALCULATIONS

We will now calculate how much tax Jim pays and his net pay. Assume Jim is on Table A, how much tax does he pay and what is his take-home pay?

Gross pay	250.00	250.00
Less SAC	10.00	
	240.00	
Less TFA	70.00	
Taxable income	170.00	
Deductions		
SAC	10.00	
Tax at 26% (of Taxable Income)	44.20	
Total Deductions		54.20
NET PAY		£195.80

Jim will pay tax of £44.20. His take-home pay will be £195.80

Pay Related Social Insurance (PRSI)

An employee also contributes to a social insurance scheme to provide funds to the Government for its social programmes, ie, unemployment benefits, free medical and dental treatment for the low paid, etc. Different PRSI rates apply to certain classes of employment. Most employees will, however, pay PRSI at 6.75%. PRSI is calculated on Gross Pay – SAC.

EXAMPLE 3 CONTINUED, SHOWING PRSI CALCULATIONS

We will now calculate Jim's PRSI deduction and net pay. Assume Jim pays PRSI at 6.75%, how much PRSI does he pay and what is his take-home pay?

Gross Pay	250.00	250.00
Less SAC	10.00	
	240.00	
Less TFA	70.00	
Taxable income	170.00	
Deductions		
SAC	10.00	
Tax at 26% (of Taxable Income)	44.20	
PRSI at 6.75% (of gross pay less SAC)	16.20	
Total Deductions		70.40
NET PAY		£179.60

Jim will pay PRSI of £16.20, and this reduces his take-home pay to £179.60.

Deductions from Wages

An employer will deduct two types of deductions from gross pay. These are:

a) *Statutory deductions:* Statutory deductions are deductions that an employee is obliged to pay by law from wages, ie, tax (known as PAYE – **P**ay **A**s **Y**ou **E**arn) and PRSI.

b) *Voluntary deductions:* Voluntary deductions are deductions that the employee is not obliged by law to pay from wages. However, many employees subscribe to group schemes to pay VHI contributions, to donate money to charities, to save or to pay their trade union subscriptions *directly* from their wages.

The accounts clerk should ensure that s/he has a signed form from the employee authorising such a deduction to be made from the his/her wages.

EXAMPLE 3 CONTINUED, SHOWING VOLUNTARY DEDUCTIONS

We will now calculate Jim's net pay assuming he pays the following voluntary deductions: VHI contribution £24.00, contribution to saving scheme £5.00.

Gross pay		250.00	250.00
Less SAC		10.00	
		240.00	
Less TFA		70.00	
Taxable income		170.00	
Deductions			
SAC	10.00		
Tax at 26%	44.20		
PRSI at 6.75% (of Gross pay less SAC)	16.20		
VHI Contribution	24.00		
Saving scheme	5.00		
Total deductions			99.40
NET PAY			£150.60

Summary of Calculation of Wages

1. Calculate gross pay: hours worked by rate per hour including overtime
2. Calculate taxable income: gross pay less SAC less TFA
3. Calculate total deductions:
   a) SAC
   b) tax: taxable income by rate of tax
   c) PRSI: gross pay less SAC by PRSI rate
   d) voluntary deductions, eg, contributions to VHI, saving schemes
4. Calculate net pay: gross pay less total deductions

Payslip

Most payslips are produced nowadays using computerised payroll packages. The details necessary for calculating pay are entered once, ie, name of employee, employee work number, RSI number, SAC contribution, TFA, Tax Table and the voluntary deductions.

At the end of each week, the accounts clerk only enters the standard and overtime hours worked and the payroll package automatically calculates the total gross pay, PAYE due, PRSI due, total deductions, net pay and provides a running total of the pay to date since the start of the tax year (begins 6 April).

Every employee is entitled to receive a pay slip which summarises the calculations of take-home pay. The pay slip for Jim would read as follows:

PAYSLIP **Jim Leahy 0008976**	**APPLEWOODS SUPPLIES**		RSI No 6743212 S Tax Period 10	
Gross Pay Analysis	**Deductions**		**Year To Date**	
Basic Pay 250.00	PAYE	44.20	Gross Pay	2500.00
O/T	PRSI	16.20	TFA to date	700.00
Holiday Pay	Superannuation	10.00	Taxable Income	1700.00
Other	Union Subs			
	VHI	24.00		
	Savings Scheme	5.00	Tax Paid	442.00
Total Gross Pay £250.00		99.40	PRSI Paid	162.00
Hourly Rate				
Hrs @			TFA per week	70.00
Hrs @			Tax Table	A
			NET PAY	150.60

Explanation of year-to-date figures

Even though the payroll package calculates the pay and the year-to-date figures, you should be aware of how these calculations work in order to check your own payslip when you gain employment.

From the top right of the payslip, we see that this is the tenth week of pay. The year-to-date figures inform the employee of his/her total pay and statutory deductions to date.

Assume Jim receives the same wage each week, the calculations are:

Year-to-date figure	Calculation	Answer
Gross Pay	Gross Pay by 10 weeks	£250.00 x 10 = £2500.00
TFA to date	TFA per week by 10 weeks	£70.00 x 10 = £700.00
Taxable Income	Gross Pay – SAC – TFA by 10 weeks	(£250.00 – £10.00 – £70.00) x 10 = £1700.00
Tax Paid	Tax Paid per week by 10 weeks	£44.20 x 10 = £442.00
PRSI Paid	PRSI Paid per week by 10 weeks	£16.20 x 10 = £162.00

Employment Legislation

Since joining the EU, Ireland has introduced a number of acts of law that protect the employee at work. The Terms of Employment Information Act (1994), the Unfair Dismissals (Amendment) Act (1993) and the Maternity Protection Act (1994) are briefly discussed below.

THE TERMS OF EMPLOYMENT INFORMATION ACT 1994

The Terms of Employment Information Act 1994 implements EC Directive 91/533 and amends the Minimum Notice of Employment Act (1973). The employee is entitled to a Contract of Employment, within 2 months of commencing work where s/he works at least eight hours per week. The contract should include the following details:

◆ Name and address of employer
◆ Name and address of employee
◆ Title of job
◆ Date of commencement of job
◆ Place(s) of work of employee
◆ Nature and duration of contract – ie, part-time, full-time permanent, contract
◆ Rates of pay, ie, pay scales
◆ Methods of payment, ie cheque, Electronic Funds Transfer (EFT), cash
◆ Frequency of pay – weekly, monthly, etc
◆ Conditions relating to holiday leave and sick leave
◆ Pension contributions and entitlements
◆ Period of notice required by employee and employer

UNFAIR DISMISSALS (AMENDMENT) ACT 1993

The Unfair Dismissals (Amendment) Act 1993 incorporates the Unfair Dismissals Act 1977 and 1991. The purpose of this Act is to protect employees from being unfairly dismissed from their jobs. The Act lays down criteria as to what is 'unfair'. If an employee believes s/he has been unfairly dismissed, s/he can bring a case against the employer to the Employee Appeals Tribunal or through the courts for adjudication.

When a case is brought to the Employee Appeals Tribunal, it is up to the employer to prove that there were substantial grounds for the dismissal.

Grounds for Dismissal

An employee can be dismissed if:

♦ The employee was not qualified or competent to do the job s/he was employed to do

♦ The conduct of the employee contravened company rules, ie, taking alcohol or other substances while at work

♦ The conduct and behaviour of the employee was a danger to other employees

♦ The dismissal was due to unavoidable redundancy

Unfair Dismissal

The dismissal is seen as unfair if it is shown that the reason for the dismissal was:

♦ Religious or political

♦ Gender or racial bias

♦ Involvement of the employee in trade union activities

♦ Pregnancy

♦ Sexual orientation

Procedures to Take if Unfairly Dismissed

If the employee believes that s/he has been unfairly dismissed, s/he must:

1. Make a claim against the employer within 6 months of dismissal by sending a special claim form (obtainable from the Department of Labour) to the Rights Commissioner.

2. Send a copy of the claim form to the employer within the same time period.

If the employee or employer does not wish to involve a Rights Commissioner, the employee sends the claim form to the Employment Appeals Tribunal. Both the Rights Commissioner and the Employment Appeals Tribunal can only make recommendations which may or may not be accepted by the employer. If the employer does not accept the recommendations, the employee can bring the case to the Circuit Court.

If it is agreed that the employee has been unfairly dismissed, the employer must:

♦ give the employee his/her old job back (re-instatement) or

♦ give the employee an alternative job at the same operational level (re-engagement) and/or

♦ arrange financial compensation to be paid (within 2 years) to the employee.

MATERNITY PROTECTION ACT 1994

This act amends the Maternity Protection of Employees Acts 1981 and 1991 and implements the European Directive 92/85/EEC. The Act provides protection at work for pregnant women and for those who have recently given birth. The act also entitles the father of the child to take leave, where the mother dies following the birth of the child.

Rights and Duties of the Expectant Mother

A female employee:

◆ is entitled to minimum maternity leave of 14 consecutive weeks.

◆ may extend her maternity leave by an extra 4 weeks, which is unpaid. She should, however, notify her employer in writing of the intention to take extra leave when applying for maternity leave, if possible.

◆ is entitled to time off work for ante-natal and post-natal care without loss of pay.

◆ must be re-instated to her original job and with her usual work colleagues, if it is reasonable to do so. Her absence from work due to maternity leave should not in any way affect her status at work and her rights as an employee.

The employee must:

◆ notify her employer in writing of her intention to take maternity leave at least 4 weeks before the maternity leave begins.

◆ present a medical certificate indicating the expected week of birth.

◆ take at least 4 weeks' maternity leave before and 4 weeks' after the birth of the child (if, of course, the pregnancy is normal).

Summary

The general duties of the secretary are to process correspondence and make arrangements for appointments, travel and conferences. The secretary will use diaries, calendars and a 'things to do' checklist to help plan his/her work and the work of the manager. The day-to-day routine activities such as opening and distributing post, collecting post and preparing it for dispatch, filing, answering the telephone and processing fax messages and copying important documentation may all take place in the working day of the secretary. The office junior assistant helps the office staff in carrying out routine clerical and administration tasks.

The receptionist's main function in the office is to operate the switchboard, receive visitors and maintain the reception area. S/he will also help out in clerical activities if necessary.

The accounts clerk is responsible for financial transactions such as petty cash and wages. In the absence of an accounts clerk, the secretary will balance the petty cash and prepare the wages, or wage calculations may be outsourced to a computer bureau.

Since joining the EU, Ireland has implemented legislation to protect employees at work. All employees working more than 8 hours per week are entitled to receive a contract of employment, stating details of their duties and entitlements at work. The Unfair Dismissals Act provides the employees with the option of taking a case to the Rights Commissioner or the Employment Appeals Tribunal if they feel that they have been unfairly dismissed. If the employee wins the case, the employer must re-instate or re-engage the employee and/or pay compensation. Female employees are entitled to paid maternity leave of 14 weeks and unpaid leave of up to four weeks. The female employee should be re-instated to her original position on her return to work.

Questions

Multiple Choice Questions

1. The Office Manager typically carries out which of the following?
   a) preparing wages for the office personnel
   b) balancing the petty cash book
   c) organising procedures for clerical activities in the office
   d) calculating the travel expenses of marketing executives
   e) maintaining the switchboard

2. An office junior would do one of the following:
   a) prepare weekly wages
   b) assist the secretary in filing and processing information
   c) report at company meetings
   d) arrange appointments for a senior executive
   e) prepare the bank reconciliation statements for the business

3. A follow-up system is used for:
   a) filing completed work
   b) filing incomplete work
   c) keeping a backup of computer files on hard copy
   d) filing confidential information
   e) filing all travel arrangements

4. If 1 km = 0.6214 miles, then 17 km =
   a) 1.056 miles
   b) 27.35 miles
   c) 10.56 miles
   d) 10.48 miles
   e) 27.56 miles

5. If 50p is paid per mile for business travel, how much is paid for a 12km journey?
   a) £19.31
   b) £9.65
   c) £43.86
   d) £6
   e) £3.72

6. When making a telephone call to Ireland, the country code is:
   a) 00
   b) 01
   c) 1
   d) 353
   e) 00 44

7. When telephoning Dublin from Wexford, the area code is:
   a) 10
   b) 01
   c) 100
   d) 010
   e) 001

8. When making an international telephone call from Ireland, the access code is:
   a) 00
   b) 01
   c) 1
   d) 353
   e) 00 44

9. An employee earns £228 per week based on 38 hours worked. If s/he works 2 hours' overtime paid at double time, his/her gross income is:
   a) £294
   b) £240
   c) £222
   d) £216
   e) £220

10. An employee works 40 hours @ £2.50 per hour and 4 hours' overtime at time-and-a-half. The gross pay for this work is:
    a) £115
    b) £120
    c) £105
    d) £130
    e) £125

11. Taxable income is:
    a) gross pay − superannuation − TFA
    b) gross pay − TFA
    c) gross pay − PRSI − PAYE
    d) gross pay − PRSI
    e) gross pay − Tax Paid

12. Net pay is:
    a) gross pay − statutory deductions
    b) gross pay − PAYE
    c) gross pay − PRSI
    d) gross pay − total deductions
    e) gross pay − tax free allowances

13. Mr Hogan earns £275 per week. He pays £25 towards a pension fund and his TFA per week is £45. His taxable income is:
    a) £250
    b) £230
    c) £275
    d) £205
    e) £250

14. Mrs Dwyer earns £300 per week and pays £55 in statutory deductions. She also pays £15 per week to Goal. Her net pay is:
    a) £285
    b) £250
    c) £160
    d) £245
    e) £230

15. An imprest for a petty cash system is:
    a) the amount of money you start off with for the period
    b) the amount of money you have left at the end of the period
    c) the total amount spent on petty cash items over the period
    d) the amount spent on a single petty cash item
    e) the amount of money restored by the Accounts Office at the end of the period
    (NCVA 1995)

16. It would be correct to use petty cash to:
    a) pay the office staff's weekly wages
    b) pay for repair of office equipment
    c) pay for items broken by the public
    d) pay for employees' telephone calls
    e) pay for postage stamps
    (NCVA 1994)

17. State four features of an electronic diary. (NCVA 1994)

18. State four important items of information that should be included when making an appointment in the diary. (NCVA 1995)

Short Questions

1. List four duties of the Office Manager.
2. In relation to office staff, what does the abbreviation PA mean?
3. List four main duties of a general secretary.
4. List the advantages and disadvantages of audio-transcription.
5. Describe four aids used by a secretary in planning and organising work.
6. List the essential points a secretary should follow when planning his/her daily work.
7. List four main features of an electronic diary.
8. When taking an appointment, state the essential information that must be recorded.
9. Why is a general appointments diary not suitable for all appointments? Give an example.
10. What steps would you follow when booking accommodation for your manager?
11. What is an itinerary and what details are generally recorded?
12. List the main duties a secretary may have when arranging for a conference to be held in another location.
13. List four main duties of a receptionist.
14. Outline a procedure for dealing with expected clients/visitors.
15. How would you deal with a client/visitor who arrived without an appointment?
16. How can the reception area be made more secure?
17. Outline a procedure for dealing with incoming calls.
18. How would you make an efficient out-going call?
19. List the essential details that should be recorded on a telephone message pad.
20. What prefixes are required when making an international call from Ireland?
21. What is the 'country code' for Ireland? When would you use it?
22. Distinguish between the standard rate and the reduced rate of STD calls dialled direct.
23. List four points to follow when dealing with complaints.
24. What is an imprest?
25. Why are petty cash vouchers necessary?
26. In the payment of wages, distinguish between a piece rate and a basic wage plus commission.
27. What is a TFA? Why is it necessary?

28. When is a P45 issued?
29. Define the following:
    (a) Taxable Income
    (b) Statutory Deductions
    (c) SAC
    (d) Gross Pay
30. What entitlement does the Terms of Employment Information Act 1994 give to employees?
31. What essential details are recorded in a Contract of Employment?
32. Under the Unfair Dismissals (Amendment) Act 1993 state:
    (a) four grounds for dismissing an employee
    (b) four cases where a dismissal is regarded as being unfair
    (c) what an employee should do, if s/he has been unfairly dismissed
    (d) what an employer must do, if it is found that an employee has been unfairly dismissed
33. Under the Maternity Protection Act 1994 state:
    (a) rights of the expectant mother
    (b) duties of the expectant mother

Assignments

1. You have just answered the telephone and it is an angry customer! Goods to be delivered have not arrived. They were due last week and the customer is still waiting for them. What do you do? Record the conversation and how you would solve the problem.
2. You are the secretary of a coach hire company. A customer rings and makes a booking for the hire of a 53-seater coach for the following week. At the same time, a customer enters the office. You jot down the details of the telephone call on a scrap of paper. You forget to enter the details of the booking in the diary and consequently do not arrange the pick-up. A very angry customer telephones the following week – they have been waiting for their coach. What do you do?
3. Check the current telephone directory and cost the following telephone calls using the standard rate.
    1. Telephone call from Kerry to Dublin (> 56 km) for 5 minutes
    2. Telephone call from Dublin to London for 3 minutes
    3. Telephone call from Galway to Limerick (> 56 km) for 6 minutes
    4 Telephone call from Stillorgan to Dun Laoghaire (<56 km) for 2 minutes

4. You are working in an office in Cork and have to make the following telephone calls. Check the current telephone directory for the correct prefix codes for:
1. Waterford city
2. Galway city
3. Tralee in Co. Kerry
4. Belfast city
5. Paris (France)

5. You have to arrange a trip for an executive who must go to London from Monday to Wednesday. Outline what needs to be done to arrange this trip. Get details from your local travel agent of the times and costs of travel by air, rail and sea.

6. Using the details in Q5, and information from travel books and brochures, plan a two-day itinerary for the executive's spouse who wishes to visit some places of interest in London.

7. A regular customer has a complaint and insists on talking to the manager. However, you have been instructed not to transfer any calls to the manager. How would you deal with this situation effectively?

8. Your company is hosting the annual conference and you have been assigned the task of organising the delegates. What would you need to consider?

9. Mr Buckley travels on a daily basis from Limerick city to Waterford city on business. At the end of the week he submits a claim form for mileage only. However, you have received his claim form and the mileage is not calculated properly. Calculate his total mileage expenses due for the week based on a rate of 55p per mile.

10. Prepare the petty cash book for the following sundry cash transactions. Imprest received from accounts for £50. Decide the columnar headings.
June 1 Paid for stationery £2.60
June 3 Purchased fax paper £5.80
June 6 Paid bus fares for office staff who worked overtime £4.50
June 8 Paid cleaning staff £12.50
June 10 Paid for emergency printing when printer broke down £4.50
June 11 Gave subscription to local charity from the office £5

11. Prepare the petty cash book for the following transactions. Use five analysis columns: Postage, Stationery, Travel, Cleaning and Sundries
Mar 3 Received £150 imprest from accounts department
Mar 3 Purchased Swiftpost labels and envelopes £4.20
Mar 4 Purchased emergency postage stamps £3.28
Mar 5 Paid train fare for interviewee from petty cash £35
Mar 6 Purchased batteries for office calculator £2.75
Mar 6 Purchased biros and pencils for the office £4.50

Mar 8 Paid for courier delivery £3.50

Mar 9 Purchased cleaning materials £6.90

Mar 10 Paid for servicing the office typewriter £12

12. Michael O'Reilly works for your construction firm, Kerry Building Ltd. Calculate his net pay from the details given below. (PRSI is calculated as a percentage of gross income.)

Gross Pay £350 per week

TFA £65 per week

Pension 5% of Gross income paid

Tax Rate 26%

PRSI 6.5%

13. Dearbhla O'Donoghue is employed in a translation agency. Her gross pay is £230 per week and she is taxed at 26%. She contributes £5 to a charity and her TFA amounts to £42. Her PRSI is 6.75%. She does not have a pension plan at present. What is Dearbhla's taxable income and net pay?

14. Martin earns £12 an hour for a 35-hour week. He works 5 hours' overtime for which he is paid double time. His weekly tax free allowance is £70. He pays PAYE at 26% and PRSI at 6.75%. He does not pay a superannuation contribution.

(a) Calculate his basic pay, overtime pay, taxable income and tax paid.

(b) If Martin were to pay £10 per week towards the Sports & Social Club at work, what would his net pay be?

15. Mary earns £4.50 an hour for a 35-hour week. She works 7 hours' overtime for which she is paid time and a half. Her weekly tax free allowance is £66.33 and she pays tax at Table A rate (26%).

Her basic pay is:

Her overtime pay is:

Her taxable pay is:

Her tax is:

(NCVA)

4. Post and Postal Services

After studying this chapter you should be able to:
- Explain how incoming post is dealt with in the office
- Explain how to prepare post for dispatch from the office
- Identify typical equipment used in handling the post
- Describe the postal and courier services provided by An Post
- Calculate the correct postage for outgoing post using the *Postal Guide*

Introduction

In every business, information is received and dispatched through the post. This correspondence is the lifeblood of the organisation. The volume and confidentiality of the post relates to the nature of the business. For example, a mail order company will deal with large volumes of incoming and outgoing post to complete the normal selling of its goods, while a unit trust company will deal with smaller volumes of post but the information will be of a much more sensitive and confidential nature.

Important documents and/or **remittances** flow through the post. A remittance is money received in some form, ie, cash, notes, cheques or bank drafts.

To prevent the delay of receiving or sending remittances or other important documentation, it is important to ensure that there is a proper procedure in place to deal with both incoming and outgoing post. Delayed or missing post results in dissatisfied customers or extra expense for the business. For example, the business will lose interest that could be earned from the bank if remittances are not lodged to the business bank account.

Dealing With Incoming Post

The following procedure is generally implemented when dealing with incoming post:
- Post is delivered to the office.
- Registered or recorded post must be signed for by the post clerk or the addressee.
- Sort the post according to:
  1. letters — general, private, confidential, personal and urgent
  2. parcels

- ◆ Open:
    1. General post.
    2. Post that is incorrectly addressed to the business. For example, an envelope may be addressed to Ms Drohan, Sales Department, but she may work in the Production Department. The letter must be opened to verify which department the letter should be distributed to.
    3. Parcels, unless marked private, confidential or personal.
- ◆ Do **not** open:
    1. Post addressed to individuals as private, confidential or personal unless authorised to do so. These items should be handed unopened to the addressee.
    2. Post that is addressed to another business, eg Allied Irish Finance, 12 Drury Street, Carlow, receives a letter addressed to Allied Irish Banks Ltd, 10 Main Street, Carlow. This letter should be returned unopened to the Post Office for redistribution.
- ◆ Date stamp the post as it is opened.
- ◆ Check envelopes for enclosures.
- ◆ Record remittances in the remittance book.
- ◆ Record missing enclosures as 'enc omitted' on documentation received.
- ◆ Secure enclosures with a paper clip or staple.
- ◆ Attach a circulation list where necessary.
- ◆ Sort post into appropriate bundles for distribution.
- ◆ Distribute post to individual trays, pigeon-holes, or department post trays.

Remittance Book

A remittance book is maintained by the secretary or post clerk to record remittances received. The remittance book logs the date the post is received, who the remittance is from, the type and amount of remittance and is signed by the person opening the post. The remittance book is evidence that the payment actually arrived at the business and thus missing payments may be detected more easily.

Date	Addressee	Remittance Type	Amount	Signed
July 7	Star Ltd	Postal Order	£35.00	M Murphy
July 7	Cambridge	Cheque	£64.00	M Murphy
July 7	Calcus Ltd	Bank Draft	£13.00	M Murphy

DISTRIBUTING POST

The person dealing with incoming post should ensure a speedy delivery of post to the various departments and individuals in the business.

The post may contain magazines which should be circulated to a number of employees. A *circulation list*, drawn up by the secretary or post clerk is attached to the magazine for distribution. A circulation list is a list of all employees wishing to read the magazine. When the magazine is read, the list is initialled, dated and the magazine is passed to the next person on the list, usually within 24 hours. A circulation list is also used to circulate other internal information such as reports.

Please read and circulate to next named person on the list within 24 hrs. Initial list and insert date when circulating.		
Name	**Initial**	**Date**
John Anslow Deirdre Browne Barry Carmody Aoife Ní Mhuirí Margaret Doyle Louise Kiernan Brendan McArdle		

A Circulation List

The post clerk should maintain a list of all employees in the business, and the area in which they work so that post can be distributed promptly and accurately. Such information may be obtained from the organisation chart or the receptionist may have compiled such a list.

Dealing with Outgoing Post

Clerical staff will usually have an **in-tray** and an **out-tray** for receiving and dispatching correspondence. The post clerk will collect outgoing post from the out-trays at specified times during the day. The following procedure is generally implemented when dealing with outgoing post:

LETTERS

- ◆ Ensure all letters are signed.
- ◆ Check all enclosures (eg, cheques, documentation) are attached.
- ◆ Check the address on the letter matches the address on the envelope.

- Fold letters and any attached enclosures neatly and place in an appropriate sized envelope. Particular attention should be paid when inserting letters into window envelopes. Ensure address is visible and confidential information (eg, amount due on account) is not in view.
- Seal envelopes if necessary.
- Sort:
  1. post for franking, batching similar sized envelopes together
  2. post requiring special attention (ie, post to be registered)
- Weigh heavy envelopes individually, and calculate the postage value. (Use the Post Guide).
- Frank Post.
- Dispatch post to the Post Office.
- Register valuable post at the Post Office and obtain receipts.

PARCELS AND PACKING

To ensure a safe delivery the following guidelines may be adopted when packing parcels for dispatch.

1. Pack the items tightly together to prevent movement. Foam or paper is often used.
2. Use protective wrapping around the parcel, ie, 'bubble wrap'.
3. Wrap the outer parcel with plain paper or place in a cardboard box.
4. Write the name and address of the recipient of the parcel clearly on the front of the parcel.
5. Write the sender's name and address clearly on the back of the parcel. Mark **'SENDER'S ADDRESS'** clearly to avoid confusion.
6. If using a bar coded label, stick the bar coded label on the left-hand side of the front of the parcel.

WEIGHING AND COSTING POSTAGE

Every office should obtain a copy of the *Post Guide* from An Post. The *Post Guide* outlines the current postage charges for all types of post, both national and international and outlines specific details of the Post Office Preferred (POP) envelope size and weights. The post clerk should refer to this guide to check that the correct value of postage is placed on all post for dispatch.

Postal charges are determined by the weight and size of the envelope or parcel. For example, the lowest charge for an ordinary sealed letter (not exceeding 120mm by 235mm) to Europe is (currently) 32p. The weight should not exceed 20 grams (approx the weight of 3 A4 pages).

If an incorrect stamp or franking value (ie, under the postal value) is placed on the post, the addressee is charged with the difference in postage and a nominal fee (currently 50p). If the addressee refuses to pay the charge, the sender is obliged to pay the postal charge.

ZONE 1
INTERNAL AND NORTHERN IRELAND

Weight not over	Letters	Printed Papers
20g (P.O.P.)	32p	28p
50g	36p	30p
100g	48p	40p
250g	72p	58p
500g	£1.20	98p
1Kg	£2.40	£1.83 (Max)
1.5Kg	£3.60	
2Kg	£4.80	
	Each Additional 500g = £1.20	
Weight Limit	No Limit	1Kg
Postcards	28p	

REGISTRATION

Fee	Maximum Compensation	Fee	Maximum Compensation
£1.05 (Min Fee)	£20.00	£1.65	£600.00
£1.15	£100.00	£1.75	£700.00
£1.25	£200.00	£1.85	£800.00
£1.35	£300.00	£1.95	£900.00
£1.45	£400.00	£2.05	£1,000.00
£1.55	£500.00		

Advice of Delivery
Requested at time of posting £1.00
Requested subsequent to posting £2.00

REDIRECTION
First 3 months (Permanent Move) .... Free
Next 6 months £15.00
Subsequent 6 months £15.00
Change of address postcards .... (Per pack of 10) £3.00
Redirection ceases at end of 3 months unless renewed.

UNPAID OR UNDERPAID POSTAGE –
Don't Guess it – Check it! Items unpaid or underpaid are surcharged 50p plus the deficiency in postage. This is collected from the addressee but in the case of refusal the sender will be obliged to pay.

PRINTED PAPERS – WHAT ARE THEY?
Printed papers include greeting cards, newspapers, books, invoices and pamphlets etc. posted in unsealed envelopes. **Other correspondence in unsealed and sealed envelopes are classed as letters.** For full details on what qualifies as printed papers contact your local Post Office.

Your envelope should not be greater than 120mm
Your envelope should be at least 90mm

Your envelope should be at least 140mm

ZONE 2
EUROPEAN UNION COUNTRIES

Weight not over	BRITAIN		OTHER E.U. COUNTRIES	
	Letters	Printed Papers	Airmail Letters	Surface Printed Papers*
20g (P.O.P.)	32p	28p	32p	28p
50g	40p	33p	75p	40p
100g	53p	44p	£1.07	55p
250g	78p	54p	£2.14	£1.10
500g	£1.32	£1.08	£4.07	£2.00
1Kg	£2.64	£2.00	£6.95	£3.20
1.5Kg	£3.96	£3.08		
2Kg	£5.28 (Max)	£4.16 (Max)	£11.24 (Max)	£4.50 (Max)
3Kg		Books Only £6.00		Books Only £6.00
4Kg		£8.00		£8.00
5Kg		£10.00		£10.00
Weight Limit	2Kg	2Kg Books 5Kg	2Kg	2Kg Books 5Kg
Postcards	28p		28p	

*There is no airmail service to Europe for printed papers. Where the quickest possible delivery is required please use the letter service.

E.U. Member Countries
Austria, Belgium, Denmark, Finland, France, Germany, Great Britain, Greece, Italy, Luxembourg, Netherlands, Portugal (inc. Azores, Madeira), Spain (inc. Canary Islands, Balearic Islands), Sweden.

BENEFIT FROM LOWEST POSTAGE RATES
POST OFFICE PREFERRED (P.O.P.)
To benefit from the lowest rate of postage for mail posted within Ireland and to any EU member country your mail should conform to Post Office Preferred (P.O.P.) weight and size standards.
■ **Weight:**
Not more than 20 grammes or approximately the weight of an envelope containing up to 3 regular (A4) size sheets of paper.
■ **Size:**
See below for handy size guide.
If your envelope is bigger or smaller than the P.O.P. outline, or weighs more than 20 grammes you must pay a higher than P.O.P. rate.

Your envelope should not be greater than 235mm

ZONE 3
THE REST OF THE WORLD

Weight not over	EUROPE (Excl. E.U.)				ALL OTHER COUNTRIES			
	Airmail Letters	Surface Printed Papers	Surface Letters	Airmail Printed Papers		Weight not over	Airmail Letters	Airmail Printed Papers
20g (P.O.P.)	44p	37p	44p	37p		20g	53p	38p
50g	73p	40p	73p	40p		30g	74p	53p
100g	£1.07	55p	£1.07	55p		40g	96p	68p
250g	£2.14	£1.10	£2.14	£1.16		50g	£1.18	83p
500g	£4.07	£2.00	£4.07	£2.00		60g	£1.40	98p
1Kg	£8.96	£3.20	£8.96	£3.70		70g	£1.62	£1.13
						80g	£1.84	£1.28
2Kg	£11.24 (Max)	£4.50 (Max)	£11.24 (Max)	£4.50 (Max)		90g	£2.06	£1.43
		Books only		Books only		100g	£2.28	£1.59
3Kg		£3.00		£6.00		Each Add. 10g	22p	15p
4Kg		£8.00		£8.00				
5Kg		£10.00		£10.00				
Weight Limit	2Kg	2Kg Books 5Kg	2Kg	2Kg Books 5Kg			2Kg	2Kg Books 5Kg
Postcards		37p		37p			38p	

INTERNATIONAL REPLY COUPONS
Price 77p. Coupons from other countries may be exchanged for an airmail stamp (minimum rate) to that country e.g. E.U. 32p, Rest of Europe 44p, Rest of World 52p.

REGISTRATION & INSURANCE (Foreign Service)
The service is available to all countries abroad except if otherwise stated in the Foreign Post Summary Eolai An Phoist Section 2.4. Ask for details at your local Post Office.
Registration: All letter services (except bulk services).

Fee	Maximum Compensation
£1.05	£20.00

Advice of Delivery.
Requested at time of posting £1.00

Insurance: Letters.

Fee	Maximum Compensation	Fee	Maximum Compensation
£1.15	£100.00	£1.55	£500.00
£1.25	£200.00	£1.65	£600.00
£1.35	£300.00	£1.75	£700.00
£1.45	£400.00	£1.85	£800.00
		£1.95	£900.00
		£2.05	£1,000.00

Post Office guide extract

EXAMPLE – PREPARING POST FOR DISPATCH

A heavy envelope arrives to the post room from Purchasing, to be dispatched to the UK. Outline procedure for dispatch.

1. Check envelope is sealed and addressed properly.
2. Place envelope on weighing scales and note weight (assume weight of 236g).
3. Check postal guide for charges to UK for post weighing not more than 250g. (Current charge is 78p.)
4. Adjust franking machine to emit a stamp to the value of 78p.
5. Stick franking machine stamp to the envelope and dispatch.

Layout of the Post Room

The layout of the post room must allow for sorting, checking and distributing the post. A clear working area is essential to avoid the mix-up of incoming and outgoing post.

Space should be allocated in the post room for the following incoming post activities:

a) **dumping** post from the post bags
b) **sorting** letters (private, confidential, personal, urgent) and parcels
c) **opening** the general post, date stamping and attaching enclosures

d) **recording** remittances

e) **sorting** post into bundles for distribution to various departments

Workstations should be cleared to allow for outgoing post procedures such as:

a) **folding** and **inserting** letters into envelopes

b) **packing** and **wrapping**

c) **sorting** into required bundles for franking

d) **weighing, stamping** and **franking**

e) **dispatching**

Equipment in the Post Room

The volume of post flowing through the business determines what type of equipment will be used in the post room. For example, a small business may not require a franking machine and may operate a manual weigh scales and a manual letter opener. A business with large volumes of post may operate up-to-the-minute electronic postal equipment. Typical equipment found in the post room includes some or all of the following:

◆ Letter openers – paper knife and automatic letter openers

◆ Date stamping machine to date-stamp incoming post

◆ Baskets and trolleys for collecting and distributing post around the organisation

◆ Jogger machine that vibrates paper to align it for stapling or binding

◆ Folding, inserting and sealing machine for placing documents into envelopes and sealing

◆ Addressing printer machine for printing addresses on large quantities of post

◆ Weighing scales for measuring weight of parcels and envelopes

◆ Franking machine, for placing the value of the postage on the post

◆ Sundry stationery, eg, stock of envelopes, rubber bands, Sellotape, glue, air mail stickers, Swiftpost stickers, etc

◆ Sundry equipment, eg, sponge for sealing and stamping (pre-gummed stamps are now available), scissors, parcel-tying materials, staplers, etc

LETTER OPENERS

A paper knife is used to open sealed letters individually. Shake the envelope to bring the contents to the bottom of the envelope to avoid damaging the contents. The sharp edge of the knife is inserted through the flap of the envelope and the envelope is opened by moving the knife under the envelope flap **away from the body**, (ie, sharp edge faced out). Care should be taken when handling the knife.

An **automatic letter** opener is used where there is a large volume of letters to open. Envelopes are fed automatically to the letter opener and a minute strip from the top of the envelope is cut by a blade. The width of the cut can be adjusted to open heavy envelopes. It is important to ensure that envelopes are faced correctly so that contents are not damaged.

Automatic letter opener

DATE STAMPING MACHINE

A date stamping machine is used to stamp all incoming post with the date as evidence of receipt on a particular date. The day, date, month and year are adjusted by external controls. It is important to remember to change the date.

THE ADDRESSING PRINTER

The addressing printer is connected to a computer and accommodates different sized envelopes and forms.

Address printing machine

Date stamping machine

The names and addresses are held on a computer file and printed on the envelopes or forms as they are fed through the addressing machine.

JOGGER MACHINE

A jogger machine aligns individual pages for stapling or for inserting into envelopes.

FOLDING AND INSERTING MACHINE

A folding and inserting machine is used to automatically fold and insert printed material into window envelopes (eg, invoices, statements). Some machines will also seal the envelopes.

WEIGHSCALES

A weighscales is used to weigh non-standard letters and parcels so that the correct postage values can be fixed on the post.

A manual weighscales is used when dealing with small volumes of non-standard sized envelopes and parcels. The post is placed on the scales and the weight is read from the display. The post clerk compares the reading with the Post Guide to ascertain the correct post charge.

An electronic postal scales is used to speed up the post calculation process when dealing with large quantities of non-standard sized post (eg, a mail order company has large volumes of post of different sizes and weights). Modern electronic postal scales can be programmed to calculate the correct postal charges and can be interfaced with a franking machine to print the appropriate frank value.

THE FRANKING MACHINE

A franking machine is used by a business that dispatches a large volume of post on a regular basis. It places an impression of the postage value on envelopes or parcels which are accepted by the postal system as stamped post.

The envelopes are stacked on a feeder tray, and the required settings, ie, date, envelope width and frank value are set. As the envelope passes through the machine, the stamp value and date of postage are imprinted (franked) on the envelope. Some businesses place an advertising slogan on their 'frank'.

Modern franking machines, eg, the Neopost 5400 series, can stamp up to 3,500 envelopes per hour and have a moistening device that seals the envelopes as they are passed through for franking.

The business purchases or leases the franking machine from the manufacturer, but must obtain a licence from the Post Office. The franking machine operates in a similar fashion to a telephone call card in that a franking card with franking units is purchased from the Post Office.

Features of the Franking Machine
- The franking machine prints an impression of a stamp on the mail.
- The date of postage is set using an external date-setting control.
- The machine can be set to various levels to record different stamp values.
- The width of the mail feeder can be adjusted to allow for different envelope sizes.
- A meter reads the franks (units) used and displays units remaining.
- Gummed postage-stamps can be printed for large parcels or bulky envelopes which cannot be fed through the machine due to their size.
- Some franking machines have a signal indicator to set a new date when switched on every day.

Advantages of the Franking Machine
1. Saves time and effort required to stamp and seal envelopes.
2. Usage is recorded by the meter, avoiding the need for manual accounts (ie, postage book).
3. Security is improved as pilfering of stamps and petty cash is avoided.
4. Free advertising with imprinted business slogan.

5. Modern franking machines have a minimum value warning to ensure the meter does not run out in a franking session.

Disadvantages of the Franking Machine

1. Wastage if the operator cannot use the machine properly, eg, forgets to set the date.
2. Units are purchased during Post Office hours.
3. Private post may pass through the system unnoticed.
4. A licence is needed from the Post Office.
5. It may take time to purchase new units from the Post Office.

Franking machine

An Post – Irish Post Office Services

When working in an office, it is essential to be familiar with the services provided by An Post and private courier firms to ensure the safe and prompt delivery of post in the most effective manner.

An Post is currently developing a **'track 'n' trace'** system to improve the delivery of post. This system incorporates bar codes and scanners and an automated receipt system to trace the route of all post from the time of delivery. At present, An Post can only trace post bound for abroad to the point of departure from this country.

Securing Post

REGISTERED POST

Letters that contain important documents or valuable items can be registered with the Post Office. Registering the letter (or parcel) entitles the customer to compensation in the case of loss or damage to the post. The amount of compensation is directly related to the value of the contents. Post can be registered using registered envelopes or registered labels.

1. Using registered envelopes

The letter is placed in a special registered envelope which is purchased at the Post Office. When a customer registers a letter, the registered envelope is handed over the Post Office counter by the customer. A receipt is completed and signed by the customer stating the address of the receiver and the value of the item registered. The receipt is date-stamped by the Post Office and returned to the customer. This receipt is called a **Certificate of Postage.**

A certificate of postage can be also be obtained from the Post Office without registering a letter. This certificate acts as proof that the letter was posted on a particular date, but the customer is not entitled to compensation if the letter is lost.

2. Using registered labels

    The registration label consists of a **receipt and identification label**, with corresponding bar codes, so that the letter may be traced through the **track 'n' trace** scanning system. The customer fills in the receipt, stating the recipient's address and the value of the contents. The receipt is date-stamped and signed by the Post Office clerk and returned to the customer as proof of posting. The customer fixes the identification label over the top of the envelope (do not fix over address) and hands the envelope to the Post Office clerk.

    A registration fee is charged ranging from £1.05 to £2.05 depending on the value of the contents (see *Post Guide*). The maximum compensation that a customer can receive is £1,000. The customer must provide the receipt to claim compensation for loss or damage to the post.

Receiving registered post

When a registered letter/ parcel is delivered to the business, the recipient checks the delivery to ensure all contents are intact and signs a **Delivery Record Card** as proof that the post was delivered successfully.

Registered label

If the bar code system is used, the postman removes the bar code sticker from the identification label and places it on the Delivery Record Card as proof of delivery.

ADVICE OF DELIVERY (RECORDED DELIVERY)

The sender of the registered post may require proof from the Post Office that the post was delivered. Using the Delivery Record Card, the Post Office can issue an Advice of Delivery receipt which will have the recipient's signature. A small fee is charged to the sender for this service.

SENDING MONEY THROUGH THE POST

Coins will generally not be accepted by the Post Office for posting through the normal posting system. Valuable coins (ie, collectors items) should be delivered by a courier service.

It is not advisable to send notes through the postal service. If the customer does so, the notes should be registered. The Post Office recommends that money sent within Ireland through the post should be in the form of:

a) postal orders or

b) money orders.

POSTAL ORDERS

Postal orders are available in denominations of:

£1s ranging from £1 – £5;

£10s ranging from £10-£50;

£75 and £100.

A **poundage** fee is charged on **every** postal order (see *Post Guide*).

More than one postal order can be used to make up the total amount required, and amounts less than £1 are made up by purchasing normal postage stamps and sticking them on the postal order.

EXAMPLE 1

A customer wishes to send postal orders to the value of £2.64 through the post. The customer will purchase a postal order for £2 (for a **poundage fee** of 55p) and two 32p ordinary postage stamps. The total cost of the purchase will be £3.19 (£2.55 +64p).

EXAMPLE 2

If the Post Office does not have a supply of postal orders in denominations of £2, then the customer must purchase two £1 postal orders at a poundage fee of 50p each. The total cost of purchase will be £3.64 (2 x £1 + (50p x 2) + 64p).

When purchasing a postal order, the name of the payee is filled in and the amount of the postal order is written in words. It is date-stamped by the post official and a counterfoil is given to the customer as proof of purchase. The postal order is valid for six months.

The payee named on the postal order can cash the postal order at any Post Office or bank in Ireland. For extra security, it should be crossed and therefore must be lodged into a bank account or Post Office savings account.

MONEY ORDERS

A money order instructs the Post Office to pay the value of the money order to the person named on the order. Money orders are the Post Office's equivalent of a bank draft and are valid for six months.

A money order can be purchased up to a maximum value of £500. If a customer wishes to send more than £500, a second money order may be purchased, or the balance may be made up with postal orders.

The customer is charged a commission on purchase of the money order. The current commission charges are £2.25 for a money order up to the value of £100 and £2.75 for a money order ranging in value from £100 – £500.

As one money order is available for any amount up to £500, it may be cheaper than purchasing postal orders.

Airmail Services

AIRMAIL – SWIFTPOST

Swiftpost is a **priority letter service** from An Post. The Swiftpost items receive special priority handling and separate sorting which ensures a faster delivery worldwide. Swiftpost envelopes or labels are easily identified and have bar codes so that letters can be traced by the **track 'n' trace** system. International Swiftpost mail is dispatched on the first available air flight to another country. However, at present, international bound post can only be traced up to the point of departure from Ireland.

An Post also operates a **Swiftpost** service within Ireland and the post receives priority sorting and distribution over mainstream post.

Using Swiftpost envelopes
1. Insert letter into Swiftpost envelope and complete the name and address of addressee on the front of the envelope.
2. Hand the envelope to the post clerk who will complete a receipt with the corresponding Swiftpost number.
3. The post clerk will date stamp the receipt and return it to you.
4. This receipt is used by the customer to query missing or delayed post.

Using Swiftpost labels
Here the procedure is similar to using Swiftpost envelopes except that an ordinary addressed envelope is used and a Swiftpost label is placed over the top of the envelope with the bar code towards the back of the envelope.

Swiftpost envelope and label

AEROGRAMMES

An aerogramme is a lightweight paper that folds into an envelope and can be purchased from the Post Office or from a stationery supplier. A customer may use an aerogramme rather than a postcard to write a brief but confidential letter to someone abroad. The cost of an aerogramme, including postage, is currently 45p worldwide.

Aerogramme

AIRMAIL

Ordinary letters that are destined for abroad, delivered through the regular postal system are denoted by a special sticker attached to the envelope stating 'par avion' or 'airmail'. Airmail stickers are used to sort airmail from ordinary national post. However, there is no priority distribution on airmail letters, thus airmail is suitable when speed of delivery is not essential. It is cheaper to send letters by airmail rather than using the Swiftpost service.

Airmail sticker

Business Response Services from An Post

An Post provides businesses with opportunities to use the postal system to allow customers reply to their business free of charge using business reply and freepost services. To avail of these two services, a business response licence is obtained from the Post Office and the business pays the postage charge plus 1p handling fee for every item that is received using these services.

The business may use the business response licence to generate sales orders, receive donations and obtain information by:

1. sending customers a postage-paid, pre-addressed reply card (business reply service)
2. allowing customers to reply to general advertisements using a special Freepost address.

BUSINESS REPLY SERVICE

The business reply service consists of special, pre-printed envelopes or cards with the business licence number, name and address, followed by the words 'Business Reply' and the post district. These are enclosed with literature sent by the business. The recipient will use the business reply envelope or card to respond. No postage is paid by the recipient and the business only pays for the replies it receives.

POSTAGE TO BE PAID BY LICENSEE	No Postage Stamp necessary if posted in the Republic of Ireland

Licence Number

Name of Company Ltd
Full Postal Address
Business Reply
Post Town (District No. if there is one)

Business reply envelope

FREEPOST

A business using the Freepost service **does not** have to enclose a pre-printed envelope or card. The customer replying to the business will use their own stationery and will address the envelope with the business Freepost address as agreed with the Post Office.

A Freepost address is used by a business that advertises in media such as newspapers, radio or TV where the inclusion of a pre-printed card or envelope is not possible. However, a business can also use a pre-printed card or envelope with the agreed Freepost address printed.

Collecting Post

POSTE RESTANTE

Poste Restante or post 'to be called for' is a facility offered by An Post for people travelling who do not have a known address. Post can be addressed to the person travelling in care of a specified Post Office. The post is held at the Post Office for three months.

PRIVATE POST BOX

An Post operates a private post box facility for customers who do not have a regular address or who do not wish correspondents to know their address. The customer/business is allocated a private box number where post can be addressed and delivered to. Private box numbers are common where employers have a job vacancy but do not wish to declare the location of the vacancy to the public. Respondents are given a box number to apply to and the employer collects the replies from the private post box.

PASSPORT EXPRESS

An Post has recently arranged with the Passport Office to allow customers obtain their passport through the Post Office. Passport application forms are available at the Post Office and the customer places the completed form in a special passport express envelope. Everything is paid at the Post Office, ie, the passport fee plus the cost of the service. All applications are sent by Swiftpost and the passport can be collected at the Post Office within 10 working days.

Direct Marketing Facilities
POSTAIM

Postaim is a service that allows a business to distribute mailshots, product samples, leaflets, brochures or other promotional material through the normal postal system to a specific target market, for example, every household that has teenagers living at home. The material to be delivered is addressed by the business, and the postmen deliver the **addressed** items as they are delivering the normal post. The fee charged depends on the number and weight of items to be distributed.

PUBLICITY POST

Publicity post is similar to Postaim, but it does not require names and addresses on the items to be delivered. The promotional material is delivered to every address in a postal district. The fee charged depends on the size of the district covered.

MICROPOST

MicroPost is an electronic postal distribution service offered by Post Gem, a separate division of An Post. The business sends the prepared document along with the desired mailing list, via a computer, to Post Gem. Post Gem prints the documents, inserts them in envelopes and puts them in the regular postal system or other services on the same day. The business is relieved of dealing with regular administration, saving time and money.

Courier Services

National and international courier services are available from private firms (eg, Securicor, Elan) and An Post. A courier will deliver parcels, letters and documents hand to hand, outside the normal postal system. Courier services are generally more expensive than the normal postal system of delivery, but on-time delivery is guaranteed.

A business will use a courier to deliver documents or parcels where:
1. the post must be received urgently
2. the post is valuable or confidential and the business does not wish to rely on normal post services
3. the business has missed the normal collection time for outgoing post

The business can arrange for such items to be collected by the courier and delivered directly to the hands of the addressee. The terms of delivery depend on the distance travelled, the value of the item and the urgency and time of delivery. Damage or loss of items is covered by transit insurance.

An Post Courier Services

The courier services provided by An Post are carried out by a separate division of An Post called SDS – Special Distribution Services. SDS provides Parcel Forward and Collect on Delivery (COD) facilities on its national and international distribution services. The maximum weight of parcels for most SDS services is 30 kg and they must not be greater than 1.5 metres in length.

PARCEL FORWARD SERVICE

A business may wish to offer customers the facility of returning parcels without the customer being charged for the postage. SDS will deliver parcels where the postal charges have not yet been paid and the postage charge is paid by the business receiving the parcel. There is an annual fee of £100 and a service charge of 10p per parcel in addition to the normal cost of delivery.

COLLECT ON DELIVERY (COD)

This service is used by a business where the customer has not yet paid for the goods purchased. The courier collects the value of the parcel (trade charge) plus the service fee from the addressee on behalf of the sender. The trade charge is then sent to the sender of the package. Each COD parcel is insured against physical loss or damage in transit. The value of the item (trade charge) cannot exceed £1,000.

SDS NATIONAL SERVICES

SDS operates three basic services within Ireland:

SDS Regular

The customer wishing to use this service brings the parcel to a Post Office within normal working hours. The parcels are collected by the courier from the Post Office and deliveries are made within an average of 24 hours nationwide, Monday to Friday.

The fees charged for delivery depend on the weight of the item, ranging from £2.40 (items under 1 kg) to £6.80 for the maximum weight of 30 kg. The parcel can be insured and an Advice of Delivery receipt obtained for an additional fee.

SDS Regular is more suited to the general public and small businesses than to a business that has extensive delivery requirements.

EMS (Express Mail Service)

EMS is a guaranteed overnight, pre-noon parcel delivery service nationwide. Parcels can be **collected on demand** from individual addresses in the following cities: Waterford, Cork, Limerick, Galway and Dublin. Customers outside these areas can bring the parcel to any Post Office for collection by the courier. A Saturday service is provided in cities only (at present) for an additional fee.

All EMS items are automatically covered by transit insurance for loss or damage and a money-back guarantee if the item is not delivered on time. The sender can obtain an Advice of Delivery receipt for an additional fee.

This service is more commonly used by a business then SDS Regular as transit insurance and a money-back guarantee are automatically included in the cost of delivery.

Business Special

Business Special is a 24-hour collection and delivery service available to the business community only. The business enters into a **contract** with Business Special for delivery of a minimum number of items. The charge for items delivered is negotiated with each business. Parcels are delivered nationwide by the close of the following working day.

Like EMS, the items are covered by transit insurance and an Advice of Delivery receipt can be obtained.

	SDS Regular	**EMS**	**Business Special**
Delivery	24 hrs average to every address Monday - Friday	Guaranteed pre-noon nationwide Monday - Saturday	24hr collection and delivery to businesses only Monday–Friday
Insurance cover	Optional	Included	Included
Advice of Delivery	On request	On request	On request
Collected by courier at	Post Office	Post Office and specified city addresses	Business Address
Time for collection by courier	Post Office working hours	Post Office working hours and before 2 pm from specified city addresses	Negotiable

Summary – SDS courier services

SDS INTERNATIONAL SERVICES

SDS also operates three worldwide courier services.

EMS (Courier) Service

This services guarantees delivery to over 200 destinations worldwide. Delivery times depend on time of postage (obtained from the local Post Office). Delivery is covered by transit insurance to the maximum value of £5000.

Priority (air)

Parcels that are delivered using the Priority (air) service should bear a special Priority label and an insurance form OE500 must be completed.

Economy (surface)

The economy service is generally used for bulk parcels that are not time-sensitive. Delivery times can vary depending on the size of the dispatch. An Economy service label is attached to the parcel.

Non-postal Services supplied by the Post Office

An Post operates many non-postal services for the general public. Customers can place money in deposit accounts and special savings accounts and can purchase lottery tickets, TV licences, dog licences, greeting cards and stationery in most Post Offices. An Post is also the state agency responsible for distributing social welfare payments to the general public.

As a result of increased competition and changes in legislation, An Post now operates a service for those customers who wish to pay their bills (eg, ESB, gas, Telecom Eireann) through the Post Office.

Summary

Businesses may adopt varying procedures for dealing with the post. In a large business, there may be a centralised post area, or separate post room. Post clerks will receive, sort and distribute incoming post to the addressee and will be responsible for outgoing post. Outgoing post must be collected, parceled, weighed and franked for dispatch. The post clerk must be trained in the procedures of dealing with post to prevent delay or the loss of post.

The typical equipment used in the post room is:

letter opening equipment, date stamp, distribution equipment such as trolleys and baskets, dispatch equipment such as weighscales, addressing printer machine, franking machine and sundries such as stationery and parcel wrapping materials

All businesses should be familiar with the services available from An Post, ie, registered mail, recorded delivery, sending money through the post, airmail services, business response services, collection services, direct marketing facilities and SDS courier services.

Questions

Multiple Choice Questions

1. **Track 'n' Trace** is a new development in An Post that:
   a) delivers post by rail
   b) records the route of post during transit using bar coded stickers and scanners
   c) records international post to point of delivery
   d) delivers post by rail **and** air for a faster service
   e) guarantees to deliver post within 48 hours

2. Which of the following is an incorrect procedure when dispatching post?
   a) Collect post for dispatch from various out-trays
   b) Check documents for signatures and enclosures
   c) Open all post, except post marked 'private'
   d) Staple enclosures securely
   e) Weigh the letters using the *Post Guide* as a reference
   f) Bring post to the Post Office

3. Which of the following types of post should the secretary **not** open?
   a) personal & confidential letters
   b) post addressed 'to whom it may concern'
   c) post addressed to 'the Company'
   d) parcels delivered by courier with no address
   e) parcels addressed to 'the Manager'

4. Recorded delivery is where a customer:
   a) requires proof of postage
   b) requires proof of delivery
   c) returns post delivered to the wrong address
   d) requests that post be delivered to a forwarding address
   e) requests that post be delivered to a private box number

5. A customer who registers a letter is given a date-stamped receipt. This receipt is called:
   a) a certificate of postage
   b) an Advice of Delivery
   c) Swiftpost
   d) *Poste Restante*
   e) a postal order

6. A franking machine is used to:
   a) open the letters individually
   b) place the value of postage on envelopes and parcels
   c) date-stamp incoming post
   d) stack incoming post in bundles for distribution
   e) record the private usage of stamps

7. A date-stamping machine would be used in the post room for:
   a) outgoing mail
   b) circulation of memos
   c) acknowledging incoming mail
   d) placing a postage stamp on an envelope
   e) outgoing Swiftpost items

8. A jogger machine is used in the post room to:
   a) open a large quantity of letters and parcels
   b) place addresses automatically on envelopes
   c) align sheets of paper together for stapling or binding
   d) measure the weight of a parcel
   e) fold and insert letters in envelopes

9. To avail of the cheapest rates of postage nationally, an ordinary sealed envelope should weigh:
   a) less than 20 grams
   b) between 30 and 35 grams
   c) between 35 and 40 grams
   d) between 40 and 50 grams
   e) 25 grams

10. A customer who wishes to send £350 from Cork to Wicklow through the post is advised to:
    a) send postal orders
    b) send a money order
    c) send notes and coins
    d) send an aerogramme
    e) send the money through Swiftpost

11. The charge on a postal order is called:
    a) commission
    b) fee
    c) poundage fee
    d) extra charge
    e) service charge

12. The PO Business Reply Service enables:
    a) customers to reply to businesses without paying postage
    b) customers to reply to businesses at a cheap rate
    c) businesses to correspond with each other using a rapid delivery service
    d) businesses to write to the Post Office without paying postage
    e) customers to reply to a business private box number

13. The direct marketing facility from An Post that allows addressed mail be delivered to customers is called:
    a) EMS
    b) Publicity Post
    c) SDS
    d) Postaim
    e) COD

14. COD applies where:
    a) the sender delivers the post personally to the addressee
    b) the sender will pay the courier in advance of delivery
    c) the Post Office will retain the post until the customer calls to the Post Office
    d) the Post Office cannot deliver the post and returns it to the sender
    e) trade charge and fee are collected by the courier from the addressee

15. A business wishes to make a special offer to its customers. Which one of these postal services would bring the best response?
    a) Express Mail
    b) Cash on Delivery
    c) *Poste Restante*
    d) Business Reply Service
    e) Recorded Delivery   (NCVA 1994)

16. What is the cost of sending a letter weighing under 20g to countries in the European Union?
    a) 28p
    b) 32p
    c) 38p
    d) 40p
    e) 52p   (NCVA 1994)

17. Which of the following is **not** a mailing service offered by An Post?
a) EMS Regular
b) Royal Mail Special Delivery
c) Swiftpost
d) Mail Mover
e) Special Distribution Service   (NCVA 1996)

Short Questions

1. List three items of equipment used to dispatch outgoing post and explain their use.
2. What is the Post Office service which is designed to encourage people to reply to advertisements in newspapers without paying postage costs?
3. How should money be sent through the post?
4. Where can you find information regarding the current rates of postage, weight and size?
5. Write short notes on the following Post Office services:
a) Recorded Delivery
b) Registered Post
c) Swiftpost
6. How do you deal with incoming post marked urgent?
7. You are in charge of incoming post and receive three cheques in the morning post, what should you do?
8. List two items of equipment used in the mail room to deal with incoming mail.
9. What checks should be made before using the franking machine?
10. Write a short note on the following Post Office services:
a) Collect on Delivery
b) *Poste Restante*
c) Parcel Forward Service
11. List three advantages and three disadvantages of the franking machine.
12. List two differences between postal orders and money orders.
13. Describe the three national courier services provided by An Post.
14. Explain the new 'track 'n' trace' service provided by An Post.
15. List at least three non-postal services provided by An Post.
16. List **four** items of equipment in the mail room and say what each is used for. (NCVA 1994)
17. List **four** items of equipment in a well equipped mail room.   (NCVA 1995)
18. Outline **four** procedures you should follow to open, sort and distribute the incoming mail.   (NCVA 1996)
19. List **four** items which are used in the preparation of outgoing mail. (NCVA 1996)

20. Prioritise the following items of mail received in the post for Mr A Murphy, Buying Manager.

(a) an order received from a customer

(b) an advertising brochure

(c) a 'personal' letter addressed to Mr Murphy

(d) an 'urgent' letter

(NCVA 1996)

Assignments

1. You have just been promoted and a new office junior will take your place in the office. Write a brief report on how to deal with incoming post.

2. Your company supplies office equipment. The following is a list of incorrectly addressed post which you must open. Decide which department should deal with the letters. The company's departments are Accounts, Personnel, Sales and Purchasing.

(a) cheque received from a customer for goods received

(b) enquiry for a quotation on prices of filing cabinets

(c) catalogues from a manufacturer of office furniture

(d) a letter from the local secretarial college enquiring about employing students on work experience

(e) form from the Revenue Commissioners requesting financial information

3. Use the *Post Guide* to cost the following:

parcel for France weighing 1 kg

parcel for England weighing 275 g

parcel for Zambia (Africa) weighing 4 kg

parcel for Roscommon weighing 159 g

5. Money and Banking

After studying this chapter you should be able to:

- ◆ Distinguish between central, merchant and commercial banks
- ◆ Explain the services provided by the commercial banks in Ireland
- ◆ Describe the features of current and deposit accounts
- ◆ Outline the procedure to follow when receiving a cheque as payment
- ◆ Explain how to prepare a lodgement for the bank
- ◆ Explain methods of payment through the electronic banking system
- ◆ Outline the methods of carrying money when abroad

Introduction

Banking in Ireland has changed dramatically over the past decade. There has been a definite move to a cashless society and to reduce the amount of form filling created by banking transactions. Modern technology has facilitated this with the introduction of electronic banking. Electronic banking simply means transferring funds from one account to another by electronic means which has reduced the necessity of carrying large quantities of cash.

The Irish Banks

The **Central Bank of Ireland** is responsible for the management of the national reserves, ie, it is the banker for the Government. Its main function to is formulate monetary policy and to protect the Irish punt from devaluation. The Central Bank controls interest rates, issues currency and acts as a lender to the commercial banks.

A business may deal with two main types of banks: a **merchant bank** and a **commercial bank**. A **merchant bank** (referred to as a 'wholesale bank') specialises in providing high level finances for business rather than personal customers. Examples of merchant banks include Hill Samuel Bank Ltd and Guinness & Mahon Ltd.

The majority of banking requirements of a business and personal customers will be catered for by a **commercial bank**. The Irish commercial banks are Allied Irish Bank, Bank of Ireland, Ulster Bank and National Irish Bank.

The following services are available for both business and personal customers:

♦ Loan Facilities
♦ Current Accounts
♦ Deposit Accounts
♦ Electronic Funds Transfer
♦ Foreign Exchange

Loan Facilities

Loans can be offered on a short-term (up to one year), medium-term (from one to five years) or long-term basis (more than five years). A business may need a short-term loan or overdraft facility if there is an immediate cash flow shortage, or loans may be required by the business on a medium or long-term basis to invest in new products, equipment, premises or other assets.

Current Accounts

Current accounts are frequently used to cater for day-to-day financial transactions (ie, lodgements and withdrawals). The bank requires two references, specimen signatures and a sum of money to be deposited before a current account can be opened.

When a current account is opened, a cheque book and cheque guarantee card are issued to facilitate the payment of bills. The cheque guarantee card is a guarantee by the bank that cheques will be paid. At present, the bank guarantees cheques up to a maximum of £100.

Features of a Current Account

♦ Money can be lodged and withdrawn on demand
♦ **Cheque books** and **cheque guarantee cards** are issued in the name of the account holder.
♦ An overdraft facility may be available.
♦ A **bank statement** is received monthly or on demand.
♦ Standing orders and direct debits can be paid to and from the current account.
♦ Eurocheques and Eurocards can be issued on a current account.
♦ Interest can be earned on current accounts if a credit balance is maintained over a period of time.

The Cheque and Cheque Guarantee Card

A cheque is a written instruction to the bank to pay the sum of money that is written both in words and figures to the person named on the cheque.

One card is now available that combines a cheque guarantee card, automatic teller machine (ATM) card and debit card.

There are three parties to a cheque:

a) **the drawer:** The account holder or person authorised to sign the cheques.

b) **the drawee:** The bank on which the cheque is drawn.

c) **the payee:** The person named on the cheque to receive the payment.

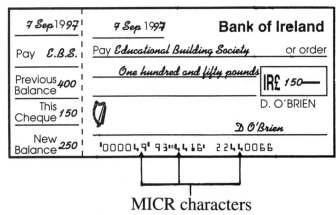

MICR characters

Cheque and stub

A cheque contains the following pre-printed information:

◆ cheque number

◆ the current account number and name of account holder

◆ the address and sorting code of the bank

◆ a space for signing, dating and writing the value of the cheque in words and figures

◆ the bank logo

COMPLETING A CHEQUE

The cheque is completed by filling in the following details:

1. Name of payee

2. Amount of the cheque in words and amount in figures.

3. The drawer's signature

4. Date

5. The drawer may cross the cheque to make it more secure. The cheque counterfoil (stub) is completed and retained by the drawer to check with his/her **bank statement.**

In practice, office personnel may fill in the cheques and obtain the signatures from management or whoever is authorised to sign the cheque for the business.

If the cheque is incorrectly completed, the bank will return it to the payee marked 'refer to drawer'. The payee must return the cheque to the drawer who may write a new cheque, or initial any alterations made on the existing cheque.

A completed cheque is legal tender and the payee can:

1. Lodge the cheque to their own bank account.
2. Bring the cheque to the bank and exchange it for cash.
3. **Endorse** the cheque to a third party (eg a retailer in exchange for goods).

Cheques that are not fully completed, but are signed, are known as **blank** cheques. Blank cheques can be given to a person to fill in the amount due. Not recommended.

SECURING THE CHEQUE

To reduce the risk of an unauthorised person cashing a cheque, the following precautions can be taken:

1. Write the amount in words and figures close together to prevent alterations being made. Use a dash (-) instead of a decimal point. (The decimal point could be changed to a comma!)
2. Keep the cheque guarantee card separate from the cheque. Most retailers will not accept a cheque unless a cheque guarantee card is also presented.
3. Cross the cheque.

Crossing a cheque

The purpose of crossing a cheque is to make it more difficult for an unauthorised person to cash the cheque as the crossed cheque must be lodged to the payee's account. Cheques that are not crossed are referred to as **open** cheques.

A cheque is crossed by drawing two parallel lines across the face of the cheque. A crossed cheque may be 'opened' by the drawer writing 'pay cash' between the parallel lines. This crossing instructs the bank to pay cash to the payee in exchange for the cheque.

There are two types of crossings:

1. <u>General crossings</u>
   a) with or without the words '& Co'. This cheque can be endorsed and lodged into any bank account.
   b) with the words 'not negotiable'. This cheque must be lodged to the payee's account.
   c) with a stated limit to safeguard against a third party adding additional figures and words to the amount written on the cheque.
   d) with the words 'a/c payee only'. This cheque must be lodged to the payee's account via any commercial bank.

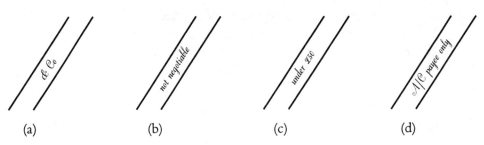

General crossings

2. Special crossings
    a) with the name of a commercial bank. This cheque can be lodged at any branch of the specified bank.
    b) with the bank and branch address specified. This cheque must be lodged at the branch specified.

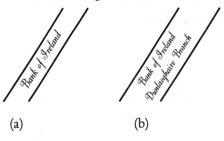

Special crossings

ENDORSING A CHEQUE

The payee can transfer a cheque to a third party by signing (endorsing) their name on the reverse of the cheque. This **endorsement** instructs the bank to pay the third party the amount of the cheque. A cheque can be endorsed many times.

THE JOURNEY OF A CHEQUE

The following example simplifies what happens to the cheque when it is presented for payment.

EXAMPLE

Mr O'Donovan writes a cheque for £350 to Ms O'Neill. Ms O'Neill's bank account is in Tralee and Mr O' Donovan's bank account is in Limerick.

1. On receipt of the cheque, Ms O'Neill lodges the cheque to her bank account in Tralee.
2. The Tralee bank **credits** (increases) Ms O'Neill's account with the value of the cheque.
3. The cheque is then sent by the Tralee Bank to the clearing bank in Dublin.
4. The clearing bank sends the cheque back to Mr O'Donovan's bank in Limerick.
5. The Limerick Bank **debits** (decreases) Mr O'Donovan's current account with the value of the cheque.

At present, the processing of a cheque may take up to three working days. Technology is currently being introduced to reduce this processing time.

RECEIVING A CHEQUE FOR PAYMENT

When a personal cheque is received over the counter:

a) request the customer's cheque guarantee card and check expiry date.

b) check payee's name and date on the cheque. **Post-dated** cheques (cheques written for a future date) and **stale** cheques (more than 6 months old) should not be accepted.

c) Check that the amount in words and the amount in figures on the cheque correspond.

d) Check that the name and signature on the card and on the cheque correspond.

e) Write the card number and expiry date on the back of the cheque. This guarantees that the cheque will be paid by the bank, if amount does not exceed £100.

BANK STATEMENT

A bank statement is sent to the account holder on a monthly basis or is available on request. The statement shows all transactions that have occurred on the account within that period, eg, lodgements made, cheques presented to the bank for payment, standing orders and direct debits processed, bank charges and any other withdrawals made from the account.

The final figure on the statement is the **bank balance**, ie, the amount of money remaining in the account. However this may not be the true balance at the time the business receives the statement. For example, there may be cheques that the business has lodged to the bank, but have not yet been processed.

When the business receives the bank statement, the account clerk should check the entries on the statement with the business records (ie, cheque stubs, lodgement and withdrawal counterfoils) to establish the current balance. A **bank reconciliation statement** is prepared, which shows what the final balance on the account should be after adjusting for lodgements or withdrawals not shown on the bank statement.

Account Statement					

Account Holder
PAT KELLY
Current Account

Bank of Ireland
DUN LAOGHAIRE, CO. DUBLIN
Tel: (01) 2800273
Fax: (01) 2800810

Post to
Mr Pat Kelly
"Woodview"
Leixlip
Co Kildare

Page   **1**   **of**   **1**

90–11–10
Branch Code

103
Statement Number

30 Dec 1996
Date of Statement

862700256
Account Number

DATE	DETAILS		DEBIT	CREDIT	BALANCE
1996					
29 Nov	Balance Forward				1120.20
2 Dec	New Ireland – Life	DD	31.90		1088.30
	Pass 29 Nov		60.00		1028.30
	Pat Kelly	SO	100.00		928.30
4 Dec	AMV00102281	DD	14.41		913.89
6 Dec	PASS 06Dec		10.00		903.89
	Banking 365 Access		296.60		607.29
9 Dec	Cheque	493	50.00		557.29
	Current Account Fees		10.80		546.49
11 Dec	Giro Credit			1500.00	2046.49
16 Dec	Pass 16Dec		150.00		1896.49
17 Dec	Cheque	495	120.00		1776.49
20 Dec	In Branch Cr			250.00	2026.49
23 Dec	Banking 365 Access		420.00		1606.49

Bank statement

OVERDRAFT FACILITY

An overdraft facility is available on a current account, ie, the bank will make extra funds available for a short period of time, usually up to one year. Cheques may be written or cash withdrawn to the limit of the overdraft.

An annual fee is charged for this facility and interest is charged on amounts overdrawn. However, the bank will retain the right to demand repayment of the advance made to the business at any time.

Deposit Accounts (or Savings Accounts)

All the commercial banks provide facilities for their customers to place money on deposit. A deposit account is a savings account where interest is earned and withdrawals can be made on demand.

To open an ordinary deposit account, the customer must bring two forms of identification to the bank and must make a lodgement of at least £1. An application form is completed and signed by the customer. The customer may be issued with a deposit book where a bank official records each lodgment and withdrawal. The customer may also apply for an ATM card to access their account.

GENERAL FEATURES OF ORDINARY DEPOSIT ACCOUNTS
- Used for customers who wish to save money.
- Interest is earned on the money on deposit.
- Interest is calculated according to the length of time the money is on deposit.
- Interest is subject to DIRT (Deposit Interest Retention Tax – 26%). This is deducted by the bank on behalf of the Government and the balance is credited to the account.
- Cheques cannot be drawn.
- Bank statements are issued.

If the business has excess money, it may invest in some of the following accounts:

SPECIAL SAVINGS ACCOUNTS (SSA)

Special savings accounts have been introduced by all banks to avail of special tax savings.
- The DIRT on interest earned is reduced to 15%.
- Interest can be paid to the account holder as income. It can be lodged to the customer's bank account or a cheque can be sent by the bank.
- There is a minimum opening balance of £1,000 and a maximum of £50,000 can be deposited.
- Notice of 30 days must be given to the bank before withdrawing money.
- No withdrawals can be made until 90 days after the account has been opened.

FIXED TERM DEPOSIT ACCOUNTS

A fixed term deposit account allows the customer to deposit lump sums for a fixed period of time. At the end of the term, the initial investment is returned plus the interest earned. Withdrawals from the account can be made, but there may be a charge attached. Interest is subject to DIRT at the standard rate.

Lodgements

Lodgements to the bank can be made by:

◆ completing a lodgment slip in the bank
◆ using the automatic teller machine (ATM)
◆ using the night-safe facility
◆ using the express lodgement facility in the bank

PREPARING A LODGEMENT

When preparing money (notes, coins and cheques) for lodgement to a bank account:

1. Count all coins and place in money bags available from the bank. Count notes and cheques separately.
2. Sort the notes into similar denominations facing upwards to facilitate counting. Place into bundles that are easy to count, eg, bundles of £100, and secure with an elastic band.
3. Record the value of the lodgement (ie, total coins, notes and cheques) on your own records, noting the value, number and drawer of each cheque.
4. Fill in the lodgement slip before you go to the bank.
5. Ensure that the bank official stamps the counterfoil on the lodgement slip and returns it to you as proof of lodgement.

Cash and security

1. Lock cash away in a safe at night and during the day if necessary.
2. Count cash in a private area, eg, a back room with the door locked.
3. Do not open the safe when there are other people in the office.
4. Request an escort while going to the bank when carrying large sums of money.
5. Vary the times and days of carrying out the lodgement.
6. Remove surplus cash from tills regularly.
7. Fill in the lodgement slips before going to the bank.

LODGEMENT SLIP

Businesses that lodge money regularly will be issued with a lodgement book containing a series of lodgement slips, with the business account number and name pre-printed on the slip. Alternatively, individual lodgement slips are obtainable at the bank. The completed lodgement slip shows:

◆ the account number, name and address of the business
◆ name of bank, branch and sorting code
◆ the amount of the lodgement in notes, coins and cheques (these may be listed on the back of the lodgement slip)
◆ the date of the lodgement
◆ the signature of the person lodging the money
◆ The lodgement counterfoil (stub) is date-stamped by the bank as a receipt

Lodgement slip   *Lodgement stub*

THE AUTOMATIC TELLER MACHINE (ATM)

The automatic teller machine allows customers to access their accounts both within and outside banking hours. The customer is issued with an ATM card and a personal identification number (PIN). It is very important that card and PIN are kept separately to prevent someone accessing the account. Cash can also be retrieved from the ATM using a credit card or Eurocard.

The ATM can be used to:
◆ withdraw cash from an account
◆ lodge money to an account
◆ pay bills such as Visa or ESB
◆ order a new cheque book, bank statement
◆ change the PIN number
◆ make an enquiry on an account balance
Some ATMs will issue foreign currency

LODGING MONEY USING THE ATM:

◆ Complete a lodgement slip
◆ Place the cash and lodgement slip in a special lodgement envelope
◆ Insert ATM card in the ATM machine and key in PIN
◆ Select lodgement option from the display screen
◆ Key in the amount to be lodged
◆ Insert the envelope in the chute and wait for receipt from ATM

ATM machine

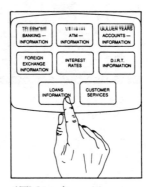

ATM touch-sensitive screen

LODGING MONEY USING THE NIGHT SAFE

The night-safe service enables a business to lodge money after banking hours. The business is issued with a lodgement book, lockable leather wallet and key to the night safe.

The completed lodgement slip and money are placed in the wallet. The wallet is locked and placed in the night vault of the bank through the night safe entrance.

The wallet is retrieved and normally opened in the presence of two bank officials the following day. The money is counted and lodged to the business account specified on the lodgement slip.

The business may request that the night lodgement is not opened until a member of the business is present to watch the contents being counted.

LODGING MONEY USING THE EXPRESS LODGEMENT FACILITY

The commercial banks have a quick lodgement mail box facility within the bank for those customers who wish to lodge money during banking hours.

◆ Place cash, notes and cheques and completed lodgement slip into the lodgement envelope and seal.

◆ Deposit the lodgement in the Express Lodgement box.

A receipt is not given immediately. The customer may request the bank to date-stamp the lodgement stub and return it to the customer when the lodgement is processed.

Withdrawals

Money can be withdrawn from bank accounts in a variety of ways:

1. by filling in a withdrawal slip at the bank
2. using the ATM machine
3. cheques
4. Electronic Funds Transfer (EFT)

Withdrawal slip

Withdrawal counterfoil

Electronic Funds Transfer (EFT)

Electronic Funds Transfer is a safe and more convenient method of paying bills, ie, transferring funds from one account to another automatically, without handling cash or cheques. Bills can be paid automatically through the bank, once the service has been agreed by the business and the bank.

Standing orders, direct debits and bank giros are common methods of paying bills using EFT.

STANDING ORDERS

A standing order is used to make payments of a **fixed** amount from one account to another account on a regular basis, eg, weekly, monthly or yearly. This facility ensures that payments are made on time.

To set up the standing order facility, the customer must complete a standing order form (mandate) giving the following details:

◆ name and account number from which payment is made
◆ name, address and branch code of the bank receiving the payment
◆ name and account number of the account receiving the payment
◆ amount of payment
◆ frequency of payment
◆ date of each payment

Standing orders are typically used to: pay insurance premiums, equipment rentals, mortgage repayments and regular lodgements to deposit accounts. The standing order can be cancelled upon the written instruction of the customer.

There is a setting-up fee and a transaction fee on each standing order. At present standing orders are not set up for sterling amounts.

Advantages of standing orders

1. Payments are automatically deducted from the customer's current account and paid into the account named on the standing order.
2. Safe method of ensuring payments of a fixed amount are paid on time.
3. Details of the standing order transactions are shown on the bank statement.
4. Special discounts may be availed of by paying bills on time.

DIRECT DEBIT

A direct debit is used to make payments of **variable** amounts from one account to another account on a regular or irregular basis. For example, Telecom Éireann and the ESB must be paid regularly, but are of irregular amounts. Usually a business offers the facility of paying bills by direct debit by sending its customers a direct debit mandate to complete. A direct debit can be cancelled on written request to the bank.

EXAMPLE

The Gas Company sends the customer a direct debit mandate to complete.

The customer signs the form, giving their account name, number and bank branch and returns the direct debit form to the gas company.

The Gas Company sends the direct debit mandate to the customer's bank authorising the bank to debit the amount of the gas bill from the customer's account.

The Gas Company is credited with the amount of the bill.

Details of the direct debit transaction are shown on the customer's bank statement.

Advantages of direct debits

1. Payments are automatically deducted from the customer's current account and paid into the account named on the direct debit mandate.
2. Safe method of ensuring payment of variable amounts on a regular or irregular basis.
3. Details of the direct debit amount are shown on the bank statement.
4. Special discounts may be availed of by paying bills on time.

BANK GIRO/CREDIT TRANSFER SYSTEM

The bank giro/credit transfer system is used to pay money directly to a bank account or several bank accounts with the minimum amount of administration, and is commonly used to pay wages.

The bank giro system is available under:

a) EFT and
b) the manual system
a) With the EFT system, a computerised payroll package (agreed with the bank) is used to calculate the wages and prepare summary details of employees. This information is sent directly to the bank via computer or by disk. The information is processed and the wages are transferred automatically to the appropriate accounts, ie, the business account is debited with the total wage bill and each employee's account is credited with the wages due. No credit card slips are prepared and therefore processing time is reduced.
b) With the manual system the wages are calculated (either manually or with a computerised payroll package) and the wages clerk prepares a summary listing of the employees' details, ie, employee's name, wage due and bank details (account number, branch and bank). These details are sent to the bank with **one** cheque for the wages bill.

Individual credit transfer slips are prepared and the wages are credited to the appropriate account. This system is slower than EFT.

Other payments such as gas bills, Mastercard bills etc can be paid through the credit transfer system by completing a bank giro form and attaching the appropriate remittances. The processing of bank giro forms may take three working days.

Bank giro form

DEBIT CARDS (LASER)

A relatively new advance in the transfer of funds by electronic means is the introduction of debit cards (eg, Laser is the Irish debit card, Switch is the UK debit card). Debit cards allow the customer to pay for goods at the point of sale or cash desk using the debit card. The retailer will run the debit card through a special 'swipe' machine which links up with the customer's current account. The cost of the goods is automatically deducted from the customer's current account and entered into the retailer's account providing the customer has sufficient funds.

Advantages of debit cards

1. Safer for the customer than carrying cash.
2. The system is on-line (ie, linked directly to the customer's current account) so the retailer is assured of payment immediately to their account if the customer has enough funds.
3. No form filling is required at the point of sale.
4. The customer and retailer receive a record of the transaction immediately.
5. The customer can obtain cash as well as paying for goods in selected retail outlets.

Disadvantages of debit cards

1. At present, very few retailers operate the system.
2. There is no credit available to the customer.
3. Customers cannot view their balance through the 'swipe' machine to ensure they have sufficient funds.
4. If the computer system breaks down, the debit card will not be accepted.

Other methods of payment

CREDIT CARDS

A credit card is used to purchase goods and services on credit. A customer who wishes to obtain a credit card must complete an application form and the bank will determine a credit limit, based on the information received. The customer receives a credit card and PIN from the banks' credit card services centre. The banks may operate a number of credit cards, eg, Allied Irish Banks offers both Visa and Mastercard. The customer should sign the back of the card immediately. This signature is used to verify the identity of the customer when they use the credit card. A bank statement is sent to the customer on a monthly basis with all transaction details, total balance due, any interest charged and minimum payment required.

CREDIT CARDS AND THE RETAILER

Retailers who wish to operate a credit card system for their customers are charged a joining fee and a percentage commission on sales. The retailer is guaranteed payment by the credit card company and will send all credit sales vouchers to the credit card centre for payment. The credit card centre will collect payment from the customer.

The retailer is issued with:

1. a manual imprinter machine to imprint details from the customer's credit card onto a sales voucher.

2. three-part sales vouchers pre-printed with the retailer's name, address and account number. The top copy is given to the customer as a receipt, the bottom copy is used to collect payment from the credit card centre. The other copy is retained by the retailer for their own records.

The retailer can operate an electronic credit card reader which authorises the credit card limit and prints out the sales voucher with the amount of sale.

ACCEPTING THE CREDIT CARD FOR PAYMENT OF GOODS

The salesperson should:

1. Check the expiry date on the credit card.

2. 'Swipe' the card through the electronic reader. This authorises the credit card and prints out a sales voucher.

    If the electronic reader is unavailable, an imprinter machine is used. As this machine cannot verify credit cards, the business will implement a policy, ie, to ring the credit card company for purchases over a specific amount. The credit card centre will also send out a listing of stolen card numbers and the salesperson should check the card number against this list.

To use the imprinter machine:

   a) place the credit card face upwards on the imprinter machine.

   b) place a sales voucher over the credit card.

   c) run the lever on the imprinter machine over the sales voucher and back until the details from the credit card are imprinted on the sales voucher.

   d) Remove the sales voucher and credit card from the machine.

   e) complete the details on sale voucher, ie, date, description of goods and value.

3. Give the sales voucher to the customer to sign and check the signature with the signature on credit card.

4. Give bottom copy of the sales voucher to the customer and retain the other copy.

5. Return the credit card to the customer.

Advantages of the credit card
◆ Guaranteed payment to the retailer.
◆ Convenient for the customer, safer than carrying cash.
◆ The major credit cards are accepted in most countries.
◆ Extended credit facilities for the customer.
◆ Customer can set up a direct debit to pay their credit card bills.
◆ Can be used to withdraw cash from ATMs.
◆ Can be used to withdraw the local currency from an ATM abroad.
◆ A business may give a business credit card to an employee who is travelling on behalf of the business.

Disadvantages of the credit card
◆ Interest rates can be high for customers who do not pay their bills on time.
◆ Retailer is charged commission on sales.
◆ Customer may allow bills to mount up and get into serious debt.
◆ Annual Government tax on the credit card – currently £15.
◆ Interest charged on cash advances from the ATM (if account is not in credit).

BANK DRAFTS

A bank draft is purchased at a bank and like a cheque it is an instruction to a bank to pay the amount of the draft to the payee. The bank guarantees payment on the draft. Bank drafts can also be purchased in foreign currencies. Bank drafts are commonly used where:

Bank draft application form

1. A customer does not have a current account upon which to draw a cheque.
2. Once-off or non-routine payments are required (eg, examination fees).
3. A business is dealing with a new customer for the first time and requests a draft rather than risking a cheque as payment.
4. The customer wishes to send money abroad.

Foreign Exchange

FOREIGN CURRENCY

Most bank branches have a foreign exchange facility. This allows the customer to trade £IR for regular 'hard' (stable) currencies such as dollars, sterling, Deutschmarks, francs, etc. Currency should be ordered in advance of travel, particularly where large amounts are required.

The exchange rates for buying and selling foreign notes and cheques are displayed daily in the bank and these rates are determined by the Central Bank and the world trading markets. The bank will have a different rate for purchasing and selling notes and cheques (including traveller's cheques). The commercial banks will not buy back coins of a foreign denomination. When buying or selling foreign currencies, remember that the banks charge commission on the transaction.

The **Sell rate** is the rate at which the bank will sell foreign currency to the customer.

The **Buy rate** is the rate at which the bank will buy foreign currency from the customer.

If you wish to sell back your foreign currency, the bank will buy it back but at a buy rate which may be lower than that at which you bought initially.

Purchasing foreign currency

When purchasing foreign currency the bank's 'sell' rate is used to calculate the amount of foreign currency sold for £IR 1. The £IR quantity is multiplied by the sell rate.

EXAMPLE 1

Ms Carty wishes to holiday in the USA and has a budget of IR£300. If the bank's 'sell rate' is 1.57, how many US$ can she buy? (Assume no commission.)
Solution
For every IR£1 purchased, Ms Carty will receive US$ 1.57.
For IR£300, Ms Carty receives US$ 471 (ie, £300 x 1.57).

Selling foreign currency

When selling back foreign currency to the bank, the 'buy' rate is used. The foreign currency amount is divided by the buy rate.

EXAMPLE 2

Ms Carty returns from her holiday and discovers a US$ 50 note in her handbag. The 'buy' rate (ie, what the bank will buy the dollars for) is 1.05. How much Irish currency does she receive in exchange for US$ 50? (Assume no commission.)
Solution
Miss Carty will receive IR£47.61 for her US$ 50 note (US$ 50 ÷ 1.05).

TRAVELLER'S CHEQUES

As part of foreign exchange services, the bank will advise customers travelling abroad to use traveller's cheques rather than carry cash. Traveller's cheques are pre-printed cheques of a fixed value which can be exchanged in most countries for purchases or local currency. Banks may not stock weaker currencies eg, African currencies. The customer may purchase traveller's cheques in sterling, dollars (US, Canadian and Australian), francs (French and Swiss), marks, pesetas, and yen. Traveller's cheques should be ordered in advance of travel.

Purchasing traveller's cheques

When purchasing the traveller's cheques, the cheques are signed at the bank by the customer. The customer is presented with a listing of the cheque numbers. This listing should be kept separate from the cheques and is used to secure a refund in case of theft.

If the cheques are stolen or lost, the customer is given a hotline number to the bank: the cheque numbers can be traced and a refund is possible.

A commission is charged when the traveller's cheques are purchased.

When purchasing an item with the traveller's cheques, the customer must countersign the cheques and personal identification is usually required (eg, passport). Change is given in local currency. A commission may be charged.

Unused traveller's cheques can be sold back to the bank at the current exchange rate or kept for future use.

EUROCHEQUES AND EUROCARDS

Eurocheques are available from all the commercial banks in Ireland. The Eurocheque operates as a normal cheque and is widely accepted in Europe. The Eurocheque card guarantees the Eurocheque up to a value (at present) of £140 and can also be used to obtain local currency from an ATM machine. The Eurocheques are processed by the National Eurocheque Clearing Centre and the customer's bank account is debited in punts. A commission is charged to cover processing costs.

OTHER SERVICES AVAILABLE FROM THE COMMERCIAL BANKS

A new development in Irish banking is the introduction of telephone banking, available 24 hours a day, seven days a week.

Customers can:

- check their account balance.
- pay bills, eg, ESB, Telecom, Visa. (Some banks allow the customer to schedule a payment for up to 28 days in advance of the bill falling due.)
- transfer funds from one account to another.
- order statements.

The commercial banks also offer a range of other facilities to provide for all the financial requirements of their customers, such as personal loans, mortgages, commercial leasing facilities, developmental loans, purchase and sales of shares on the stock exchange, treasury services (foreign currency accounts, foreign currency loans, documentary credits for export and importing companies, etc) and an advice service.

Summary

All businesses will use the services provided by the commercial banks. The most common account used is the current account which caters for day-to-day transactions, such as a regular flow of lodgements and withdrawals. Customers are provided with cheques and cheque guarantee cards when a current account is opened. Cheques are a safer method of paying bills than sending money through the post. They can be crossed to make them more secure.

Another safe method of paying bills is through the electronic funds transfer system (EFT), ie, using standing orders, direct debits and bank giro/credit transfers to lodge money to another account.

Payments for retail purchases or services can be made with a credit card or debit card. These are safe methods of buying goods as no cash changes hands.

All details of account transactions can be seen from the bank statement. The customer/business should retain all receipts and check the bank statement to establish the correct balance.

Each of the commercial banks offers a variety of deposit or savings accounts. However, the conditions attached to each account will vary, eg, minimum and maximum investment, rules of withdrawal, interest attached. The customer should shop around to obtain the interest rates and conditions of use that suit their individual requirements.

Building societies (eg, the EBS) and An Post can now offer competitive savings and deposit accounts, some of which can avail of tax reductions on interest earned. The commercial banks have therefore broadened their range of products to include specialist services such as special savings accounts, stock market introductions, home loan centres and financial advice centres.

From both a business and personal point of view, it is important to build up a good relationship with your bank to negotiate terms and conditions of loans and overdraft facilities.

Questions

Multiple Choice Questions

1. Which one of the following banks is **not** a commercial bank?
   a) Allied Irish Banks
   b) Central Bank
   c) Ulster Bank
   d) Bank of Ireland
   e) National Irish Bank

2. Which of the following features is **not** applicable to the deposit account?
   a) a bank statement can be obtained
   b) a cheque book and cheque card are issued to the customer
   c) an ATM card is issued
   d) a deposit book is issued to record lodgements and withdrawals
   e) interest can be earned

3. The minimum amount for investment in a special savings account is:
   a) £50,000
   b) £1,000
   c) £10,000
   d) £5,000
   e) £100

4. An overdraft facility:
   a) allows the customer to withdraw more money from their current account
   b) allows the customer to withdraw more money from their deposit account
   c) is granted automatically with the credit card
   d) is an account overdrawn
   e) allows the customer to withdraw more money from their credit card account

5. The person who signs a cheque is called:
   a) the drawer
   b) the drawee
   c) the payee
   d) the bank official
   e) the bank manager

6. Which of the following is not an example of electronic banking?
   a) direct debit
   b) using the ATM to pay bills
   c) standing order
   d) using the deposit book to lodge money
   e) using a debit card to pay for goods purchased at the EPOS

7. DIRT is charged on special savings accounts at a reduced rate of:
   a) 26%
   b) 48%
   c) 10%
   d) 15%
   e) 25%

8. When lodging a cheque made payable to you, the bank will:
   a) debit your account and credit the account of the drawer
   b) credit your account and debit the account of the drawer
   c) credit your account and credit the account of the drawer
   d) debit your account and debit the account of the drawer
   e) credit your account and debit the bank branch's cheque account

9. Which of the following features is **not** applicable to a current account?
   a) an overdraft facility is available
   b) a cheque book and cheque card are issued to the customer
   c) an ATM card is issued
   d) a deposit book is issued to record lodgements and withdrawals
   e) interest can be earned

10. A cheque which is dated more than six months previously is known as:
    a) a post-dated cheque
    b) a crossed cheque
    c) a stale cheque
    d) a current cheque
    e) an open cheque

11. A credit card allows the customer to:
    a) pay for goods directly from their bank account
    b) receive goods immediately but pay for them later
    c) give the retailer a cheque in payment for the goods
    d) cash Eurocheques
    e) exchange traveller's cheques in a foreign country

12. Which one of the following bank services could be used by an employer to pay employees?
    a) standing order
    b) direct debit
    c) credit transfer
    d) bank statement
    e) ATM

13. A bank draft is used when:
    a) a new customer wishes to open a current account
    b) a customer wishes to pay a bill and does not have a cheque book
    c) a customer wishes to close their current account
    d) a customer is withdrawing money from their deposit account
    e) a customer is lodging money to their deposit account

14. Which of the following is out of sequence when accepting payment by credit card?
    a) check expiry date on the credit card
    b) ask the customer to sign the sales voucher
    c) authorise the payment with the credit card company
    d) fill in the details of the sale
    e) return a copy of the sales voucher to the customer

15. When you are travelling to America, the bank will advise you to take:
    a) a cheque book
    b) cash
    c) traveller's cheques
    d) Eurocheques
    e) a bank draft

16. When a customer is buying foreign currency at a bank, the bank will:
    a) use the buy rate to sell the currency
    b) use the sell rate to buy the currency
    c) use the buy rate to buy the currency
    d) use the sell rate to sell the currency
    e) issue the customer with a Eurocheque book

17. Your boss wishes to take 500 dollars with him to America. The rate of exchange is 2.5 dollars to the Irish pound. How much money will you need to buy 500 dollars?
    a) £200
    b) £1,250
    c) £250
    d) £2,500
    e) £125

18. If the sell rate for sterling is 1.06 and you wish to exchange £IR50, how much sterling would you get?
    a) £53
    b) £47.16
    c) £51.06
    d) £48.94
    e) £50

19. The banking service used for the payment of several creditors without the drawer having to prepare separate cheques for each is:
    a) a standing order
    b) credit transfer
    c) direct debit
    d) a banker's draft
    e) credit card

(NCVA 1996)

Short Questions

1. Describe the parties to a cheque.
2. How can a customer's cheque be guaranteed up to the value of £100?
3. Give four examples of a crossed cheque and briefly explain differences.
4. Distinguish between:
   (a) blank cheque
   (b) open cheque
   (c) endorsed cheque
   (d) stale cheque
   (e) post-dated cheque
5. What happens a cheque when it is presented to the bank for payment?
6. Distinguish between a special savings account and an ordinary savings account.
7. Describe the typical uses of an ATM machine.
8. What is the Express Lodgement Facility? How would you use it?
9. List the details that must be filled in on a lodgement slip.
10. What precautions should be taken when lodging cash in the bank?
11. Describe the procedure to follow when cashing traveller's cheques.
12. What is meant by EFT? Give three examples.
13. Describe a typical use of the bank giro/credit transfer as used under EFT.
14. Distinguish between a standing order and a direct debit.
15. How does a bank giro/credit transfer under EFT differ from the manual system?
16. When would a bank draft be used?
17. List three advantages and three disadvantages of the Laser card.
18. What are the checks that should be made when receiving a credit card as payment for goods?
19. Why do retailers operate a credit card system when they are charged a fee?
20. Distinguish between a credit card and a debit card.
21. Distinguish between:
    (a) Eurocheque and a normal cheque.
    (b) Eurocheque and a traveller's cheque.
22. Outline the essential procedures to be followed when preparing cash for a bank lodgement. (NCVA 1994)
23. What are the four main advantages of the credit transfer system? (NCVA 1994)
24. Outline four procedures to be followed when accepting a cheque payment from a customer. (NCVA 1994)
25. List four checks you would make before accepting payment by cheque. (NCVA 1995)
26. Outline procedures to adopt when preparing a bank lodgement. (NCVA 1995)
27. Describe security measures to take when collecting cash from bank and in making up wage packets. (NCVA 1995)

28. Describe four steps one should take to guarantee a cheque received with a cheque card. (NCVA 1996)
29. Outline four procedures one should follow when preparing and making a lodgement of cash in the bank's night safe. (NCVA 1996)

Assignments

1. You are authorised to pay a bill by cheque for stationery received for the value of £240.94 from Cross Stationery Suppliers Ltd. Using the cheque provided at the back of this book, fill in the necessary details on behalf of the company with today's date.

2. The following problems have arisen, now that your firm is expanding:
   (a) Paying employees by cash is becoming too risky and preparing cheques for each employee is time-consuming.
   (b) Fixed rate mortgage payable monthly is often overlooked owing to pressure of work, and the cheque sent to building society is often late.
   (c) Insurance premiums seem to rise each year, and again are overlooked, as renewal notices are sent in about a month before due date.

   Your employer has therefore asked you to look into the possibility of using other banking services, which would result in greater efficiency and economy. For each of the problems, indicate the service you would recommend, followed by a full description of the steps to be taken in order to make use of each of these recommended services.

3. The bank statement for Murphy's Deli Ltd has arrived in the office. You notice that your balance and the balance on the bank statement are different. Explain why this may have happened.

4. You have £2,500 to invest in the bank for a long-term period. Check out the rates of interest applicable to the various savings accounts offered by the commercial banks and calculate which account will give the best rate of return after a period of five years.

5. Check today's foreign currency buy and sell rates for notes and cheques for the following countries: UK, America, Switzerland, France, Spain, Portugal, Germany, Australia, Canada and Japan.

6. Identify three methods of withdrawing funds from a bank. Compare the methods in terms of security and speed of withdrawal.

6. Business Transactions

After studying this chapter you should be able to:

♦ Identify basic documentation relating to business transactions
♦ Explain terms and conditions in standard business documents
♦ Describe the sequence of activities involved in processing a business transaction
♦ Produce business documents
♦ Carry out business calculations
♦ Describe the procedure for ordering and dealing with incoming stock
♦ Describe how a stock-take is carried out

Introduction

business transaction takes place between two organisations, one of which is purchasing goods or services, the other selling. From the time of the initial enquiry to the dispatch of the goods, several **stages** are involved in the process.

In a small business the whole process may be carried out by one person. For example, in a sole trader or partnership one person may be responsible for monitoring stock levels, procuring an order, assessing quotations and placing the **order**. When the goods are received the same person may be responsible for checking the goods received against the **delivery document** that comes with the goods. S/he will also cross-check the goods received against the copy of the order to ensure that the goods were actually ordered. When the business is billed for payment by means of an **invoice**, the invoice will be checked against the record of the goods received to ensure that the goods have actually been received before payment is made and that the correct amount has been charged.

In a large business this process will be split among several individuals who work in different departments. This process is described in this chapter.

Stages of a Business Transaction

The stages of a business transaction are as follows.

PURCHASE REQUISITION

A purchase requisition form is an **internal request** for goods to be purchased. It is signed by the head of a department and sent to the Purchasing Department. If details such as supplier's name, catalogue number and price are not known, a brief description of what is required is recorded. The purchasing department will source the information required.

In the purchase requisition shown here the supplier's name, price and catalogue numbers are unknown.

Distribution of Purchase Requisition:
◆ Top Copy to Purchasing Department
◆ Copy in the Department's file

PURCHASE REQUISITION		Ref No AB231	
Department **Sales Department**			
Supplier's name (if known) _____			
Address _____			
Qty	**Details**	**Cat No**	**Unit Price**
20	**Reams of A4 laser printer paper (White)**		
10	**Copier transparencies (Box 100)**		
2	**Toner cartridges (black)**		
Signature *John Murray*		Date **12 October 1996**	

Purchase requisition form

LETTER OF ENQUIRY

The buyer in the purchasing department sources the supply and the price of goods by contacting appropriate suppliers. The buyer can track down possible sources of supply by looking up the items in particular directories, for example, the *Golden Pages*, trade journals and files on past suppliers. S/he may contact the supplier by telephone, letter of enquiry, fax, e-mail, etc. Details for the enquiry are taken from the Purchase Requisition.

A letter of enquiry (see overleaf) is a written request from a buyer to a seller requesting details of goods required. Such details would include price, trade discounts, cash discounts, delivery dates and whether carriage is paid or not. All the terms and conditions received from various suppliers will be compared before any particular supplier is decided upon.

Distribution of Letter of Enquiry by the Buyer:
◆ Top copies to various suppliers
◆ Copy in Buyer's File

Office Supplies Ltd

34 Main St

Blackrock   **Tel No: 01 2875640**

Co Dublin   **Fax No: 01 2876543**

12 October 1996

Photocopy Ltd
Wexford Industrial Estate
Wexford

Dear Sir/Madam

We would like you to quote for the following items which we will
need on a regular basis:

20	Reams of A4 laser printer paper (White)
10	Copier transparencies (Box 100)
2	Toner cartridges (Black) Model Express 30

Please send me your catalogue and a quotation for the above items
including your most favourable terms and delivery arrangements.

Yours faithfully

Brendan Kelly
Purchasing Dept

Letter of enquiry

QUOTATION

The enquiry will be handled by the **Sales Department** of the supplier. This
department will give the buyer information about the price and terms of sale, ie,
trade discount, cash discount, delivery dates and delivery terms.

This information may take the form of a price list or a catalogue and an
order form is generally sent with the price details. For more complex items or
where the buyer has asked for a special price, a quotation is sent.

A quotation is an offer to supply goods at the stated price and under the
terms and conditions stated in the quotation.

Distribution of Quotation by the Seller:

◆ Top copy to Customer

◆ Copy in File (Sales Department of Supplier)

Quotation No. 1460

Photocopy Ltd   **Tel No: 053 564396**
Wexford Industrial Estate   **Fax No: 053 564987**
Wexford

                                                         VAT No: 159 4321 67

16 October 1996

Attention of Mr Brendan Kelly

Office Supplies Ltd
34 Main St
Blackrock
Co Dublin

In reply to your enquiry dated 12 October, we have pleasure in quoting as follows:

Qty	Description	Cat No	Unit Price
20	Reams of A4 laser printer paper (White)	B2345	£7.75
10	Copier transparencies (Box 100)	B3347	£27.30
2	Toner cartridges (Black) Model Express 30	F1037	£118.32

VAT – Standard Rate of 21%

Terms: Trade Discount 25% for orders over £300 (before VAT)
        Cash Discount 5% for payment within 10 days of invoice date
                2½% within 1 month

Delivery: by our van within 7 days of receipt of order – carriage paid

We look forward to receiving your order.

Quotation

INFORMATION ON BUSINESS DOCUMENTS

Some of the terms and conditions stated in a quotation may be trade discount, cash discount, transport costs (such as carriage paid and carriage forward) and methods of payment such as cash with order (CWO).

Trade discount: an allowance given by a manufacturer to a wholesaler or by a wholesaler to a retailer, for bulk purchasing to encourage customers to buy in large quantities. It is deducted on the invoice and **does not** depend on the time of payment.

Cash discount: an allowance given in **addition** to trade discount to encourage prompt settlement of an account. The supplier may offer different rates for accounts settled within a stated period, for example, s/he may offer 5% for accounts settled within 10 days of the invoice date and 2½% for accounts settled within 1 month. It is deducted by the buyer when payment is being made.

If the terms of sale were stated as 3% one month, this means that the purchaser can deduct 3% from the invoice total if the invoice is paid within one month. If the terms of sale were stated as **net two months**, this means that no cash discount will be given and payment must be made within two months.

The benefits of offering a cash discount are:

a) The risk of bad debts may be reduced as the buyer is encouraged to settle payments promptly.

b) The firm may be able to pay its own debts promptly, and thus avail of the cash discount terms offered by its own suppliers.

c) It improves the cash position of the business.

Carriage paid: cost of transporting the goods to the purchaser's premises is included in the price quoted, ie, it is paid by the supplier.

Carriage forward: cost of transporting the goods is **not** included in the price quoted, ie, it is paid by the buyer.

CWO: (cash with order). The purchaser must forward the payment with the order before the order will be processed.

VAT number: Registered businesses must quote their VAT (value-added tax) registration number on **all** business documents.

The trader submits a VAT return to the Government every two months detailing the VAT on sales and the VAT on purchases. If the VAT on sales exceeds the VAT on purchases the trader pays the difference, otherwise a refund is claimed.

Reference number: is used to trace correspondence. For example, the quotation above has a reference number of 1460 and this will be quoted by the buyer when placing an order. It enables the seller to trace the order received to the quotation given. It also serves a useful function when enquiries have to be made. For example, if a business has placed many orders with the same firm, a query about a particular order can be traced immediately by quoting the order reference number.

E&OE: means 'errors and omissions excepted'. This means that the seller has the right to correct the information stated on the documentation. For example, if there is an error in arithmetic or if an item has not been charged for, the seller can send a supplementary invoice (usually called a debit note) to correct the mistake.

ORDER

When the purchasing officer receives the quotations from the various suppliers, s/he will evaluate them. The cheapest may not necessarily be the best – delivery dates, quality and the terms of sale are other important factors to take into account. An order will be placed with the supplier that offers the best overall package.

The buyer will use the pre-printed order form received or an order form will be prepared using NCR (no carbon required) paper, computer application templates or an accounting package.

An order is sent by the buyer in the Purchasing Department to the Sales Department of the supplier. The details for the order are taken from the quotation received from the seller. It is signed by the buyer in the Purchasing Department. The order gives full details of the goods to be supplied including catalogue references, quantity, quality, colour, size and unit cost. Total cost is included on some order forms. A delivery address is included if the goods are to be delivered to a different building. Distribution of Order by the Buyer:

- Top copy to the Sales Department of the supplier
- The buyer will keep a copy (Purchase Department)
- Stores (notification of goods to be received, for checking with Delivery Note and for writing up the Goods Received Note)
- Accounts Department (for checking with Goods Received Note from Stores and the invoice from the supplier before making payment)

Order No. A221

Office Supplies Ltd   **Tel No: 01 2875640**
34 Main St   **Fax No: 01 2876543**
Blackrock
Co Dublin   **VAT No: 284 3455 89**

Quotation No: 1460

20 October 1996

Photocopy Ltd
Wexford Industrial Estate
Wexford

Please supply the following:

Qty	Description	Cat No	Unit Price	Total Price
20	Reams of A4 laser printer paper (White)	B2345	£7.75	£155.00
10	Copier transparencies (Box 100)	B3347	£27.30	£273.00
2	Toner cartridges (Black) Model Express 30	F1037	£118.32	£236.64
				£664.64

Terms: of Sale
Trade Discount 25%
Cash Discount   5% within 10 days
                     2½% within 1 month
Carriage paid

Brendan Kelly
Purchasing Department

Order form

Procedure for Dealing with Incoming Orders (Supplier Firm)

1. Orders are date-stamped.
2. Orders are sent to the Accounts Department for credit approval.
3. If the order is approved, an invoice with duplicate copies is prepared.

CREDIT CHECKS

When a large order is received, and if the seller has not previously dealt with the purchaser, the seller will take one or more of the following steps before executing the order to minimise the risk of non-payment:

The seller invites the buyer to submit references. These may be from:

(i) **a bank official.** The buyer submits the name of their bank official with whom the seller can communicate. The communication of references between the bank official and the trader is treated as highly confidential.

(ii) **a trader.** The buyer gives the name of a business with whom s/he has previously dealt .

The seller requests payment by one of the following:

(i) requesting cash with the order (CWO).

(ii) submitting a pro-forma invoice which is an imitation invoice rather than a real invoice. It is used to request payment in advance of delivery from a first-time customer or where no credit facility is allowed. (A pro-forma invoice is also used when goods are sent 'on approval', eg, in a mail order business. If the goods are retained, payment is made in accordance with the pro-forma invoice.)

(iii) requesting the buyer to furnish a percentage of the cost of the order before delivery is made and the balance on delivery.

PREPARATION OF INVOICE

If the order is approved by the supplier, an invoice is prepared by the Sales Department in duplicate form for distribution.

An invoice is a bill requesting payment; it is sent by the sales department of the supplying firm to the Accounts Department of the purchasing firm. It is usually sent **after** the dispatch of the goods, though in some cases the invoice is enclosed with the goods.

An invoice will contain the following information:

◆ name and address of both the buyer and the seller
◆ date and VAT registration number
◆ quantity, description and catalogue/reference number of product
◆ the unit cost of each item, the total cost of each item and the overall total cost
◆ trade discount
◆ the VAT rate and VAT amount shown separately

- terms of sale such as cash discounts, carriage details as quoted on quotation
- E&OE at the bottom of the invoice

Distribution of Invoice by the Seller:

- Top copy to customer (Accounts Department)
- Copy held in Sales Department to answer queries
- Copy to Accounts Department to record the sale on the customer's account
- Copies to Stores

COPIES TO STORES

When an order is received and approved by the supplier, an invoice is prepared in duplicate form for distribution. However, the copies prepared for Stores will **not** state the price details.

The duplicate copies may be prepared by printing onto NCR paper. Alternatively, the templates (pre-designed documents) available with computer application packages or an accounting package may be used.

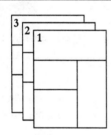 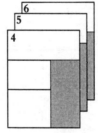

1. Customer's copy
2. Sales Department's copy
3. Accounts Department's copy

4. Stores' copy
5. & 6. Delivery notes (also sent to stores)

The details printed on the top copy appear on the other copies, except where there are shaded areas, ie, the price details do not appear on the shaded areas.

Carbonised (NCR) invoice

Three copies are normally sent to Stores. Stores will keep one copy as proof of authorisation to release the goods. The other two copies are sent with the goods when they are dispatched to the customer. These two copies are labelled as a delivery note or an advice note depending on the firm's delivery policy. If the business has its own transportation system the copies are labelled as delivery notes. If the goods are not dispatched by the supplier's own transport, ie, the goods are sent by post or rail, the copies are labelled as an advice note.

DELIVERY NOTE

A delivery note is prepared at the same time as the invoice and therefore contains the same particulars as the invoice, except the price of the goods.

The goods are normally sent before the invoice. A delivery note accompanies the goods and the delivery person requests the customer to sign the delivery note. S/he gives the top copy to the customer and returns the signed copy as proof of delivery.

Before signing, the customer (Stores Department) checks the goods against the delivery note ensuring that all goods listed on the delivery note are received. If the goods are found to be faulty or goods are missing this is recorded on the delivery note before signing.

It is rarely possible to examine goods in detail immediately they are delivered. The most that can normally be done is to check that the correct number of boxes are received and that there is no obvious damage. In this case 'not examined' should be recorded on the delivery note.

Distribution of Delivery Note by Seller:

◆ Top copy given to customer

◆ Duplicate copy held by delivery person who returns it to the organisation

---

Delivery Note D1675

Photocopy Ltd   **Tel No: 053 564396**
Wexford Industrial Estate   **Fax No: 053 564987**
Wexford

                                                VAT No: 159 4321 67

Order No: A221

27 October 1996

Office Supplies Ltd
34 Main St
Blackrock
Co Dublin

Qty	Description	Cat No	
20	Reams of A4 laser printer paper (White)	B2345	
10	Copier transparencies (Box 100)	B3347	
2	Toner cartridges (Black) Model Express 30	F1037	

Not Examined

Received by: *John Hegarty*

Delivery note

ADVICE NOTE

An advice note contains the same information as a delivery note. It is used when the goods are not sent by the supplier's transport, for example, the goods are sent by post or rail. It is packed with the goods to enable the receiver to check them upon arrival. It does not have to be signed. An advice note may also be sent in advance of the goods, to inform the buyer that the goods are being dispatched.

Procedure for Dealing with Incoming Goods (Purchasing Firm)

When the goods are delivered to Stores, the following procedure is carried out:
1. The packet is opened, unpacked and the contents are checked against the delivery note or advice note. Any discrepancies are noted, for example, shortages, damaged goods or incorrect goods.
2. The goods are then checked against the copy of the order to ensure that the goods received were ordered, and also that all the goods ordered were received.
3. A goods received note is prepared by Stores.

GOODS RECEIVED NOTE

When the goods are received a goods received note is prepared by Stores noting any discrepancies such as shortages, damages or incorrect goods received. A copy will be sent to the Accounts Department to be compared with the copy of the order form and the incoming invoice before payment is processed.

Distribution of Goods Received Note by Buyer:

◆ Top Copy to Accounts Department (to check against copy of order and incoming invoice)
◆ Copy held in Stores to update stock records

Goods Received Note No: 12343

Office Supplies Ltd

Supplier: Photocopy Ltd
Date Received: 27 October 1996
Delivery/Advice Note No: D1675

Order No	Description	Qty Received
A221	Reams of A4 laser printer paper (White) Copier transparencies (Box 100) Toner cartridges (Black) Model Express	20 10 2

Received by:	Date:	Entered in stock by:	Date:
D. Foyle	27/10/96	P. Connolly	27/10/96

Inspected by: Harry Dineen	Date: 27/10/96

Shortages:
Damage recorded:
1 ream of A4 laser printer paper damaged

Goods received note

CHECKING INVOICE RECEIVED

The invoice is usually sent **after** the dispatch of the goods, though in some cases the invoice is enclosed with the goods.

When the invoice is received by the Accounts Department of the purchasing firm the following checks are made:

1. Check invoice against the copy of the order to ensure the correct goods have been invoiced.
2. Check the prices, discounts and terms of sales against the quotation.
3. Check invoice against the goods received note (from Stores) to ensure that goods have actually been received before making payment.
4. Check all calculations, total unit cost, trade discount and total cost.

Distribution of Received Invoice by Buyer:

◆ Original copy held in Accounts Department

Invoice No: 1675

Photocopy Ltd   **Tel No: 053 564396**
Wexford Industrial Estate   **Fax No: 053 564987**
Wexford

                                           VAT No: 159 4321 67

Delivery Note No: D1675
Order No: A221

28 October 1996

Office Supplies Ltd
34 Main St
Blackrock
Co Dublin

Qty	Description	Cat No	Unit Price £	Total Cost £
20	Reams of A4 laser printer paper (White)	B2345	7.75	155.00
10	Copier transparencies (Box 100)	B3347	27.30	273.00
2	Toner cartridges (Black) Model Express 30	F1037	118.32	236.64
				£664.64
	Deduct: 25% Trade Discount			166.16
	Net goods value		Sub Total	498.48
	ADD: VAT @ 21%		VAT	104.68
			Total	£603.16
	Terms: 5% within 10 days			
	2½% within 1 month			
E&OE	Carriage Paid			

Invoice

Procedure for Dealing with Errors on Invoice

If errors are discovered on the received invoice by the purchasing firm, the Accounts Department will contact the supplier and negotiate the return of the goods where necessary. The supplier will rectify the error by sending a credit note or a debit note as appropriate.

CREDIT NOTE

A credit note is sent by the seller to the Accounts Department of the purchasing firm when goods were overcharged, goods were charged for but not received, goods are returned or packing cases are returned. It is an allowance given by the supplier, reducing the original invoice charge.

When damaged goods needing replacement are returned, the normal practice is to issue a credit note for the returns. The seller then issues a new invoice for the replaced items.

The seller reduces the amount owing in its books by the amount of the credit note and the buyer pays the original invoice less the amount of the credit note.

Distribution of Credit Note by Seller:

◆ Top copy to Customer (Accounts Department)
◆ Copy to Sales Department
◆ Copy held in Accounts Department to record on customer's account

---

Credit Note No: C2343

Photocopy Ltd   **Tel No: 053 564396**
Wexford Industrial Estate   **Fax No: 053 564987**
Wexford

VAT No: 159 4321 67

Invoice No: 1675
Order No: A221

30 October 1996

Office Supplies Ltd
34 Main St
Blackrock
Co Dublin

Qty	Description	Cat No	Unit Price £	Total Cost
1	Reams of A4 laser printer paper (White)	B2345	7.750	7.75
	Deduct: 25% Trade Discount			1.94
	Net goods value		**Sub Total**	5.81
	ADD: VAT @ 21%		**VAT**	1.22
			Total	**£7.03**
E&OE				

Credit note

DEBIT NOTE

An error in an invoice resulting in an **undercharge** is corrected by means of a debit note. It is sent by the seller to the Accounts Department of the purchasing firm for the additional charge. It has the same effect as an invoice. Nowadays, many firms just send an additional invoice for the additional charge instead of a debit note. For example, assume that the VAT rate on Invoice No 1675 was charged at 18% instead of 21%. There is an undercharge of £14.96 (£498.48 x 18% = £89.72. £104.68 – £89.72 = £14.96).

Distribution of Debit Note by Seller:

◆ Top copy to Customer (Accounts Department)
◆ Copy held in Accounts Department to record on customer's account

---

Debit Note No: D343

Photocopy Ltd   **Tel No: 053 564396**
Wexford Industrial Estate   **Fax No: 053 564987**
Wexford

                                                       VAT No: 159 4321 67

Invoice No: 1675
Order No: A221

30 October 1996

Office Supplies Ltd
34 Main St
Blackrock
Co Dublin

Ref	Description	Amount £
Invoice No 1675	VAT charged at 18% instead of 21% Undercharge	£14.96
E&OE		

Debit note

Requesting Payment

Most businesses do not expect every invoice to be paid separately by the buyer as this would cause considerable clerical work. The usual practice is for a statement to be sent out at intervals (monthly in most cases) and for payment to be requested by a specified date.

STATEMENT

At the end of the month the Accounts Department of the supplier firm sends a Statement of Account to the customer. The statement of account is a copy of the customer's account in the sales ledger, also known as the debtor's ledger. (The customer is known as a debtor – a person who owes you money.)

The statement does not contain particulars of the goods supplied but will show the balance at the beginning of the month, all transactions during the month and the balance due. The transactions during the month may include invoices, debit notes and credit notes sent and cheques received.

Statement

Photocopy Ltd   **Tel No: 053 564396**

Wexford Industrial Estate   **Fax No: 053 564987**

Wexford   **VAT No: 159 4321 67**

---

31 October 1996

Office Supplies Ltd
34 Main St
Blackrock
Co Dublin

Shows all increases in amounts owed, eg, invoices, debit notes.

Shows all decreases in amounts owed, eg, credit notes and cheques received.

Date	Ref No	Details	Debits	Credits	Balance
28 Oct	1675	Invoice	603.16		603.16
30 Oct	C2343	Credit Note		7.03	596.13

Terms: 5% within 10 days
2½% within 1 month

Statement

Procedure for Dealing with Incoming Statements

When the statement is received by the Accounts Department of the purchasing firm the following checks are made:

1. Details of the statement are compared with the details entered for the creditor in the purchaser's ledger.
2. Calculations on the statement are checked.

3. The cash discount at the appropriate rate is deducted and the payment is sent to the Accounts Department of the supplier before expiration of credit period, to avail of the discount. For example, if Office Supplies Ltd settles its account within 10 days of the statement date, it will pay £566.33 (£596.13 minus 5%).

DEALING WITH CASH DISCOUNT

To avail of cash discount, the statement must be paid within the time specified by the terms of trade. The date is taken to be the date of the statement.

EXAMPLE 1

The following statement is sent to a customer, John Moran. How much will John pay if he pays the statement on:
a) 12 February 1996?
b) 19 February 1996?
c) 28 February 1996?
d) 20 March 1996?

Date: 5 February 1996

Date	Details	Debit	Credit	Balance
2 Jan 96	Balance b/f			895
15 Jan 96	Invoice No 1232	420		1315
18 Jan 96	Credit Note No 341		25	1290
20 Jan 96	Cheque		895	395

Terms: 3% within 2 weeks
Net one month

Solution:
a) The balance due is £395. As the trader pays the statement on 12 February which is within two weeks of the statement date, he is entitled to deduct a discount of 3%. He will therefore pay £395 less 3% which is £383.15. The amount £383.15 clears John Moran's account in full as the seller has allowed him a discount for prompt payment.
b) The answer is the same as for (a) as John Moran has paid the statement within the two-week period.
c) As the statement is not paid until 28 February which is after the date when a discount is allowed, John Moran is not entitled to any discount. He must therefore pay the full amount owing of £395.
d) The statement is not paid until 20 March which is after the date when a discount is allowed and after the date when the statement should be paid. John

Moran is not entitled to any discount and he pays the full amount owing of £395. However, as John did not pay his statement on time, he may not be given any credit in the future. Some suppliers also charge interest if the statement is not paid on time.

How solution (a) would be recorded in the seller's books (not required for answer)

The seller keeps a record of the transaction details in its debtor's ledger. These details are entered from source documents such as invoices, credit notes and debit notes sent to the customer and cheques received from the customer. On 5 February, the seller will have recorded the following details for John Moran in the debtor's ledger.

John Moran a/c					
Dr			**Cr**		
Date	*Details*	*£*	*Date*	*Details*	*£*
2 Jan	Balance b/f	895	18 Jan	Returns – Cr No 341	25
15 Jan	Sales – Inv No 1232	420	20 Jan	Cheque	895
			31 Jan	Balance c/d	395
		1315			1315
1 Feb	Balance b/f	395			

When the seller receives the cheque from John Moran on 12 February s/he enters the amount of the cheque plus the amount of discount allowed as shown below.

John Moran a/c					
Dr			**Cr**		
Date	*Details*	*£*	*Date*	*Details*	*£*
12 Feb	Balance b/f	395	12 Feb	Cheque	383.15
			12 Feb	Discount	11.85

Stock Control

Stock control means controlling the level of stock held in a business. It is used to ensure that the business has sufficient stock to meet anticipated needs, while at the same time not holding more than is necessary.

No business wants to hold large stocks of items. Stock represents money tied up in the business. It also costs the business in terms of insurance, storage space (ie, rent) and security. Indeed, some stock items may go out of date, lose their value or deteriorate. On the other hand, having insufficient stock available ('stock-out') when it is needed is also unsatisfactory. Delays ('bottlenecks') will occur in production, customer orders will not be processed on time and there will be a consequent loss of goodwill. The business may have to buy stock from a different source (if available) and this generally means higher prices. What is needed is a balance between these two extremes.

In a small business the stock of stationery and supplies may be the responsibility of the secretary. S/he will be responsible for monitoring stock levels, ordering supplies and dealing with incoming supplies. In a large organisation, stock control will be the responsibility of the Stores Department which will monitor stock levels and notify the Purchasing Department when new supplies are required.

Stock Control System

A business will set a minimum stock level, a re-order level and a maximum stock level for each item of stock based on the rate at which stocks are used over a given period and the time it takes for the order to be processed. Mathematical formulas may be used in complex situations to determine the economic order quantity (EOQ). A stock control card (also known as a bin card) is maintained for every item in stock.

Minimum stock level. Stock cannot safely be allowed to drop **below** this level. To avoid this happening, a 're-order level' is set above the minimum stock level. The minimum stock level is the 'buffer stock' and it is used in case of emergencies. It is set at a level so that the order will be received before the buffer stock is depleted.

Re-order level. When stock falls to the re-order level an order is placed. The quantity ordered is the difference between the re-order level and the maximum stock level. It is set at a level such that the order will be received before the minimum stock level is reached.

Maximum stock level: This is the maximum amount of stock that should be stored. Above this level it is uneconomical to hold stock.

For example, illustrated overleaf is a stock control card for dot matrix printer ribbons. The firm has set the maximum level at 30 ribbons, the re-order level at 10 ribbons and the minimum level at 7 ribbons based on knowledge of usage and the **lead time.** (Lead time is the time it takes from ordering the stock to the actual delivery of the stock.) The unit size of 1 means that the ribbons can be ordered as a single item.

The balance on 1 July was 17 ribbons. On 3 July and 10 July, ribbons were issued to departments, reducing the stock to 9 ribbons on 10 July. As 9 ribbons is below the re-order level, an order was placed to replenish the stock. The quantity ordered was 20 ribbons which is the difference between the re-order level of 10 and the maximum level of 30. The stock was received on 15 July and brought the stock level to 29 ribbons. Another issue took place on 17 July. This system ensures that the business holds an economical amount of stock.

Stock Control Card

Item:	Dot Matrix Printer Ribbon		
Code No:	D0034	Maximum Level:	30
Unit Size: 1	Re-order	Re-Order Level :	10
Location:	A34	Minimum Level:	7

Date	Issued to/ received from	Quantity issued	Quantity received	Balance
1-7-96				17
3-7-96	Marketing Dept	3		14
10-7-96	Accounts Dept	5		9
15-7-96	Johnstown Supplies		20	29
17-7-96	Office Admin	1		28

Stock control card

To avoid losses due to obsolete or perished goods, the First In First Out (FIFO) system of issuing stock is used. The FIFO system operates by distributing the goods according to the earliest date at which they were delivered.

For example: assume 20 items were received on 4 June and 25 items on 28 June. If a requisition for goods was received on 8 July for 25 items, the stock will be issued from the delivery received on 4 June first, and the balance of 5 items will be issued from the later delivery.

SOURCE DOCUMENTS FOR STOCK CONTROL CARD

The issue and receipt of stock are entered from the source documents received by the Stores Department.

The source documents for **issues** of stock are:

a) A **stock requisition form** which is issued by another department within the business requesting stock for internal use. It is laid out in a similar fashion to the purchase requisition form.

b) A **copy of invoice received.** When an order has been received, an invoice is prepared in duplicate form by the Sales Department of the supplier. Copies of the invoice go to the Stores Department. The top copy is used to record the issue of stock from Stores. The other copies, known as delivery notes or advice notes, are sent with the goods.

The source document for **receipt** of stock is:

a) The **goods received note.** A delivery note or an advice note accompanies all stock received. The stock is checked against the details recorded on the delivery note. The contents of the packet are then checked against the delivery note and further discrepancies may be noted. A goods received note is then prepared. The top copy goes to the Accounts Department for checking against the incoming invoice. The copy held in Stores is used to write up the stock control card.

COMPUTERISED STOCK CONTROL

Today, the stock control procedure is normally automated using an accounting/stock control computer package. This package will display stock control cards for each item of stock in a manner similar to the manual system.

The accounting/stock control package will be set up initially with details of each stock item and the minimum, re-order and maximum levels entered. The issue and receipt of stock are entered from the source documents received by the Stores Department and the balance of stock is automatically calculated. The system will provide warnings when the re-order level or the minimum level is reached. The warning could be an audible bleep or a message that appears on the screen. Alternatively, an automatic search can be made to check all items when the re-order or minimum level is reached. The items in question are displayed on the screen and can be printed if required.

Stock control systems can be incorporated at the point of sale. This type of control system is used typically in supermarkets where there is a high volume of stock passing through the point of sale. All stock received is entered on the computer and as each item is purchased, the amount of related stock decreases. This is achieved by a bar code scanner linked to a computer. Thus an up-to-date list of the amount of stock remaining can be obtained on demand.

Computerised stock control systems simplify the process of **stock-taking** as a complete list of all items in stock can be printed. The stock-taker only needs to record the actual amount of physical stock.

Stock-taking

While a stock control system ensures that the business holds an economical amount of stock and will not suffer a stock-out, procedures also need to be put in place to check that the amount of stock stated on the records actually is in stock. To confirm the accuracy of the stock records a stock-take is carried out.

A stock-take is simply a physical count of the stock that remains in the storeroom. A stock-take is carried out once a year or more frequently depending on the nature of the business and value involved. The business may operate a constant stock-take where areas of stock are checked periodically throughout the year, or it may operate random 'spot checks' on certain items of stock to ensure that stock records are being maintained properly and to reduce the risk of pilfering.

When a stock-take is carried out, the physical stock is counted and recorded on a **stock list**. The stock list will have the following information pre-recorded: reference number of stock item, item description, location of stock item and value of the item. The stock-taker **only** records the **actual count** of each stock item. If a manual stock control system is in use, the stock-taker will also calculate and record at a later date the total value of each stock item for financial accounting purposes. Where a computerised system is in operation, the stock-taker records the actual count of each stock item. This information is then entered into an accounting/stock package or a spreadsheet where the value of stock remaining is automatically calculated.

The quantity of stock recorded for each item is compared to the balances stated on the individual stock control cards. Discrepancies are investigated; these can arise for the following reasons: (a) stock was stolen; (b) stock was issued and not recorded; (c) stock was received and not recorded; (d) breakages or spillages were not recorded.

Rally's Mail Order Ltd
Main Street
Wexford

Stock of Stationery as at 17 July 1996

This column is completed by the stock-taker.

This column is completed by the stock-taker or automatically calculated by the computer.

Ref No	Item Description	Location	Quantity in stock	Value per item £	Total value	Signature
P675	A4 Bond Paper	A45	40	6.00	240.00	
D0034	Dot Matrix Printer Ribbon	A34	28	7.50	210.00	
E89	DL Envelopes	B23	30	3.50	105.00	
	etc					
total						

Stock-take list

Summary

A business transaction takes place between two organisations, one purchasing and the other selling goods or services. From the time of the initial enquiry to the dispatch of the goods, several stages are involved in managing the process. In a small business the whole process may be carried out by one person, but in a large organisation the process will be split among several individuals who work in different departments.

The purchaser's main stages in the transaction are: sending letters of enquiry; receiving and assessing quotations; sending an order to the supplier that offers the best overall deal. When the goods are received they are checked against the delivery note to ensure that all goods listed are there; any damaged goods or discrepancies are noted before signing. The goods received are then checked against the order to ensure that the goods received were the goods ordered. A goods received note is prepared by Stores and sent to the Accounts Department. The Accounts Department checks the goods received note against the order and invoice before making payment.

The seller's main stages in a transaction are: sending out a quotation in reply to a letter of enquiry; receiving the order; checking the credit-worthiness of the customer; making out duplicate invoices. Copies of the invoice are sent to Stores to authorise the release of the goods. The other copies given to Stores are either delivery notes or advice notes depending on the firm's transportation policy. The delivery note is given to the courier when the goods are being delivered. The customer checks the goods and notes any discrepancies on the delivery note before signing. The signed delivery note is returned and the invoice sent to the customer.

If errors are discovered on the received invoice by the purchasing firm, the Accounts Department contacts the supplier and returns the goods where necessary. The supplier rectifies the error by sending a credit note or a debit note as appropriate.

At the end of the month the supplier sends a statement to the purchaser requesting payment. The supplier may offer a cash discount for prompt payment. If the purchaser pays the statement on time s/he deducts the cash discount from the balance shown on the statement before paying.

A business must ensure that it carries enough stock to meet its expected demand. It must balance the need to have stock available against the cost of carrying too much stock. This is achieved by a stock control system.

A stock control system will have a minimum, maximum and re-order level set for each item of stock. These levels are based on the rate at which stocks are used over a given period and the time it takes for the order to be processed.

In order to ascertain whether the stock control cards are accurate, a stock-take is carried out. A stock-take is simply a physical count of the stock that remains in the storeroom which is recorded on a stock list. Stock-takes are carried out once a year or more often depending on the nature of the business and value involved. Any discrepancies between the number recorded on the stock control card and the physical stock should be investigated. Today, the stock control procedure is normally automated using an accounting/stock computer package or the stock control systems can be incorporated at the point of sale.

Summary — Stages in Business Transactions

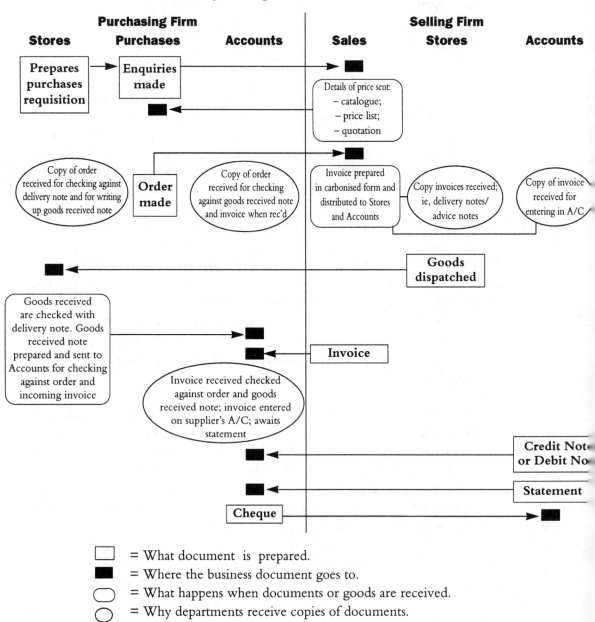

Questions

Multiple Choice Questions

1. Which of the following stages of a business transaction is out of sequence?
   a) order
   b) credit note
   c) invoice
   d) statement

2. A request from a department to the Purchasing Department to buy items usually takes the form of:
   a) a memo
   b) a letter of enquiry
   c) a requisition
   d) an order

3. A buyer may pay an invoice before the credit period expires to avail of:
   a) trade discount
   b) cash discount
   c) carriage paid
   d) carriage forward

4. If the seller undercharges the buyer on an invoice, s/he will send:
   a) a credit note
   b) a debit note
   c) an advice note
   d) a statement

5. The term of sale 'net two months' means:
   a) No trade discount is allowed but payment is due within two months.
   b) No cash discount is allowed but payment is due within two months.
   c) Trade discount is allowed if payment is received within two months.
   d) Cash discount is allowed if payment is received within two months.

6. Trade discount is deducted:
   a) when making out the invoice
   b) when making out the statement
   c) when paying the statement
   d) when paying the invoice

7. Carriage forward means:
   a) the purchaser must pay the transport costs
   b) the seller will pay the transport costs
   c) the goods are delivered before the purchaser pays
   d) the purchaser must pay before delivery of the goods

8. Which of the following documents is signed when the goods are received?
   a) requisition
   b) advice note
   c) delivery note
   d) invoice

9. An advice note is sent:
   a) to inform the purchaser of an overcharge on an invoice
   b) to inform the purchaser of an undercharge on an invoice
   c) to inform the purchaser that the goods have been dispatched
   d) to inform the seller that goods have been returned

10. The document that details the goods sold on credit is:
    a) a credit note
    b) an advice note
    c) an invoice
    d) a goods received note

11. If goods are sent on approval the seller will send:
    a) an advice note
    b) a letter of enquiry
    c) a pro-forma invoice
    d) a quotation

12. On 10 August an invoice for £900 marked with the terms 2½% within 7 days was received. If you paid this invoice on 13 August, you would pay:
    a) £900.00
    b) £877.50
    c) £922.50
    d) £855.00

13. If a customer's account is reduced because of an adjustment, the seller must send:
    a) a debit note
    b) a credit note
    c) a quotation
    d) a statement

14. A statement is sent by the Accounts Department of the supplying firm to which department of the purchasing firm?
    a) Sales Department
    b) Purchasing Department
    c) Accounts Department
    d) Dispatch Department

15. A statement is sent out:
    a) after each transaction
    b) before the goods are dispatched
    c) at fixed intervals, usually monthly
    d) when the goods are paid for

16. A stock control card is used:
    a) to request stock from Stores
    b) to record the issue and receipt of stock
    c) to calculate the minimum and maximum stock levels
    d) to count the physical stock

17. The term 'stock-out' means:
    a) conducting a stock-take
    b) ordering stock
    c) bottlenecks in production
    d) having insufficient stock available

18. Under a stock control system, the quantity ordered is:
    a) the difference between the minimum and the maximum stock levels
    b) the difference between the re-order level and the minimum stock level
    c) the difference between the maximum and the re-order levels
    d) the difference between the lead time and the re-order level

19. What is the new balance on a stock control card with the following details?
    Balance 46, Requisition 18, Requisition 20, Receipt 30, Requisition 29
    a) 47
    b) 83
    c) 37
    d) 9

20. To minimise the loss of holding obsolete or perishable goods the business will:
    a) use the First In, First Out (FIFO) method
    b) sell the cheapest stock first
    c) use the Last In, First Out (LIFO) method
    d) sell the dearest stock first

21. Lead time refers to:
    a) the time taken from ordering stock to actual delivery of the stock
    b) the amount of stock that should be ordered to minimise costs
    c) the level of stock to maintain to avoid stock-outs
    d) the minimum buffer stock to maintain

22. A business document sent by the seller to the buyer when damaged goods are returned is called:
    a) an advice note
    b) a credit note
    c) a statement
    d) an invoice
    e) a delivery note   (NCVA 1994)

23. A requisition form is needed when:
    a) goods are being loaded onto a ship
    b) tax is being paid on imported goods
    c) a shortage has been discovered in stock
    d) goods are needed from Stores
    e) faulty goods are returned   (NCVA 1994)

24. An invoice shows a total amount of £3,500 less 5% if paid within thirty days. The customer availing of this discount should make out a cheque for:
    a) £3,450
    b) £3,430
    c) £3,335
    d) £3,325
    e) £3,305   (NCVA 1994)

25. The business document sent by the Stores Department to the Purchasing Department asking it to buy additional supplies of stock is:
    a) a delivery note
    b) a purchases order
    c) a purchases requisition
    d) a debit note
    e) a remittance   (NCVA 1995)

Short Answer Questions

1. What are the main stages in a transaction when you are buying goods, from the initial enquiry up to the time when the goods are paid for?
2. What are the main stages in a transaction when you are selling goods, from the receipt of the enquiry to the time when payment is received?
3. When the sales invoice is made out, how are the copies distributed?

4. What information would you expect to be on an invoice?

5. What information would you expect to find on a delivery note? Is it the same as an invoice and why?

6. Distinguish between trade discount and cash discount and briefly explain when each discount is offered.

7. What does E&OE mean on business documents?

8. Distinguish between a credit note and a debit note.

9. Give two functions of a delivery note.

10. When is an advice note sent?

11. Give three reasons for the issue of a credit note.

12. What is the function of a goods received note?

13. What does the term 'net' mean on business documents?

14. What is the procedure for dealing with goods received?

15. What checks are made on an incoming invoice?

16. What is a pro-forma invoice and when is it used?

17. Distinguish between a credit and a debit entry on a statement.

18. What checks are made on an incoming statement?

19. What is meant by a stock control system? Why is it used?

20. List four reasons why holding too much stock may cost the business money.

21. If a business has recorded a minimum, maximum and re-order level for stock control, what quantity will be re-ordered?

22. Distinguish between stock control and stock-take.

23. List the source documents used to record the issue and receipt of stock when a stock control system is used.

24. The sub-total of goods on an invoice is £420. Trade discount of 10% has yet to be deducted and VAT of 21% has to be added. Calculate:
    a) the trade discount
    b) the VAT
    c) the invoice total

25. What items of information are essential on a statement of account?

    (NCVA 1994)

26. List **four** common terms of trade offered by a supplier to a buyer when sending a quotation for goods.   (NCVA 1996)

Assignments

Blank documents are provided at the back of the book for the following exercises. These should be photocopied.

1. Joan Butler is employed as an office clerk in M & M Construction Ltd, Dundrum, Co Dublin. She requests the following items to be purchased by the Purchasing Department.

2 Sigma Purchase Orders

2 Sigma Delivery Notes

1 Paper Mate 2000 Fine (Blue)

a) Complete the necessary document she will send to Michael McGrath, the Purchasing Officer.

b) Complete the order (Order No. O231) sent to Collins Stationery Supplies Ltd, Monasterevin, Co Kildare. (Refer to price list in Question 12.)

2. From the information provided compile the quotation that is sent by Mr John Doyle, Stationery Supplies, 44 White Street, Cavan in reply to a letter of enquiry received from Ms Jane Hanley, 5 High Street, Cavan.

Quotation number Q531

Cat No 231   40 lever-arch files @ £1.20 each

Cat No 235   20 box files @ £3.50 each

Cat No 211   10 boxes of manilla folders at £5.00 per box

Delivery 1 week from receipt of order

Cash discount 5% within 1 week

a) When does a seller send out a quotation?

b) What department sends out the quotation?

c) What action does a prospective buyer take when s/he receives a quotation?

3. A buyer is offered goods by the following suppliers. What factors will the buyer have to take into account in deciding which of the quotations to accept?

Supplier 1	**Supplier 2**
15% trade discount	25% trade discount
Ready delivery	1 month delivery
Cash – one month net	5% cash discount within 10 days

4. Complete the tabulation for the three items.

Description	Item 1 £	Item 2 £	Item 3 £
Sales	1370	47.65	2,875.00
Trade Discount 15%			
Sub Total			
VAT 21%			
Amount Due			

5 (i) Show how the following items will appear in a statement.

a)	2/2/96	Balance b/f	895
	15/2/96	Sales Invoice	420
	18/2/96	Credit Note – Returns	25
	27/2/96	Cheque	895
b)	1/3/96	Balance b/f	20
	3/3/96	Sales Invoice	840
	10/3/96	Debit Note – Undercharge	20
c)	1/4/96	Balance b/f	–
	6/4/96	Sales Invoice	25
	20/4/96	Credit Note – Returns	10
d)	1/5/96	Balance b/f	55
	4/5/96	Sales Invoice	975
	8/5/96	Sales Invoice	1,420
	15/5/96	Credit Note – Returns	70
	27/5/96	Cheque	55

(ii) If the terms of sale arc: Cash Discount: 3% within 2 weeks, net one month, state how much the cheques payable will be if a cheque is sent:
within 2 weeks;
after 2 weeks but within 1 month;
after 1 month.

6. On 11 March, Printer Supplies Ltd, 12 Main Street, Kildare, supplied to Copypress, Westgate, Wexford, the items ordered on Order No. O451. On 18 March, Copypress returned 1 can of damaged cleaning fluid.

Order No. O451

10 cans of cleaning fluid at £5.50 per can excluding VAT of 21%.

Terms of sale were: 10% trade discount and 2½% cash discount within 1 month.

a) Complete the invoice number I231 sent on 11 March.

b) Complete the credit note number C390 sent on 20 March.

c) Complete the statement number S200 sent on 31 March.

d) How much will Copypress pay if the statement is paid on 27 April?

7. Complete the statement sent on 31 October by Office Supplies Ltd, Hume Place, Dublin 1 to Mr Mark O'Reilly, Roxboro Rd, Limerick from the extracts of the documents given below.

Office Supplies Ltd **Invoice No 9876**	Office Supplies Ltd **Invoice No 9882**	Office Supplies Ltd **Invoice No 9891**
23/10/96 ref: Order No 3451 Goods £55.00 VAT 21% **Terms** Trade Discount 10% Cash Discount 5% 1 month	27/10/96 ref: Order No 3462 Goods £155.00 VAT 21% **Terms** Trade Discount 10% Cash Discount 5% 1 month	13/11/96 ref: Order No 3471 Goods £100.00 VAT 21% **Terms** Trade Discount 10% Cash Discount 5% 1 month

Office Supplies Ltd **Credit Note 4521**	Office Supplies Ltd **Credit Note 4571**	Office Supplies Ltd **Cheque No: 123211**
29/10/96 ref: Invoice No 9876 Goods £5.00 Trade Discount 10% VAT 21%	16/11/96 ref: Invoice No 9891 Goods £10.00 Trade Discount 10% VAT 21%	31/10/96 Value £200

8. Joseph Moran is the Manager of the Purchasing Department in MEC Office Supplies Ltd. He receives the following quotation on 3 August 1996.

Quotation
Curragh Envelopes Ltd
Kilcullen
Co Kildare

Tel: 045 852329
Fax: 045 852330

VAT Reg No: 883294U
Date: 3 August 1996

MEC Office Supplies Ltd
Industrial Estate
Co Laois

Terms: 5% 1 Month   Carriage Paid

Qty	Code	Description	Unit Price £
20	3000	Treasury tags (box size 100)	2.27
4	4012	Two ring A4 binders (packet 10) 2.27	12.00
2	3002	Dl 8⅝" x 4¼" window gummed	32.10
Vat 21 %			

a) Complete the delivery note sent with the goods by Curragh Envelopes Ltd.

b) Complete the invoice sent by Curragh Envelopes Ltd.

c) Complete the cheque that Joseph Moran sends on 20 August 1996.

9. You work for Office Equipment Supplies Ltd and the following goods were ordered by Marcol Systems Limited.

Order No: x11

Marcol Systems Limited
Eagle House
Naas
Co Kildare

Tel: 045 852000   **VAT Reg No:** 659844d
Fax: 045 852001   **Date:** 13 October 1996

Office Equipment Supplies Ltd
Evin Blue Industrial Estate
Dublin 1

Qty	Code	Description	Unit Price £
5	1933	3.5" DS/DD IBM PS2	£9.70
3	1934	3.5" DS/HD IBM PS2	£8.90
5	1827	3.5" DS/DD Applemac	£9.70
1	1600	3.5" 3 Drawer Unit	£64.00

Terms: Trade Discount 15%, VAT 21%, Cash Discount 1 Month, Delivery 14 days

---

a) Complete the invoice sent by you on 25 October. All goods ordered were delivered.

b) Complete the cheque sent on 10 November.

c) Complete the statement sent by your firm on 30 November.

10. Examine the invoice below.
    a) An invoice was sent by Office Supplies Limited on 12 January 1997 for goods ordered. Examine the invoice and correct any errors.
    b) What document would Office Supplies Limited send you to confirm the mistake and correct it? Prepare this document.
    c) Complete the statement sent by Office Supplies Limited on 30 January 1997.

No 135B

Invoice

Office Supplies Limited
Evin Blue Industrial Estate
Dublin 1

Tel: 01 5533321   **VAT Reg No:** 9935841
Fax: 01 5547711   **Date:** 12 January 1997

Marcol Systems Limited
Eagle House
Naas
Co Kildare

Qty	Code	Description	Unit Price £	Total £
3	2010	5 Star Fabric Ribbons	25.20	75.60
5	2011	Kores High Density Nylon	12.10	65.00
10	2050	5 Star Correctable Film	7.15	71.50
			Sub Total	212.10
			VAT	44.54
			Total	256.64

---

11. The supplier is Shannon's Supplies Ltd, Kilrush, Co Clare and the purchaser is Kathleen Carty, Church Street, Athlone, Co Westmeath. The terms of sale are 5% cash discount if payment is received with 30 days of the statement date.

		£
Balance outstanding from last month		425.50
4 Mar	Goods supplied on Invoice P2341	70.15
6	Goods returned – Credit Note CN523	20.10
7	Goods supplied on Invoice P2352	60.05
9	Cheque received	425.50
16	Goods supplied on Invoice P2370	15.00
18	Cases returned – Credit Note	5.00
26	CN547 Goods supplied on Invoice P2381	45.00

a) Complete the statement sent on 30 March from the details above.
b) Complete the cheque sent on 10 April.

12. On 30 June 1996, Hegarty & Co Ltd, Delgany, Co Wicklow received a statement from Collins Stationery Supplies Ltd, Monasterevin, Co Kildare. The balance due was £527.

On 2 July 1996, Nuala Lennon, the Purchasing Manager in Hegarty & Co Ltd, ordered the following goods from the price list she received.

10 Bic Crystal Medium (Black)

15 Bic Crystal Fine (Red)

20 Bic Crystal Medium (Blue)

5 Bic Clic Stic Ball Pen (Blue)

Price List

Collins Stationery Supplies Ltd
Monasterevin
Co Kildare

Means £7.30 for a pack of 50.

Code	Description	Unit Price £
0124	Paper Mate 2000 Fine (Blue/Black)	7.30/50
0125	Paper Mate 2000 Fine (Red)	1.70/12
0126	Paper Mate 2000 Medium (Blue/Black)	7.30/50
0127	Paper Mate 2000 Medium (Red)	1.77/12
0128	Zebra Ball Pen (Black/Blue/Red)	6.12/10
0129	Zebra Refills (Black/Blue/Red)	2.06/10
0130	Bic Clic Stic Ball Pen (Blue/Black/Red)	8.00/25
0131	Bic Soft Feel Stic (Blue/Black/Red)	4.25/12
0132	Bic Crystal Fine (Blue/Black/Red/Green)	3.10/20
0133	Bic Crystal Medium (Blue/Black/Red/Green)	3.20/20
0136	Pentel Fountain (Black/Blue/Red/Green)	18.70/12
0137	Pentel Ultra Fine (Black/Blue/Red/Green)	12.90/12
0200	Sigma Purchase Orders	6.86/50
0201	Sigma Delivery Notes	5.40 /50
0202	Sigma Invoice Sets	5.40/50
0203	Sigma Statements	6.80/50
0204	Sigma Memos	6.25/100

All Prices are excluding VAT at 21%

Terms: Trade Discount 15%, Cash Discount 2% 2 weeks

Net 1 Month

Required:

a) Complete the order form sent by Nuala Lennon on 2 July.

b) Complete the delivery note sent by Collins Stationery Supplies Ltd on 6 July.

c) Complete the invoice sent by Collins Stationery Supplies Ltd on 6 July.

d) On 8 July, Nuala Lennon wrote to Collins Stationery Supplies Ltd stating that Bic Crystal Fine (Green) were forwarded instead of Bic Crystal Fine (Red). Complete the Credit Note sent to Hegarty & Co Ltd.

e) Complete the cheque sent on 20 July by Hegarty & Co Ltd to clear their account.

f) Complete the statement sent by Collins Stationery Supplies Ltd on 31 July 1996.

13. You are secretary to the Purchasing Manager, and she has asked you to accept the responsibility of purchasing and controlling all items of stationery used in the business.

a) How would you ensure that stock levels are maintained and accurate?

b) What system would you use to record the receipt of stock and control the issuing of stock to various departments?

14. The details for receipt and issue of computer diskettes are given below. The unit size is 1 packet (20 disks per packet). Draw up an appropriate stock card recording the details.

July 1   25 packets in stock

      6   4 packets issued to Personnel Department

      9   6 packets issued to typing pool

      9   2 packets issued to Accounts Department

    12   1 packet issued to Advertising Department

    13   20 packets purchased

    20   8 packets issued to accounts

15. You have just taken over a position as stationery clerk, and have found that your predecessor kept records on scraps of paper. Your job is to set up a stock control system. From the information recorded on the scraps of paper given below:

a) show how you would record the details for overhead transparencies.

a) state when you will place an order for more supplies.

Inkjet overhead transparencies: min and max level – 5 and 25 boxes

Unit size of 1 box (50 sheets per box)

Balance on 2 June was 10 boxes

1 box issued to D on 5 June

5 boxes issued to Office Services Department on 9 June

Received from Star Stationery Limited on 11 June – 20 boxes

4 boxes issued to Marketing Department on 23 June

16. a) Complete the stock control card (figure 1) below.

b) Identify the items on the stock list (figure 2) which must be re-ordered immediately. For the items identified, decide what quantity should be re-ordered.

c) Complete the materials requisition form (figure 3) issued by the Sales Department to Stores for the items identified.

Stock Control Card

Item:	Star Economy Envelopes		
Code No:	E900	Maximum Level:	50
Unit Size:	1 packet	Re-order Level:	15
Location:	A31	Minimum Level:	10

Date	Issued to/ received from	Quantity issued	Quantity received	Balance
May 30	Sales			35
June 1	Personnel	5		
5	Purchasing	10		
12	Stationery Ltd	5		
15	Accounts		35	
20	Office Services	15		
25	Quantity Issued	10		

Figure 1– Stock control card

Stationery Stock List			12 September 1996			
Item	Location	Unit Size	Re-order Level	Max Level	Min Level	Balance
Plain Subject Dividers	D12	25/pkt	12	30	10	15
Manilla A-Z Indexes	D14	8/pkt	35	50	30	32
Myler Tabbed Index	D15	5/pkt	15	45	10	15
Punched Pocket Dividers	D12	2/pkt	25	40	20	27
Wallet Folders	E3	25/box	10	20	4	4
Clifton File	E4	25/box	6	10	4	7
Sorterlace Files	E5	10/box	7	12	5	6

Figure 2 – Stock list

Materials Requisition	No_____
From _____	
To: _____	

Qty	Details

Signature	Date

Figure 3 – Materials requisition form

NCVA 1996

1. An invoice was sent by Astra Business Systems to Ideal Office Supplies on 14 April 1996, for goods on Order No A125. All goods ordered were delivered. You are required to **complete the invoice**.

2. Ideal Office Supplies returned two Olivetti Inkjet JP370 printers which were damaged in transit. **Complete the credit note** that was issued on 20 April 1996 in response to these returns.

3. An opening unpaid balance of £2,579.50 was brought forward on the statement from March 1996. On 18 April 1996 a cheque for £2,450.52 was received from Ideal Office Supplies. Cash discount of 5% had been deducted from the amount owing. **Complete the statement of account** that was sent to Ideal Office Supplies on 30 April 1996, showing details of **all** transactions that occurred during the month of April 1996.

4. A cheque was received from Ideal Office Supplies in full settlement of the balance due on the April statement. **Complete the cheque and the stub** dated 12 May 1996.

Astra Business Systems

Santry Hall Industrial Estate
Dublin 9

Price List

Code	Description	Unit Price
672/1091	IBM Aptiva Cyrix 586 computer	1,429.00
672/1125	IBM Aptiva P75 Mini Tower computer	1,599.00
672/0755	Apple Performa 6200	1,329.00
671/2031	Citizen ABC mono printer	119.00
671/1324	Citizen inkjet Projet 2c colour printer	248.50
671/2000	Olivetti inkjet JP370 printer	299.00
671/2017	Sharp JX 9200 laser printer	349.00

Terms: Trade Discount 15%, Delivery 14 days, VAT 21%, Cash Discount 5% 1 month.

Order

Ideal Office Supplies
Silver Springs
Delgany
Co. Wicklow

No. A125

To:

Date: 2 April 1996

Astra Business Systems
Santry Hall Industrial Estate
Dublin 9

Please supply:

Qty	Code	Description	Unit Price
3	672/1125	IBM Aptiva P75 Mini Tower computer	1,599.00
2	672/0755	Apple Performa 6200	1,329.00
5	671/2000	Olivetti inkjet JP370 printer	299.00
1	671/2017	Sharp JX 9200 laser printer	349.00

Terms: Trade Discount 15%, VAT 21%, 5% Cash Discount 1 month, Delivery 14 days.

No. 215B		**Invoice**		
		Astra Business Systems		
		Santry Hall Industrial Estate		
		Dublin 9		
To:			Date:	

Terms: 5% 1 Month   **Delivery** 14 days   **VAT** 21%

Qty	Code	Description	Unit Price £	Total Price £
			Subtotal	
			VAT	
			Total	

No. 43C		**Credit Note**		
To:			Date:	

Credited by Astra Business Systems

Qty	Code	Description	Unit Price £	Total Price £
			Subtotal	
			VAT	
			Total	

Statement

Astra Business Systems
Santry Hall Industrial Estate
Dublin 9

To: Date:

Date	Ref	Details	Debit	Credit	Balance

3419	**Associate Banks Ltd**		
19	**Delgany, Co. Wicklow**	_____ 19 ___	
To:	Pay	OR ORDER	
For:		IR£	
Balance:	3419 18-69-43 48529162 Ideal Office Supplies		

7. Computer Hardware

After studying this chapter you should be able to:
- Identify the items of hardware in a computer system
- Distinguish between the types of printers available
- Describe what a network is and distinguish between a LAN and a WAN
- Explain how a typical network operates
- Explain the function of a modem

Introduction

Computers have created a revolution in the production, processing and transfer of information, primarily because of their ability to handle enormous amounts of data quickly. Over the years, business computing has changed dramatically. It was once completely dominated by large computers but now small, powerful personal computers (PCs) are available.

Computer users today often are not computer professionals, rather, they are people who need information and tools to do their jobs effectively.

In this chapter, we look at the various components of a computer and the additional devices which can be used to make working in the office easier, such as scanners for entering data, touch screens for displaying information and networks to allow users to communicate with each other via computer.

Hardware

Hardware refers to the physical components that make up a computer system, such as the central processor unit (CPU), visual display unit (VDU), keyboard, mouse and printer.

The Components of a Computer

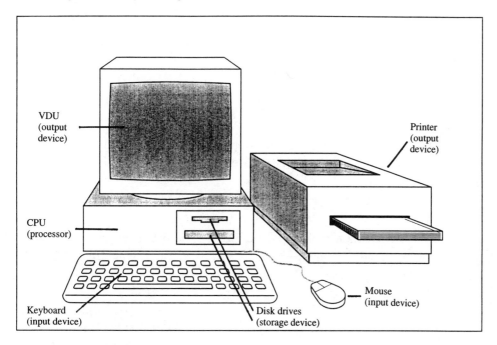

Components of a computer

The basic components of a computer system are:

Input devices: such as the keyboard, mouse and scanner which accept data for processing.

Processor: known as the central processing unit (CPU), this is the brain of the computer. The CPU performs the data processing as instructed by the software program in use. It accepts data from an input device and/or storage device, processes it and transfers the data to an output device.

Storage devices: such as the 'memory' which holds the data being processed and the disks, tapes and other devices which hold the data and programs for future use.

Output devices: such as the screen or visual display unit (VDU) which displays the results of processing and the printer which provides a 'hardcopy' (printed copy) of the data.

The word '**peripheral**' is also used to refer to components of the computer system other than the CPU.

Input Devices

Data is entered into a computer through an input device. The traditional method is to use the keyboard, but nowadays data can also be entered in less laborious ways. For example, data can be entered by talking to the computer using a headset and special software or data can be scanned directly into the computer using a scanner. Input devices can be classified into four broad categories:

1 Manual input devices
2 Pointing devices
3 Reading devices
4 Voice input devices

Manual Input Devices

Manual input devices are devices where the user types or writes the data to be entered into the computer. Examples of manual input devices are the keyboard and an electronic pen.

KEYBOARD

This is the most common tool for entering data. The data is manually entered by typing using the keyboard. Entering large volumes of data through the keyboard is laborious and prone to error.

A typical keyboard consists of:

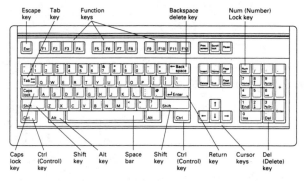

QWERTY keyboard.

Ordinary typing keys which are used to enter data and to give instructions to the computer in conjunction with **special keys** called **CTRL** and **ALT.** For example, pressing the key **'p'** would type the letter **'p'** but pressing CTRL at the same time as the key **'p'** might print a page.

Cursor control keys are up/down/left/right arrow keys to move the cursor (writing point) on the screen.

A numeric keypad is used like a calculator to enter numbers and also doubles as cursor control keys when the 'NUM LOCK key' is off.

Function keys are keys labelled F1 to F12 and are programmed to perform certain functions in each application package. For example, pressing the F1 key provides HELP.

ELECTRONIC PEN

An electronic pen is used with some handheld computers. The data is manually entered by writing on the screen and **handwriting recognition** software translates the handwriting into text.

Handwriting recognition software analyses the strokes as they are formed with the pen, and compares them with a predefined set of character shapes. Unrecognisable characters are sent to a 'context analyser' (dictionary) which looks at the surrounding characters in a word and guesses the unrecognisable character based on its position in the word.

This area is still being developed, and unless the user writes clearly his/her handwriting will not be recognised. A tutorial program which comes with the handheld computer illustrates how the user should write.

Handheld computers are used by people in jobs that involve taking notes while on the move, for example, sales representatives, auctioneers and couriers. The information recorded can be transferred to the main computer system, avoiding the duplication of effort involved in recording the information on paper first and then entering it into a computer.

Handheld computer with pen

Pointing Devices

Pointing devices are an alternative to the cursor keys on the keyboard. They are used to access menus and for selecting text or options in a program. Examples of pointing devices are the mouse, electronic pen and touch screens.

MOUSE

A mouse is an alternative to the cursor keys. It is a handheld device connected to the computer and contains a ball-type roller underneath with one or more buttons on top. It is placed on a special mat for ease of movement. When the mouse is moved, a signal is sent to the computer which moves the cursor on the screen.

A mouse does not eliminate the need to use a keyboard for entering text. It is used to move the cursor around the screen, to select text to be moved, copied or deleted and for selecting options from menus by clicking the left button. It can be difficult to use modern software applications without a mouse.

ELECTRONIC PEN

An electronic pen used with some handheld computers is also a pointing device. Text is selected by drawing brackets around the text and items are selected from a menu by pointing the pen at the required option in the menu.

TOUCH SCREENS

Touch screens are special VDUs that sense the location of your finger when it is placed on the screen.

The screen displays a menu with several listed options or **icons** (pictures). When you touch a particular icon, the program takes you to that option and may display a further list of options or the requested information in text and graphical format. Touch screens are used in large stores, amusement parks, tourist offices, banks etc to provide general information to the public.

Reading Devices

Reading devices involve the use of a scanner which takes an image of the data and inputs it into the computer. A scanner eliminates the need for keying-in data and thereby reduces the risk of input error.

The type of scanner used depends on the technology behind the source document, ie, whether the source information is in bar code format, text format, etc. Examples of reading devices are bar code scanners and office scanners.

BAR CODE SCANNERS

Many products have bar codes which consist of thick and thin lines with variable space between the lines and a unique number. A bar code is used to record details of the product such as the manufacturer, size, weight, and name of the product.

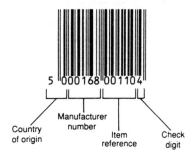

Bar code symbol

The bar code is read by a bar code scanner. There are various models of bar code scanners on the market, ranging from handheld models to models that are built into a checkout terminal.

Most grocery stores use bar code scanners for their checkout procedure. The scanner reads the bar code details and retrieves the product's price from the computer. Therefore, the price of the product does not have to be keyed in which minimises the time it take to complete a transaction and avoids input errors.

Bar coding is used to:
◆ implement EPOS and EFTPOS (see below).
◆ implement a stock control system.
◆ track items in transit.
For example, it is used in the mail service called 'Swiftpost', available from An Post. The customer purchases a Swiftpost envelope or label which contains a bar code. The bar code is scanned at each stage in its journey so that the letter or parcel can

be traced. The customer is given a receipt which details the bar code number; this number is quoted if there is an enquiry at a later stage.

EPOS

Electronic point of sale (EPOS) is a system in which a sales terminal such as a cash register provides the input to a computer. EPOS is used in supermarkets where the bar codes on products are scanned and the data in the bar codes is transmitted to the in-store computer. The computer provides the price of the item being scanned which is displayed on the screen of the cashier's register.

Advantages of EPOS

1. Eliminates data entry errors.
2. Changes in the price of products are made via the computer, eliminating the need to stick price tags on individual products.
3. Faster queues at the checkout.
4. A fully itemised receipt is produced for the customer.
5. Sales details, analysis and stock control information are made available.

EFTPOS

The retailer can link the EPOS system with an electronic payment system. An electronic payment system at the point of sale is known as an electronic funds transfer at point of sale (EFTPOS).

◆ The retailer's system is linked to a central computer which authorises the use of the customer's debit card (eg, a Laser card). This debit card authorises the transfer of funds from the customer's current account to the retailer's account. (It differs from a credit card where the purchases are charged to the customer's credit card account, for example, Access or Visa.)

MAGNETIC INK CHARACTER RECOGNITION SCANNER (MICR)

A MICR scanner reads stylish characters printed in magnetic ink, details printed at the bottom of a cheque. MICR is very accurate but documents are expensive to produce so MICR has limited application and is used mainly in banking. Cheques are encoded with the customer's account number, branch code and cheque number. When the cheques are returned to the bank, a clerk types the amount of the cheque on the bottom of the cheque using a special machine called a random endorsing machine.

The cheques are then passed through the MICR scanner which sorts the cheques by the branch sort-code. The cheques relating to the branch are stored on magnetic disk for later processing, and the non-branch cheques are sent to the central bank for processing.

OFFICE SCANNERS

A scanner takes an **image** of a page and inputs it into a computer. The scanned image is known as a **bitmap** image and cannot be edited. Special software, known as **optical character recognition** (OCR), is used to convert the bitmap image into a format that the computer can understand and therefore allow editing of the document. OCR software can recognise a wide range of fonts and generally retains the format of the documents, ie, columns and styles such as bold, italics, etc.

Uses of scanners:
1. Books, magazines, documents etc, can be scanned, eliminating the process of manually retyping the data.
2. The amount of paper to be filed is reduced. Information received in paper format can be scanned into the computer to be edited and/or filed for further reference.
3. Pictures, photographs or diagrams to be used in documentation can be input.

There are three types of scanners available on the market and the choice depends on the requirements of the user; these may include the volume of data to be scanned, the quality required, the type of items to be scanned (ie, pages versus articles from books or magazines).

Handheld scanner. This is the most affordable type of scanner capable of scanning documents or articles from books or magazines. It is suitable for low

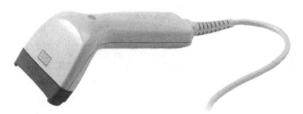

Handheld scanner

volume scanning or where high quality reproduction is not required. As the scan head is no larger than 3" wide, the document is scanned by physically moving the scanner down one side of the page at a time. The software uses a stitching process to combine the scanned image into a single file.

Sheet feed scanner. This is an affordable scanner offering better quality output than a handheld scanner. However, it is only suitable for scanning pages; articles from magazines must first be photocopied.

Flatbed scanner. This is the most versatile of scanners and is suitable for all types of jobs. It operates in a similar fashion to a photocopier.

Voice Input Devices

It is possible to enter data into a computer by talking to it, using a headset (earphones and microphone) and **voice recognition software** which converts the spoken words to text. The text displayed on the screen can be played back and heard through the earphones of the headset.

Voice recognition software analyses speech using an 'acoustic model' and a 'language model'. The acoustic model compares the user's speech to samples of speech patterns. It contains the most frequently used words, but additional words can be added by spelling them out. The language model is used to distinguish  between words that sound alike, such as 'to', 'two', 'too' and '2'.

As with handwriting recognition software, the user must train the system; the user's speech pattern (known as a template) is recorded and used to recognise his/her speech. However, the system responds only to the person who recorded the template. Therefore other users must also train the system to understand their speech pattern.

There are various versions of voice recognition software on the market, ranging from general packages with a limited vocabulary to packages with a comprehensive vocabulary and professional packages for particular occupations, such as business, medical and legal.

Uses of voice recognition:
1. To dictate directly into most window applications and to execute commands, such as open file, save, spell-check etc.
2. Used by employees who need to record information **directly** (unlike audio dictation which must be transcribed) into a computer while carrying out their work. For example, a stock control clerk can enter stock details while opening boxes and checking contents. A laboratory technician can record results while viewing items under a microscope.
3. Used by the visually impaired.

Output Devices

There are endless varieties of special purpose output devices such as airline ticket printers, ATMs (automatic teller machines) which print a transaction slip, cash registers, etc. However, output devices can be classified into two broad categories:
a) printers
b) visual display units (VDUs)

Printers

There are many different types of printers available on the market. When selecting a printer consider the following points:
- Where will the printer be located (consider the noise level and size of printer)?
- What will the printer be used for (consider fonts supported, colour capability, quality, paper types and sizes supported)?

- Is speed important?
- What volume of work is expected from the printer per time period (ie, week/month)?
- What are the maintenance cost (ribbons, toner, ink)?
- Budget constraints?

A printed copy is known as a **hardcopy**. Printers are categorised into two groups according to their method of printing:

> **Impact printers.** The print head makes contact with the ribbon and paper producing the characters on the paper and because of the contact, they are noisy.
>
> **Non-impact printers.** The print head does not make contact with the paper. These printers rely on other technology such as inkjet and laser and are virtually silent.

Impact Printers

DAISYWHEEL PRINTER

The printing mechanism is a wheel which contains a character, both uppercase and lowercase on each of its petals. During printing, the wheel rotates to position the correct character at the printing point which then strikes the ribbon and paper to produce the character. With the advent of the relatively inexpensive dot matrix printer, the daisywheel printer has become rare in the office environment today.

DOT MATRIX PRINTER

This is the most widely used impact printer. The printhead contains a series of pins in a straight line. The characters are constructed by the printhead pressing a combination of the pins against the ribbon as the printhead moves across the page. The characters appear as a matrix of dots.

Dot matrix printers come in 9-pin, 18-pin and 24-pin versions. The greater the number of pins in the printhead, the better the quality. Fabric or carbon ribbons can be used. Fabric ribbons can be used continuously until they eventually wear out, while carbon ribbons are used once, but provide better quality print.

Colour ribbons can be used with some models. A colour ribbon has four primary colours arranged horizontally, and the ribbon moves up and down while printing to produce the colour output.

Unlike non-impact printers, a dot matrix can print on multi-part stationery (also known as **NCR** – No Carbon Required). Multi-part stationery is the alternative to carbon paper used in earlier years. The output is printed only once, but two or more copies are produced at the same time. This is invaluable if the primary output is receipts, invoices and statements.

A dot matrix can print from more than one paper path (ie, it can select from different types of paper), such as:

a) **Tractor feed path**: which holds continuous stationery. Continuous stationery consists of pages which are joined together by perforations, allowing the pages to be separated easily when printed. It has holes (known as sprocket holes) on either side of the page to hold the paper in the tractor feed mechanism as the paper is pulled through while printing. A tractor feed path is not available on non-impact printers.

b) **Envelope feeder**: which holds and prints envelopes.

c) **Hopper feeder**: which holds single sheets of paper, 50 or more depending on model.

DOT matrix printer

Dot Matrix Printers	
ADVANTAGES	**DISADVANTAGES**
1. Initial cost is low.	1. Noisy.
2. Running costs are low: replacement cost of a ribbon.	2. Print quality is inferior to the non-impact models.
3. Prints on continuous stationery and multi-part stationery.	3. Not very good at printing graphics.
4. Provides near letter quality (NLQ) which may suit the job at hand.	4. Colour models are inferior to the non-impact models.
5. Extremely reliable.	5. Slower than the non-impact models.
6. Suitable for medium to high work load where quality is not important.	

Non-impact Printers

INKJET PRINTER

The inkjet is a very popular non-impact printer. The printhead consists of a series of nozzles which squirt tiny jets of ink onto the paper to form each character. As the printhead does not touch the paper, printing is virtually silent.

Colour models are available with some models using two cartridges (one for black and another for colour), while other models use one cartridge (for both black and colour). The one-cartridge model is cheaper to buy but very expensive to run, as the black ink is formed by mixing colours. Ink cartridges can be refilled but the quality may not be as good and the printer may not be guaranteed if the manufacturer's ink is not used.

The output produced is slightly moist, therefore the pages should be allowed to dry for a few seconds to avoid smudging. A variation of an inkjet printer is a bubblejet printer.

Inkjet Printers	
ADVANTAGES	**DISADVANTAGES**
1. Initial cost is relatively low: more expensive than a dot matrix but cheaper than a laser printer.	1. Expensive to run due to replacement cost of ink cartridge.
2. Virtually silent in operation.	2. Does not accommodate continuous or multi-part stationery.
3. Print quality approaching that of a laser printer.	3. Slower than a laser printer.
4. Provides good quality colour output at an affordable price.	4. Smudging can occur if printout is not left to dry for a few seconds.
5. Can be faster than a dot matrix printer.	
6. Suitable for medium work load where quality is important.	

LASER PRINTER

A laser printer works much like a photocopier. The data to be printed is sent to the printer's memory where a bitmap image of the page is formed on a charged drum by a laser beam. Where the image area is to be dark the charge is left on the drum and toner, which is powdered ink, is attracted to the charged 'dark' area forming an image of the original page which is printed.

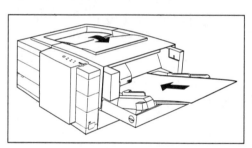

Laser printer

Colour models are very expensive and the cost is only justified where an organisation requires very high quality colour output.

Laser Printers	
ADVANTAGES	**DISADVANTAGES**
1. Top-of-the-range quality output.	1. Initial cost is higher than an inkjet.
2. Almost silent in operation.	2. Colour model extremely expensive.
3. Very fast output, faster than inkjets.	3. Does not accommodate continuous or multi-part stationery.
4. Can support a high workload.	4. Expensive to run due to replacement cost of toner.

Features of Printers

FEATURES	IMPACT PRINTERS		NON-IMPACT PRINTERS	
	DAISYWHEEL	DOT MATRIX	INKJET	LASER
Noise Level	High	High (Acoustic covers may be necessary)	Virtually silent	Almost silent
Fonts Supported	One type, as on daisywheel	Determined by application software	Determined by application software	Determined by application software
Prints Graphics	No	Yes	Yes	Yes
Colour Capability	Not available	Yes, some models, but poor quality	Yes, some models, good quality and cheaper than a laser	Yes, some models, excellent quality but very expensive
Quality – measured in dpi (dots per inch)	Letter quality	Draft to near letter quality (NLQ)	NLQ to letter quality	Letter quality
Paper Types	Bond paper Multi-part stationery Can't use continuous stationery Labels/envelopes Can't print on transparencies	Bond paper Multi-part stationery Continuous stationery Labels/envelopes Can't print on transparencies	Bond paper Can't use multi-part stationery Can't use continuous stationery Labels/envelopes Inkjet transparencies	Bond paper Can't use multi-part stationery Can't use continuous stationery Labels/envelopes Laser or photocopiable transparencies
Paper Sizes	Smaller and greater than A4 depending on carriage width	Smaller and greater than A4 depending on carriage width	Smaller and greater than A4 depending on cassette holders	Smaller and greater than A4 depending on cassette holders
Paper Paths	One path – cut sheet	Depends on model Tractor feed Hopper feed & manual feed Envelope feeder	Depends on model Tractor feed not available Cassette holder/hopper feed Envelope feeder	Depends on model Tractor feed not available Cassette holder and manual Envelope feeder
Speed	Prints one character at a time Slow	Prints one character at a time Slow	Prints one character at a time Relatively fast	Prints one page at a time Very fast
Maintenance Cost	Ribbon (cheap) Fabric ribbons which can be reused Carbon ribbons are used once, but give better quality	Ribbon (cheap) Fabric ribbons which can be reused Carbon ribbons are used once, but give better quality	Ink cartridges (expensive) Refills available	Toner (expensive) Toner cartridges can be refilled
Initial Cost	Relatively cheap, also used as a typewriter	Cheapest printer to buy today	Relatively cheap and middle of the range printer	Expensive and top of the range

Visual Display Unit – VDU

The visual display unit (VDU) is the screen or monitor of the computer.

The quality of the VDU display depends on the graphics card inserted in the computer. The quality is known as the **resolution**, which is the number of pixels (spots/dots of light) per inch displayed across and down the screen. The greater the number of pixels, the sharper the quality of the display.

The minimum recommended graphics card is an SVGA (Super Video Graphics Array) card which allows resolutions of 800 x 600 pixels or 1024 x 768 pixels.

It is important to work with a sharp image and a high 'refresh rate' to prevent eye strain. The 'refresh rate' is the rate at which the image is redrawn on the screen. The standard recommended by the Health & Safety legislation is 72Hz (cycles per second). With lower rate refresh rates a flicker will be noticeable on the screen which will causes headaches and eye strain.

The Central Processing Unit (CPU)

The central processing unit is the brain of the computer. It is a 'chip' which carries out the processing tasks by interpreting and executing the instructions in a program. The speed of the computer depends on the computer chip used.

Processors are made by many companies, but the most common is the Intel architecture (286, 386, 486 and Pentium). There are various speeds of Pentium chip (measured in MHz — millions of cycles per second): 66, 75, 90, 100, 133, 166 and 200; the greater the number, the faster the processor.

To run today's applications the minimum recommended chip specification is generally a 486. However, if you are considering purchasing a new computer, the entry level is a 'Pentium 90' or a 'Pentium 100'.

Storage Devices

The storage devices of a computer consist of temporary storage, which is the computer memory, and permanent storage, ie, disks where files are stored for future use. Data stored on an alterable medium, ie, disk, is known as **softcopy**.

Memory

The memory of a computer is a collection of chips and is referred to as random access memory (RAM). It is the computer's temporary working area which stores the programs and data while the CPU is carrying out its processing tasks. The programs are loaded from disk into memory, and the data is retrieved from disk or typed at the keyboard into memory.

The data stored in memory will be lost if the computer is turned off. Therefore, in order to keep your work for future use, it must be saved to permanent storage, ie, disk.

If the computer does not have enough memory, the machine will be slow as the programs and data will have to be swapped from memory back to disk many times. The minimum size of memory recommended is 8 megabytes, abbreviated to 8 MB. (A byte equals one character, mega equals one million, therefore, 8 MB equals 8 million characters.)

Permanent Storage

The media on which files are stored for future use are: magnetic disks, magnetic tapes and special compact disks.

MAGNETIC DISKS

Magnetic disks are the most widely used storage medium today. A disk is a circular platter on which a magnetic recording surface has been applied. There are two types of magnetic disks: a hard disk and a floppy disk.

A hard disk is a pack of disks stored inside the computer and is available in capacities ranging from 500 megabytes to 9 gigabytes (a gigabyte is a million million characters).

Floppy disks are portable 3.5" disks available in two capacities, 720 KB and 1.44 MB. A new floppy disk due on the market soon is the LS 120 MB. A new floppy disk drive must be installed in the computer as a laser beam is used to read and write data to the disk, hence the LS prefix. However, the LS drive will read both a 1.44 MB and a 720 KB disk.

Both types of magnetic disks provide **random access storage**. This means that the computer can directly go to where the information is stored on the disk and retrieve it; it does not have to read from the start of the disk until it finds the information.

CARE OF FLOPPY DISKS

Disks are fairly durable but they can be damaged, making the data stored on them unusable.

a) **Do not** expose the disks to magnetic fields, ie, put them near a telephone, a TV or photocopier.

b) **Do not** use any cleaning liquids on them.

c) **Do not** spill liquids or drop food on them.

d) **Do not** leave disks in the heat, sunlight, or in the cold. Disks can

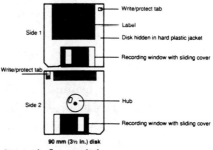

3½ inch floppy disk

become distorted by extremes of temperatures and become unusable, a disk will become warped with extreme heat.

e) **Do** store disks in a box. It prevents objects being piled on them and protects them from dust.

f) To prevent data on a disk from being erased accidentally, **write-protect** it. A 3½" disk has a built-in write-protect tab which when opened prevents data being written to or deleted from the disk.

MAGNETIC TAPE

Magnetic tape is not used as a principal storage medium today as it is slow in retrieving files. Magnetic tape is a **serial access medium**, which means that the system cannot retrieve the file directly but must work its way up to the file in a manner similar to a musical tape. If the information you want is at the end of a tape, it will take a while to spool through the tape and retrieve it.

Magnetic tape is used to off-load files that are seldom used from the hard disk, making the filing system on the hard disk more manageable. This is similar to weeding out the filing cabinet where files that are not in current use are transferred to some other location.

Magnetic tape is also used to make copies of files on the hard disk in case the files become corrupted or are deleted by mistake. This process of copying the files is known as **backing up** the system. A back-up is carried out by attaching a tape drive to the computer and the software is set so that the selected files can be transferred from the hard disk to tape. The files can be transferred back to disk when required.

Tape technology has improved immensely, and the DAT (Digital Audio Tape), which is a mini-cassette, is very popular. Depending on the model it can hold from 400 MB to 4 GB.

OPTICAL DISKS

Optical disks, also known as compact disks (abbreviated to CD) offer greater capacity than hard disks. There are three types of compact disks available:

CD-ROMs (compact disk read-only memory), are currently the most widely used, and can store more than 680 MB of data, equivalent to hundreds of floppy disks. Because of this capacity they are ideal for storing large volumes of data such as program and multimedia applications. (Multimedia is a phrase coined to mean just that – multiple media, ie, text, graphics, sound and video, the last three requiring huge amounts of storage capacity.) CD-ROMs are purchased with the data pre-encoded; data **cannot** be saved to them.

CD-ROMs are widely used in the office today. *MsBookshelf* is an office reference tool which includes a dictionary, thesaurus, almanac, atlas and encyclopedia. Many reference books, manuals, catalogues, telephone directories, databases and training programs are available on CD-ROMs. A search for information takes far less time than searching in books, filing cabinets or catalogues.

Software also comes on CD-ROMs. This has simplified the task of installing software on the computer. In the past many floppy disks were used which was time consuming.

CD-WORMs (compact disk, write once, read many times) are used for recording data. However, once the information has been recorded it cannot be **deleted**. To change information, a user would have to save the new version of the file to a new area on the disk. CD-WORMs are used by businesses that need to maintain vast archives.

CD-Rs (compact disk recordable) are a recordable medium similar to CD-WORMs. However, unlike a CD-WORM the data on a CD-R can be deleted or updated. CD-Rs can store more than 2 GB of data. CD-Rs are the way forward as regards data storage technology. Although they are not yet standardised, they have the greatest potential for augmenting or replacing magnetic disks mainly because of their huge capacity and the fact that data can be written, deleted and re-written to them.

To write to a CD-WORM or a CD-R, a special CD drive is needed. These drives are expensive and are only cost-effective where the volume of data to be stored can justify the expense. However, both types of disks can be read by a standard CD-ROM drive available with most computers.

Both the CD-WORM and the CD-R are in direct competition with microform (see Chapter 9).

Uses of CD-Rs:
1. To store and access large quantities of data.
2. To store files that contain pictures or graphics as these require a lot of disk space.
3. To store scanned images, eg, insurance companies may store their claim applications and insurance policies on CDs.
4. To back up the system.
5. To archive data.

Optical disk

Networks

A network consists of computers and peripherals (such as printers) linked together and network software to operate the configuration. It allows the devices on the network to be shared among users as well as allowing the users to share files and communicate with each other. Networks can vary in size from a small local area network, known as a LAN, to a wide area network known as a WAN.

LAN (Local Area Network)

A LAN is a collection of computers and peripherals connected by cables within a limited geographical area, ie, within a **single site** such as an airport, office building, university campus or manufacturing complex. A variety of devices can be attached to the LAN and the equipment size, brand or make can vary. As the network is local, a telephone line is **not** necessary to transmit data.

COMPONENTS OF A LAN

All LANs have the following basic components:

1. **File server**: a powerful dedicated computer which serves the rest of the network. Software and files to be shared are stored on the file server.
2. **Network cards**: which are inserted into each computer on the network. Each card has a unique identity to distinguish it from other devices on the network.
3. **Cable**: which is attached to the network cards and is used to link the computers together.
4. **Network software**: which monitors the network operations, allowing programs, files and peripheral such as printers to be shared. Modern operating systems such as *Windows 95* and *Windows NT* have network software built in.
5. **Multi-user software**: multi-user software applications are installed on the file server and can be accessed by the other computers, eliminating the need for the other computers to have separate copies of the software, thus saving space on each computer's hard disk. A multi-user licence for a certain number of users is purchased.

Some LANs have two or more file servers. This allows a back-up (ie, copies) of the data to be taken at regular intervals from one file server to the other. If the main file server goes down (stops working), the other file server can take over with the loss of only a few minutes' work.

TOPOLOGY

The configuration of a LAN (how the computers are connected together) can be shown in the three basic topologies (diagrammatical representation): star, ring and bus. This does not mean that the computers must be laid out as shown below. For example, the star topology just means that each computer must be connected to the central file server.

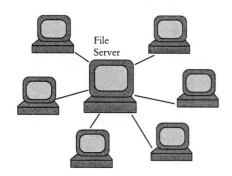

The star topology

The **star topology** is where each computer is connected to a central file server. Each computer communicates with the central file server in order to access another computer on the network. This topology is ideal for networks where ease of expansion is required.

In the **ring topology** the computers are connected to form a complete closed circuit and there is no central controlling computer. Messages are passed from one computer to the next until they arrive at the correct location. A token (signal) is required to send a message. Only one token is on the network at any one time, therefore two computers cannot send a message at the same time.

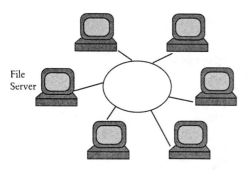

The ring topology

The **bus topology** is where each computer is connected to a single cable. To send a message, the computers listen to the line (cable) and if the line is free (ie, another message is not being sent) the computer is free to send its message.

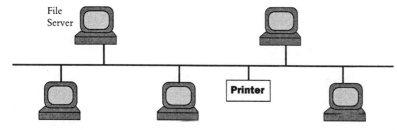

The bus topology

WAN (Wide Area Network)

A WAN is a network which covers a wide geographical area, for example, one which spreads across a country or between countries. Communication is through the telephone network and the use of satellites where necessary.

A WAN differs from a LAN in that:

1. A WAN covers a large geographical area.
2. The data is sent over the telephone network.
3. A modem (see section below) is required to transfer data from one computer to another over the telephone lines.

A WAN may use either the public telephone lines or a private network. A private network is where a business leases telecommunication lines to set up a permanent connection between areas. The choice depends on the volume of usage and security required. Where the volume of usage is high, a private network may be cheaper.

A WAN is installed where there is a high volume of inter-office communication. For example, a firm with many branches spread throughout the country would install a WAN network to facilitate inter-office communication such as: sending e-mail messages, allowing the branches to access the head office database and to transfer files between branches.

A typical set-up for inter-office communication could be as follows: each branch has a LAN installed and each LAN is connected to Head Office via the telephone network

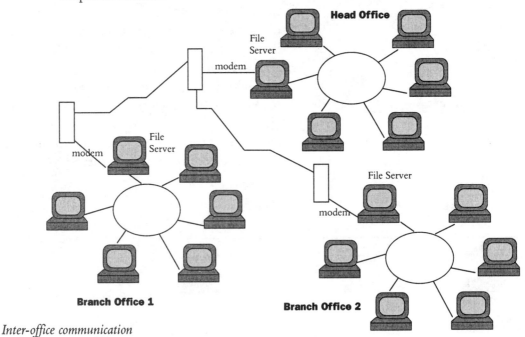

Inter-office communication

HOW A NETWORK OPERATES

A **client/server** configuration is the most popular network configuration. It consists of a file server and one or more computers known as **clients** attached to the network, hence the name client/server.

A client is a computer that sends a message requesting a service from the server on the network and the server responds to the request on behalf of the client. For example, the client could request the use of a particular software application, a document to be printed or information from a database stored on the server.

Advantages of Networks

1. **Peripheral device sharing**. Few users need their own printer, therefore it is cost-effective to put a printer on a network for all users to share. Users simply send their output to the network printer where it will queue and be printed.
2. **Software sharing**. LANs enable organisations to save money on software licences. A multi-user licence is purchased to support the maximum anticipated number of concurrent users of the package. This eliminates the need to purchase a personal copy of the software for each user.
3. **Data sharing**. Data can be stored on the LAN file server where it can be accessed by others.
4. **Communication**. Users on the network can use an internal e-mail package to communicate with each other.
5. **Inter-office connection**. This is achieved with a public network, ie, a WAN.

Modems (Modulator/Demodulator)

The telephone line was designed to carry voice, not data. In order for data from a computer to be transmitted over the telephone line a modem is required at each computer. A modem is a device which is connected to both the computer and the telephone line. The modem converts the digital signals from a computer into a format known as an **analog signal** which can be carried on the telephone line (MOdulation). The receiving modem converts the signal from analog to digital (DEModulation).

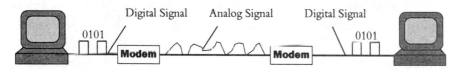

TYPES OF MODEM

Some modems can also transmit and receive facsimile (fax) transmissions (see Chapter 10).

Card modems fit into expansion slots in the computer and are connected to both the computer and the telephone system.

External modems sit alongside the computer and are connected to both the computer and the telephone system.

Summary

The hardware of a computer is the physical components of the system. It consists of: an input device, processor, storage device and output device. The word 'peripheral' is often used to mean the components of the computer system other than the processor. When selecting a computer several factors need to be taken into account.

1. **Processor**. The speed of the processor is important; to run today's applications the minimum recommended chip specification is a 486.

2. **Memory**. The minimum memory size recommended is 8 MB. If the computer does not have enough memory the machine will be slow, as the programs and data will have to be swapped from the computer's memory back to disk many times.

3. **VDU**. The VDU should have a refresh rate of 72Hz. If it is less than this, a flicker will be noticeable which will cause eye strain and headaches.

4. **Storage media.** The capacity of hard disk and required CD drive, ie, CD-ROM, CD-WORM or CD-Rs.

Magnetic disks such as a **hard disk** or a **floppy disk** are widely used to store data. Magnetic tape is used to off-load seldom-used files from the hard disk and to back up the system. CD-WORM and CD-Rs are the way forward as regards data storage technology. Data recorded on a CD-R can be deleted or updated unlike a CD-WORM which allows data to be recorded but not deleted.

Computers have an impact on all aspects of our everyday life. In supermarkets we have EPOS systems which speed up the checkout process. With EFTPOS purchases can be paid for without handling cash. Information is provided to the general public on touch-screen computers.

In the office, the keyboard is the most widely used input device. However, the mouse has made the manipulation of programs and data easier. Scanners have found a prominent position in the office eliminating the process of entering data manually. Voice input devices are now finding their way into the office and are being used by employees who need to record information while carrying out their work.

The two main types of printers used in the office are impact printers (dot matrix) and non-impact printers (inkjet and laser). The choice depends on many factors such as printer size, noise level, quality of output, speed, paper types and sizes supported, volume of work, maintenance cost and initial cost. It is not uncommon to find all types of printers in an office, the dot matrix being used for draft output or printing onto multi-part stationery, the inkjet being used for colour output and the laser being used for high quality and speedy output.

A network allows devices on the network to be shared among users and enables users to share files and to communicate with each other. A network operates by a client requesting information from the server and the server responding to that request. A network which spans a limited geographical area is known as a local area network (LAN) and does not use the telephone system. There are three typical configurations of a LAN: the star, ring and bus topologies. A wide area network (WAN) covers a wide geographical area. The computers on a WAN require a modem to allow the information to travel over the telephone system.

Questions

Multiple Choice Questions

1. Which one of the following is not a peripheral?
   a) input device
   b) output device
   c) processor
   d) hardware
   e) storage device

2. An example of an output device is:
   a) VDU
   b) scanner
   c) cursor key
   d) electronic pen
   e) mouse

3. EPOS means:
   a) Electronic Pen Operating System
   b) Electronic Point of Scanning
   c) Electronic Point of Sale
   d) Easy Pointing Optical Scanner
   e) Easy Pointing Operating System

4. The codes at the bottom of a cheque are read by:
   a) a Laser card
   b) a bar code scanner
   c) an MICR scanner
   d) an office scanner
   e) a sheet feed scanner

5. Which of the following devices is used to provide general information to the public?
   a) a VDU
   b) a scanner
   c) a touch screen

d) a bar code scanner

e) EPOS

6. Voice recognition software analyses speech using:

a) an acoustic model and a language model

b) an acoustic model and OCR

c) an acoustic model and MICR

d) an acoustic model and word processing

e) an acoustic model and a scanner

7. Which of the following scanners will not read text?

a) an office scanner

b) a flatbed scanner

c) a sheet feed scanner

d) a handheld scanner

e) a bar code scanner

8. A hardcopy is:

a) a copy of a file

b) a copy displayed on the screen

c) a bitmap copy

d) a printed copy

e) a copy of a disk

9. An example of an impact printer is:

a) a laser printer

b) a desktop printer

c) a dot matrix printer

d) an inkjet printer

e) a bubblejet printer

10. Which of the following printers support multi-part stationery?

a) a laser printer

b) a desktop printer

c) a dot matrix printer

d) an inkjet printer

e) a bubblejet printer

11. Which of the following printers cannot produce letter quality print?

a) a laser printer

b) a dot matrix printer

c) a bubblejet printer

d) an inkjet printer

e) a desktop printer

12. The quality of the VDU display is called:
    a) near letter quality
    b) letter quality
    c) display quality
    d) resolution
    e) draft quality

13. The standard refresh rate to avoid flicker on the screen is:
    a) 72 Hz
    b) 72 MB
    c) 72 z
    d) 72 KB
    e) 72 H

14. The minimum recommended processor specification is:
    a) 8 MB
    b) 8 KB
    c) 8 GB
    d) 486
    e) 386

15. Which of the following storage devices is a serial access medium?
    a) magnetic hard disk
    b) magnetic floppy disk
    c) magnetic tape
    d) CD-WORM
    e) CD-ROM

16. With a CD-WORM data can be:
    a) read but not written to
    b) read, deleted, but not written to
    c) read, written to, but not deleted
    d) read, deleted, and written to
    e) read only

17. MB means:
    a) 1 million megabytes
    b) 1 million megabits
    c) 1 million bytes
    d) 1 million bits
    e) 1 million million bytes

18. Which of the following will hold the most information?
    a) 3.5" disk
    b) hard disk
    c) magnetic tape
    d) CD-WORM
    e) CD-R

19. A file server is:
    a) a disk which serves up files
    b) a copy of the hard disk which serves as a back-up
    c) a computer which serves the network
    d) a CD-ROM which serves up vast amounts of information
    e) a back-up copy on magnetic tape

20. Which of the following printers will produce the best quality work with the greatest variety of typefaces?
    a) dot matrix
    b) daisywheel
    c) inkjet
    d) laser
    e) deskjet   (NCVA 1994)

21. Which of the following reprographic systems offers the best quality print at highest speeds?
    a) inkjet printer
    b) daisywheel printer
    c) photocopier
    d) offset lithographic duplicator
    e) laser printer   (NCVA 1996)

Short Answer Questions
1. List the four components of a computer system and give one example of each.
2. Distinguish between hardware, software and peripherals.
3. What are function keys?
4. What software is used to translate data entered with an electronic pen into text?
5. List three pointing devices.
6. List three uses of a mouse.
7. What is a touch screen?
8. What are bar codes?
9. State four advantages of EPOS.
10. Distinguish between EPOS and EFTPOS.
11. What is MICR?

12. What software is used with an office scanner to convert the image to text?
13. List three types of office scanners available on the market.
14. What is voice input?
15. What factors should be taken into account when selecting a printer?
16. Distinguish between an impact printer and a non–impact printer.
17. How does a dot matrix printer produce characters?
18. What are the advantages of a dot matrix printer over an inkjet or laser?
19. List four disadvantages of a dot matrix printer.
20. What is meant by a paper path? List three types.
21. What factors should be considered when selecting a colour inkjet printer?
22. List four advantages and four disadvantages of an inkjet printer.
23. How does a laser printer produce a page?
24. List four advantages and four disadvantages of a laser printer.
25. What are the maintenance costs of a dot matrix, an inkjet and a laser printer?
26. What is meant by an SVGA card?
27. List two chip specifications for a central processing unit.
28. What is the memory of a computer used for?
29. List four storage devices on which files can be saved.
30. Distinguish between a hard disk and a floppy disk.
31. How does magnetic tape differ from a disk? When would magnetic tape be used?
32. List four points for the care of a floppy disk.
33. List three types of compact disks and distinguish between them.
34. What is an optical disk?
35. What is a network?
36. Distinguish between a LAN and a WAN.
37. List five items necessary to install a LAN.
38. Distinguish between ring, bus and star topology.
39. Briefly describe how a client/server configuration operates.
40. List four advantages of a network.
41. What is the purpose of a modem?
42. List four considerations if asked to recommend a printer for the office.
    (NCVA 1995)

8. Computer Applications

After studying this chapter you should be able to:
◆ Distinguish between integrated packages and application suites
◆ Identify the features and uses of common generic computer application packages
◆ Identify the equipment and software necessary for in-house publishing

Introduction

Computer application packages are programs (software) written to carry out specific tasks. These tools help to make office workers more productive. For example, a firm might hold its rules and procedures manual or its price list on disk. When these documents need updating, they are retrieved from disk, updated, saved and printed. Thus the task is accomplished quickly and with a low error rate.

Typical computer application packages used by businesses are: word processing, spreadsheets, databases and desktop publishing.

Computer application packages vary in the functionality they offer depending on whether they are integrated or single packages.

Integrated Package

An integrated package is **one program** which will have more than one application, normally word processing, spreadsheets, databases and graphics. Integrated packages cover the basics in each application and are suitable for small businesses, home users or new users. Examples of integrated packages are MsWorks and ClarisWorks.

Single Package

A single package is a program which provides just one application, but which includes very advanced features not available in an integrated package. Single packages are normally purchased by businesses that require sophisticated tools (packages) to perform their work. Examples of single packages available on the market are: MsWord (word processing), WordPerfect (word processing), MsExcel (spreadsheets), Lotus 123 (spreadsheets), MsAccess (database).

Integrated Packages	
ADVANTAGES	**DISADVANTAGES**
1. Cost-effective way of purchasing software. 2. Easier to learn and use. Only the essential features are included, therefore the learning curve is short. 3. Integration between modules, eg, a spreadsheet can be copied into a word processing document with ease. 4. Less space required on hard disk to store the program.	1. Not as feature-rich as single packages 2. Complicated tasks are more difficult to accomplish.

Application Suite

An application suite is a bundle of single packages from the same software developer sold together as one unit. Businesses normally purchase an application suite rather than single packages as it is more cost-effective. Examples are:

MsOffice which includes MsWord, MsExcel, MsPowerpoint (presentation package), and Scheduler (electronic diary).

MsOffice Pro which includes MsOffice and MsAccess.

Lotus Smart Suite which includes Lotus 123, AmiPro (word processing), Approach (database), Freelance (presentation package) and Organiser (electronic diary).

Corel Office Professional 7 which includes Word Perfect, QuatroPro (spreadsheet), Paradox (database), Presentation and InfoCentral (electronic diary).

Application Suites	
ADVANTAGES	**DISADVANTAGES**
1. Cost-effective way of purchasing advanced, feature-rich programs. 2. Advanced features included in each application. 3. Integration between modules.	1. Can be difficult to learn without some previous knowledge of application. 2. Place heavy demands on the computer resources.

Word Processing (WP)

Office workers whose jobs once required many hours a day of typing and retyping documents now spend less time at this task because of word processing. There is no longer a need to completely retype a document when mistakes are made or when a document needs to be updated., saving considerable time and effort.

Word processing may be carried out on a dedicated machine for word processing only or on a general purpose computer using a word processing package such as WordPerfect, MsWord or AmiPro.

Uses

- General office correspondence (letters, memos, reports, etc)
- Sending personalised letters to individuals on a mailing list
- Producing booklets and leaflets
- Producing a table of contents automatically
- Producing newsletters with columns and graphics

Features

CREATING DOCUMENTS

When you create a new document you are presented with a blank screen and a small blinking line, called a **cursor**, which marks the position where the character will be entered. When the end of a line is reached, the cursor will automatically move down to the next line and any words extending past the right margin will automatically drop to the next line. This feature is called **word wrap**; it allows you to continue typing without having to press the 'enter key' ('return key') at the end of each line. The 'enter key' is only pressed to start a new paragraph.

EDITING FUNCTIONS

Editing means making revisions. The document will be automatically adjusted to take account of the revisions made. Editing may involve:

- **Deletion and/or insertion** of text.
- **Moving or copying.** Text can be moved or copied from one part of a document to another or from one document to another.
- **Search and replace function.** Repeated errors or text to be updated can be found and corrected automatically throughout the document using this function. This saves the time involved in scrolling through the document looking for the specific text to be changed.

FORMATTING FUNCTIONS

Formatting means changing the appearance and layout of a document and may involve changing:

- **Fonts.** A font is a set of characters in a particular typeface, style and size.

    A *typeface* is a set of characters in a particular design, for example, this text is in 'M Bembo' typeface.

    Font *size*. Fonts are measured in **points** rather than inches. There are 72 points to an inch, so a typeface with a font size of 12 points equals one sixth of an inch.

    Font *styles*. Font styles are used to enhance a document or emphasise particular words in a document using, for example: underline, **bold**, *italics*, superscript (where the character is above the typing line, eg, 10^2) and subscript (where the character is below the typing line, eg, H_2O).

Examples of some fonts available:

An example of the typeface 'H Franklin Gothic Heavy' in size 11 point

An example of the typeface 'Helvetica' with the style italics, in size 14 point

`An example of the typeface 'Courier' in size 16 point`

- **Line spacing.** The spacing between lines of text can be changed from single to line and a half, double or treble spacing.

- **Justification.** Refers to the alignment of the text on the page. There are four main types: left, right, full and centred as illustrated below.

Left justification (also known as ragged right). Text is automatically aligned flush with the left margin producing a ragged right margin.	**Right** justification. Text can be aligned flush with the right margin producing an even right margin but a ragged left margin. Used to type the date on the right-hand side of a letter.
Full (even) justification. Text can be aligned flush with both the left and right margins producing an even look. It is used in printed material.	**Centred** justification. Text is centred horizontally across the page. Used for displaying text .

- **Bullets.** A bullet is a symbol used to separate and emphasise items in a list. Examples of bullets are:

    -
    ⇨
    ◆

- **Page layout and orientation.** This involves changing the layout of the document, ie, the margins, the orientation of the paper (portrait or landscape) and the paper size.
- **Tabulation.** WP packages have pre-set tab stops at half-inch intervals. Tabs are used to align columns of text. When the tab key is pressed, the cursor is taken from point 'A' to point 'B'. Four types of alignments are available:

  left – extends text to the right from the tab stop.

  right – extends text to the left from the tab stop. Used to align non-decimal numbers.

  decimal – aligns decimal numbers on the decimal point.

  centred – centres text at the tab stop.

Left	Right	Decimal	Centred
there	10,234	12.34	there
the	23	123.56	the

OTHER FUNCTIONS

Other valuable functions in producing documents include the following:

- **Headers.** A header is text which is keyed in **only once**, but is inserted by the program at the top of every page, for example, chapter headings.
- **Footers.** A footer is text which is keyed in **only once**, but is inserted by the program at the bottom of every page. An example is page numbering, where a symbol is entered and this will print the appropriate page number on each page.
- **Orphans.** Facility to ensure that the **first line** of a paragraph does not start at the end of a column or page.
- **Widows.** Facility to ensure that the **last line** of a paragraph is not brought onto a new column or page.
- **Automatic numbering.** A function which automatically types the next number in sequence, when the enter key is pressed. If you add, delete, or re-order the items in a numbered list, the program updates the numbers in the correct sequence.
- **Spell-checker.** A spell-checker program is included in most word processing packages and is used to check the spelling of a document against an in-built dictionary. The spell-checker program stops at any word it does not recognise. The operator has the choice of ignoring the word (if it is not in the dictionary, but correctly spelt), adding it to the dictionary (if it is correctly spelt and much used), correcting the error by substituting a word from a list of suggested words or typing the word again.
- **Clip Art.** This is a library of pictures incorporated into modern application programs and can be imported into a document to add visual impact. Clip Art can also be purchased on CD-ROMs.

◆ **Mail Merge.** A facility used to create personalised standard letters sent to more than one person. It is achieved by combining the standard letter with another file (known as the data source) which contains the names and addresses. The combined output is known as the merged document.

The following features are generally not available in an integrated package:

◆ **Grammar.** The grammar program identifies a sentence that contains possible grammatical errors and suggests ways to improve the sentence. You can determine how strictly the program observes grammar by using formal, business or casual rules.

◆ **Calculation facilities.** A calculation facility allows simple mathematical functions, such as addition, subtraction, multiplication, division, percentages and averages to be carried out. This allows numerical data to be calculated without using a calculator or a spreadsheet program.

◆ **Graphics facility.** Graphics facilities enable lines, boxes and circles to be drawn. The objects drawn can be shaded using patterns and colour.

◆ **D**rop cap. Paragraphs can be formatted to have a large initial, or dropped capital letter at the beginning of the paragraph as illustrated here.

◆ **Paragraph styles.** A collection of formats – typeface, point size, indents, etc, that can be named and stored. When the named style is applied to selected text, the program applies all the formatting attributes in the named style to the selected text at once.

For example, a style could be stored to have all sub-headings in the following format: Arial 14 point, underlined, bold and centred. When the style is selected, all of the above formats will be applied to the sub-heading at once. This speeds up formatting, as each individual format does not have to be applied separately. In addition, any changes made to the style will automatically change all the paragraphs formatted with that style.

◆ **Templates.** A template is a standard layout which is set up for documents. Most packages provide templates for several common types of documents, such as memos, reports, curricula vitae, business letters, invoices, etc. Templates can be modified to suit the user's needs. Organisations use templates to ensure that all correspondence sent out by different secretaries has the same format.

◆ **Table of contents.** When styles are created, a table of contents can be created automatically. A table of contents is used to give a summary of the contents in a book with the corresponding page numbers.

Spreadsheets

A spreadsheet is a software package for financial modelling, such as the preparation of budgets, income and expense statements, forecasts and essentially any documentation that requires a lot of computational work. The major advantage is the automatic recalculation of results when a number used in the calculation is changed.

Office work that involves dealing with numerical calculations such as managing the petty cash is simplified with the use of spreadsheets. For example, the petty cash book is created in a spreadsheet. At the end of each week, the office clerk enters the details from the petty cash vouchers and the totals of each expense item and the balance left is automatically calculated.

Examples of Spreadsheet programs are: MsExcel, Lotus 123, QuatroPro.

Uses

- To carry out 'what if' questions, eg, how will the savings change if you spend more on rent
- To process numerical data
- To prepare budgets and forecasts
- To produce job cost estimates
- To produce graphical representations of figures, ie, pie chart, bar chart, etc
- To analyse results of surveys

Layout

A spreadsheet consists of rows and columns. Rows are numbered 1, 2, 3, etc, and the columns lettered A, B, C, up to Z. After Z, AA, AB, AC and so on are used. The intersection of a row and a column is known as a **cell**. Each cell is referenced by a column letter and a row number. Cell F4 is the intersection of column F, row 4 as indicated below.

1	A	B	C	D	E	F	
2		January	February	March	April	May	
3	**Income**						Cell F4
4	Wages	500	500	500	500	500	
5	Interest	10	0	0	15	0	
6		=SUM(B4:B5)	=SUM(C4:C5)	500	515	500	
7							
8	**Expenses**						
9	Rent	100	100	100	100	100	
10	Food	120	120	120	120	120	
11	Clothes	50	0	0	30	0	
12	Miscellaneous	80	80	80	80	80	
13		=B9+B10+B11+B12	=SUM(C9:C12)	300	330	300	
14							
15	**SAVINGS**	=B6-B13	0	200	185	200	

Figure 8–1

To perform calculations automatically, a **formula** is placed in the cell where the answer is required. A formula is indicated by an equals sign and the cell references are used rather than the actual data in the cells.

For example, to add the expenses for January, the cursor is placed in cell B13 (where the answer is to appear) and the following **addition formula** is entered: =B9+B10+B11+B12. Therefore if the numbers in the columns are changed, the answer is automatically recalculated.

Spreadsheets also have built-in formulas called **functions**. The SUM function is used in cell C13; **=SUM(C9:C12)** means add all the numbers in the range C9 to C12. This is similar to the addition formula of **=C9+C10+C11+C12** but a lot quicker to enter.

The results of the formulas are *actually displayed* as in columns D, E and F. For example, if the wages figure for April was changed to £600, the total income figure for April would automatically be updated to £615 and savings for April to £285. This spreadsheet shows the effect on savings if the income or expenditure pattern changed.

Features

The **editing** and **formatting** functions as described under Word Processing (except bullets and tabulation) are also available in a spreadsheet.

- **Insert a row or column** at a desired spot and the formulas will automatically adjust to take account of the figures entered.
- **Copying formulas.** A formula entered for one column or row can be copied to other columns or rows and the cell references in the formulas will adjust automatically. For example, in Figure 8–1, if the formula for the January savings =B6-B13 is copied to February it will read =C6-C13. This is known as a **relative reference** as the formula adjusts when it is moved.

  A formula with an **absolute reference** always points to the same cell, even when the formula is copied. An absolute reference is indicated by typing a dollar sign ($) in front of the column letter and/or row number that you want to make absolute. For example, in the multiplication chart below, we always want the formulas to refer to column B and row 20. In cell reference C21, the formula is entered and when it is copied to cell D21 it stills refers to column B and row 20, as a dollar sign is placed before both of these.

	B	C	D	E	F
20		1	2	3	4
21	1	=$B21*C$20	=$B21*D$20	3	4
22	2	=$B22*C$20	-$B22*D$20	6	8
23	3	=$B23*C$20	6	9	12
24	4	4	=$B24*D$20	12	16

- **Format.** The width of the columns can be changed, as can the number of decimal places displayed for numbers.
- **Sort.** Data can be sorted alphabetically or numerically.
- **Charting facility.** Spreadsheet packages offer charting facilities so that data can be displayed in a bar chart, line graph, pie chart, etc.
- **Protect facility.** A command to ensure that the contents of a specified range of cells cannot be changed. This is a useful feature, as it allows others to view your information without making changes to it, accidentally or otherwise.

Database

A database is a computerised filing cabinet storing a collection of related records. A database program provides a structure for storing data in such a way that it can be searched automatically for specific information. For example, a business could search a database of customers by county or age to target a specific segment of the market to promote their products. This is a lot quicker than searching through a manual filing system. Examples of databases in use are MsAccess, Paradox, Approach.

It is important to understand the terminology used in a database. Shown below is the structure of a database to record information about staff.

PERSONNEL FILE

Title:	Mr
First Name:	Jerry
Surname:	Kelly
Address 1:	15 Main Street
Address 2:	Blackrock
County:	Dublin
Date of Birth:	10/11/65
Position:	Sales Assistant
Salary:	£13,000

Field. Each separate item of information in the personnel file is known as a **field**, eg, 'title': is a field, 'first name': is a field, etc.

Each separate item of information is entered into a field to facilitate searching the database. The Personnel file can now be searched based on any field, ie, a search could be performed to locate all employees who earn above £15,000.

Record. A record is collection of related data items; it consists of all the fields for one unit of information. The record for Jerry Kelly is shown.

File. A file is a collection of related records. In the Personnel file, there will be many records giving similar details of other employees.

Uses

- ◆ telephone directories
- ◆ library databases
- ◆ personnel records
- ◆ details of employees, customers, suppliers, etc
- ◆ stock records

Features

The **editing** and **formatting** functions as described in Word Processing (except bullets and tabulation) are also available in a database.

- ◆ **File interrogation.** The user is able to construct a query detailing what s/he is searching for. The required subset of information will then be displayed.
- ◆ **Reports.** A report facility allows the user to construct professional reports incorporating the necessary information.
- ◆ **Multi-user.** Some database packages are multi-user which enables many users to look at the same information at the same time. Controls can be set up so that particular users only see certain areas of the database. As the database is stored in one location (ie, on the file server – see Chapter 7) this means that there will be only one version of the file, ensuring that the information that users view is up to date.
- ◆ **Security.** Multi-user databases offer both a system of passwords to block access to the system and 'access rights' which control what that user can view or alter within the system.

Sort and protect facilities available with spreadsheets are also available with databases.

Merging information. Information stored in a database can be merged with other applications. For examples, names and addresses stored in a database can be merged with a word processing package to produce personalised letters.

Desktop Publishing (DTP)

A desktop publishing application is used to layout pages. Text and graphics can be assembled on a page and sophisticated formatting tools are used to change the appearance of the layout of the document. DTP is used to produce posters, magazines, newspapers, books or other printed material.

Today's high-powered dedicated word processing packages offer functions similar to those available in a desktop publishing package, but they are not intended to replace desktop publishing packages as they fulfil different roles. In a word processing package pages are formed in a linear fashion, ie, lines of text follow each other. In a desktop publishing application, documents are built from objects like blocks of text and pictures. These objects can be placed anywhere on the page: side by side, overlapping, stretched vertically down a page, horizontally across a page or wrapped around diagrams or pictures.

Creating a Document using DTP

The procedure for creating a document with a DTP package is different to word processing.

DTP techniques require the **layout of a page** to be planned in advance, by creating 'frames' which are boxes drawn to allocate to headlines, text, pictures, etc. Once the page layout has been planned, data can be entered directly into the frames or imported from other application packages such as word processing and graphics packages.

Uses

To produce output with a professional look:

♦ The capabilities of a DTP package mean that organisations wishing to produce a wide range of documents no longer require the services of outside printers.

♦ Annual reports, sales catalogues, marketing brochures, newsletters, press releases, etc, can be produced in-house.

♦ Printing businesses use DTP to produce books, magazines, newspapers etc.

Features

All features offered by word processing packages are available in DTP. However, the terminology varies, ie, 'leading' refers to line spacing, and frames must be created before data can be entered. Additional features include:

♦ **Frames.** The layout of a page is designed using frames. The correct frame must be selected for text, word art, pictures etc.

♦ **Word Art.** This offers a variety of fonts, point sizes, and unusual ways to position text on the page. For example, you can create a publication title in 48 point and position it vertically down the page, stretch the letters to make them wider or taller, add patterns, colours, and shadows to Word Art text.

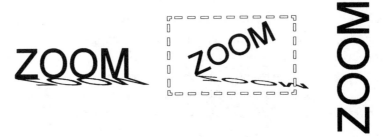

A sample of the effects allowed with Word Art

- **Leading.** This is the amount of space left between each line. It is similar to line spacing in word processing except that one is not tied to single line, line-and-a-half or double-line-spacing as in most word processing packages. In DTP the spacing between lines is adjusted in points, allowing immense flexibility (72 points equals 1 inch).

- **Kerning.** A function to reduce or increase the amount of 'white space' between letters in a word. When text is justified, the text is stretched across the page by inserting spaces between the letters in a word. When using small columns the amount of 'white space' can be very noticeable.

- **Style galleries.** These are master documents set up for particular displays, such as brochures, mail shots, banners, cards, etc similar to templates available in word processing. The format of a document selected from a style gallery can be modified and saved as your own style sheet. Using a document from a style gallery rather than designing your own style sheet will save considerable time.

- **Paragraph styles.** (as described under Word Processing).

- **Reverse video.** Text is normally printed with black characters on a white background, but this can be changed (reversed) to white text on a black background. Other colours can be used. **Reverse Video**

Advantages of DTP

- Professional-looking material can be produced.
- The range of publishing that can be undertaken 'in-house' increases.
- Cost reduction in new or revised publications, manuals, leaflets, pamphlets, etc.
- Tremendous savings can be made by using 'in-house' DTP systems instead of sending work out to printing firms. However, a trained operator is required.

Equipment necessary to produce documents in-house:

- A microcomputer (PC) with the following specifications:

  A 486 processor or higher specification, ie, a Pentium. A fast processor is necessary to run modern desktop publishing packages.

  SVGA card so that the image displayed on the screen is sharp and clear, allowing the user to work with ease.

  A minimum of 8 MB of memory to hold the data and program during processing.

  A mouse to draw frames, manipulate and format the document.

- A good quality colour inkjet printer. Colour laser printers are very expensive and are only necessary for professional output.

- A scanner to incorporate photographs, drawings, etc, into a document.

- DTP software. A medium to full-size package depending on the level of functionality required. DTP software is quite complex for an unfamiliar user, and training will be necessary.

Summary

Software packages are required to carry out specific tasks on a computer. The most widely used software packages are word processing, spreadsheets, databases and desktop publishing.

Software packages can be integrated or single packages. An integrated package is **a single program** which will have more than one application, normally word processing, spreadsheets, databases and graphics. An integrated package covers the basics in each application and is suitable for small businesses, home users or newcomers.

A single package is one program which has just one application, eg, MsWord word processing, but which includes very advanced features not available in an integrated package. Single packages are normally sold as a 'suite' which is a bundle of single packages from the same software developer, for example, Ms Office.

Questions

Multiple Choice Questions

1. A program which has more than one application is called:
   a) an application suite
   b) a general purpose package
   c) a bundle of packages
   d) an integrated package
   e) a single package

2. Which of the following is not an application suite?
   a) MsOffice
   b) MsOffice Pro
   c) Lotus Smart Suite
   d) MsWorks
   e) Perfect Office

3. Justification refers to:
   a) a symbol used to separate items in a list
   b) the page layout
   c) the spacing between the lines
   d) the alignment of text on the page
   e) the orientation of the page

4. A facility to ensure that the first line of a paragraph does not start at the end of a page is called:
   a) a footer
   b) a widow
   c) an orphan
   d) a header
   e) a paragraph style

5. A facility used to personalise standard letters is called:
   a) templates
   b) styles
   c) search and replace
   d) Mail Merge
   e) header

6. An absolute reference in a spreadsheet is:
   a) a formula that cannot be copied
   b) a formula that can be copied
   c) a formula that always points to the same cell when copied
   d) a formula that points to a different cell when copied
   e) a formula where the answer changes when copied

7. Which of the following is not a suitable spreadsheet application?
   a) currency exchange rates
   b) loan repayment schedules
   c) telephone directory
   d) projection of accounts
   e) financial budgets

8. A record in a database is:
   a) a field
   b) a collection of related fields
   c) a file
   d) a collection of files
   e) any field in the database

9. The term Word Art refers to:
   a) a library of pictures
   b) unusual ways to position text
   c) large font sizes
   d) the spacing between letters
   e) a drawing facility

10. The facility used to adjust the spacing between each line is called:
    a) leading
    b) kerning
    c) frames
    d) reverse video
    e) paragraph styles

11. A desktop publishing system will:
    a) enable a person to lay out a page for printing
    b) calculate the net profit for printing a newspaper
    c) store lists of customers and their phone numbers
    d) make out the wages payable to printers each week
    e) draw diagrams of a well designed office   (NCVA 1994)

12. A spreadsheet computer package is usually used to:
    a) write letters and reports
    b) store lists of names and addresses
    c) make calculations of business data
    d) draw diagrams of machinery
    e) make contact with firms abroad   (NCVA 1994)

Short Questions

1. Distinguish between an integrated package and an application suite.
2. State the advantages and disadvantages of an application suite.
3. Describe what the following features in word processing mean:
    a) search and replace
    b) justification
    c) headers and footers
    d) widows and orphans
4. Describe what the following features in word processing do:
    a) Clip Art
    b) Mail Merge
    c) right tabs
    d) paragraph styles
5. What is a font?
6. Describe what the following features in spreadsheets do:
    a) absolute reference
    b) relative reference
    c) protect facility
    d) charting
7. Distinguish between a field and a record as used in a database.
8. What is a multi-user database?

9. How are documents created in a desktop publishing package?
10. What is Word Art?
11. Distinguish between leading and kerning.
12. What is a style gallery?
13. What is the advantage of using paragraph styles?
14. What are the advantages of desktop publishing?
15. List four items of equipment required to perform desktop publishing.

(NCVA 1995)

16. List four common computer software applications packages and in each case state one purpose for which they might be used.   (NCVA 1996)

9. Storing and Retrieving Information

After studying this chapter you should be able to:

◆ Evaluate the differences between centralised and decentralised filing
◆ Describe the various systems of filing: manual, micro-filming and computerised
◆ Distinguish between the methods of storing files: vertical, lateral and horizontal
◆ Explain the methods of classification used in filing systems
◆ Identify the various indexing equipment available
◆ Describe the procedure for filing and retrieving documents
◆ Explain the follow-up system
◆ Identify the essentials of a good filing system
◆ Explain the Data Protection Act 1988 and how it relates to filing

It is recommended that you read the sections on storage media and networks in Chapter 7. These provide the knowledge to fully understand the storage media for computerised filing and methods of operation.

Introduction

s organisations are constantly involved in business transactions, they generate a great deal of correspondence through various media: letters, memorandums, faxes, telephone conversations and electronic mail.

The business needs a filing system to store all records for future reference. Filing is a methodical way of storing information so that it is kept safe and can be found when required.

An efficient filing system will ensure:

a) files are not lost or misplaced
b) files are up to date and complete
c) files are accurate (avoid duplication)
d) no time is wasted in locating files
e) confidential information is secure

Devising a Filing System

The location of the filing system, equipment used, methods of classification, filing and retrieval procedures will vary from one business to another depending on volume of information, number of users, frequency of access and confidentiality of the information.

When a filing system is being devised, the following factors are taken into account:

a) location of the files (centralised or decentralised)
b) type of filing system to be used (manual, computerised, microform, or a combination)
c) equipment to be used
d) categories of information to be set up (eg, customers, suppliers, products, etc)
e) methods of classification within chosen categories (eg, alphabetical, numerical, subject)
f) procedure for filing and retrieving documents
g) retention policy
h) security and access rights
i) assignment of responsibility to individuals to manage and control the system

Location of Files

An important question in designing a filing system for a business is, where should the files be located? The choices available are:

a) **centralised filing** where all the files for the whole business are stored in one central location.
b) **decentralised filing** where all the files used by a department are stored centrally within that department.
c) **individual filing** where individuals store their own files.
d) a combination of the above. Where information is used by several individuals, it is not advisable for each individual to have their own private copies. The duplication of information may lead to different versions of the same file as different amendments may be made to each copy. For example, centralised filing could be implemented in respect of documents which are not in constant use and those which are not specific to any one department. Decentralised filing could be implemented in respect of documents that are specific to a department, while files that are specific to an individual's work may be stored by that individual.

The choice between centralised filing and decentralised filing is a management decision and each has advantages and disadvantages.

Centralised Filing

ADVANTAGES

1. The staff involved will be trained in the filing system.
2. Security of records is guaranteed as strict procedures will be devised regarding access to files. Records will be kept of files borrowed so that files can be traced.
3. Related matters from all departments will be filed together or appropriately cross-referenced. This reduces the need to duplicate documents in separate files.
4. The information will be up to date as there will not be different versions of the same information in different departments.
5. Sophisticated filing equipment can be purchased.
6. Less equipment is required as centralisation ensures better utilisation of equipment, thus saving space and costs.

Computerisation has made centralised filing easier and more convenient for users. Files which are shared by individuals are stored on a central computer and can be accessed by individuals sitting at their own computer, thus avoiding duplication of files. The delays involved in requesting files are eliminated as many users can view the same file simultaneously.

DISADVANTAGES

1. There may be a delay in obtaining files as the Filing Department may be located some distance away and/or the file requested may be with another user.
2. The classification system chosen may not suit the needs of all departments, yet they have to conform to the standardised system. For example, if files are classified alphabetically by customer name, this may not suit the Sales Department which may prefer to have its files classified by geographical regions.

Decentralised Filing

ADVANTAGES

1. Information relating to a department is stored within that department. This reduces the delays involved in obtaining files.
2. The department can implement a classification system suitable for its needs. It does not have to conform to a standardised method.

DISADVANTAGES

1. Strict procedures regarding the removal of files may not be implemented. For example, a file may be removed without anyone indicating who has the file, a new file may be set up where one already exists, files may be mis-filed and therefore effectively lost.
2. More filing equipment is required for the organisation as a whole as full utilisation of equipment is not possible. This increases the space required and costs involved.

Filing Systems

A business must choose the filing system that best suits its needs. Files can be stored in the following ways or the business may choose to use a combination of all three systems:

1. Manual system, ie, paper format
2. Microform system, ie, reduced film format
3. Computerised system, ie, on computer

The choice of filing system depends on:

- space available
- budget constraints
- the number of users
- the volume of information to be stored
- the type of information to be stored (ie, active files, non-active files, confidential files)
- the size of information to be stored (ie, drawings, maps, A4/A3 pages, etc)
- frequency of access to the information
- how the information enters the business (ie, e-mail, fax, computer networks, post, etc)
- the security required
- training requirements

Manual Filing System

A manual filing system means that the files are stored in paper format in appropriately sized filing cabinets or folders. Filing equipment used in a manual system ranges from folders to cabinets.

- **Box file.** A box with a strong spring clip inside the top of the box to hold the items inserted. It is used to hold *miscellaneous* items such as leaflets, catalogues or information which is not referred to frequently. The information is filed in **chronological order,** ie, date order where the most recent item is placed on top of the pile.

Lever arch binder   *Box file*

- **Ring binder.** A ring binder is a folder with two or more rings used for filing *frequently referenced information*, such as price lists, lists of spare parts, etc. Dividers which are pre-punched with holes are used to separate the information in the folder. The document is punched with holes so that it can be placed into the rings of the binder. The ring binder is opened by pulling the rings apart.
- **Lever arch binder.** This is similar to a ring binder except that there is a lever for opening and closing the rings. A lever arch binder is generally larger than a ring binder.
- **Concertina folder.** A folder that consists of a succession of pockets which open out: each pocket can be labelled by subject order or date order depending on its use. It is used for storing items which have yet to be processed (see the follow-up system).
- **Filing cabinets.** A wide range of different filing cabinets is available on the market. The models differ in size and in the way files are arranged in the filing cabinet (see Storing files).

Storing Files

The method of storing files refers to the arrangement or layout of the filing equipment. This is an important consideration as it determines the space required and affects access to the files.

There are four main storage arrangements:

1. Vertical storage
2. Lateral storage
3 Horizontal storage
4. Combination of the above

For example, what is the best arrangement for storing box files or lever arch binders? Storing them side by side like books in a library (lateral storage arrangement) or one behind the other (vertical storage arrangement) or flat, one on top of the other (horizontal storage arrangement)? The most obvious answer to this question is to use the lateral storage arrangement, as this allows easy access. However, it may take up more space than a horizontal arrangement. The balance between space, ease of access and fitness for purpose must be weighed. A cabinet with a combination of all three storage arrangements may be purchased to implement a versatile arrangement.

Where filing cabinets are used, the question is, what model to purchase, as these vary in the way files are arranged in the filing cabinet, ie, vertically, laterally or horizontally. The choice depends on space available, suitability of access, cost and fitness for purpose.

VERTICAL STORAGE ARRANGEMENT

In a vertical storage arrangement, files are stored upright one behind the other. This is the method used in a traditional filing cabinet. The filing cabinet is fitted with metal frames which are placed on either side of the drawer. 'Suspension folders' which are fitted with hooks rest on the frames one behind the other. Tabs or title strips which indicate the name or number of the file are placed on the top of each suspension folder. To sub-divide the information which is held in a suspension folder, **manilla folders** are used. The drawers of the filing cabinet are also labelled for ease of reference.

Vertical filing cabinet

Vertical Storage	
ADVANTAGES	**DISADVANTAGES**
1. All files in a drawer can be seen at a glance. 2. Files are stored at a height which is accessible. 3. Files are protected from dust by being enclosed in the cabinet. 4. Files can be made secure by locking the cabinet.	1. Utilises a large amount of floor space as extra space is required for opening the drawers. 2. Wasted storage space. There is a limit to the height of the cabinets for safety reasons. Weight is unevenly distributed when a drawer is opened 3. Only one person can use a drawer at a time. Two drawers cannot be opened at the same time for safety reasons. 4. Staff have to wait their turn to use the system which can lead to bottlenecks at the filing cabinet. 5. Not suitable for a large filing system.

LATERAL STORAGE ARRANGEMENT

In a lateral storage arrangement, files are stored **side by side** like books on a shelf. It is a suitable arrangement for a large filing system. The filing equipment selected may be closed (ie, with doors or sliding shooters), opened or a carousel which is a rotary filing cabinet.

Where the filing cabinet is used to store suspension folders, the filing cabinet is fitted with metal frames which are placed to the front and back of the shelf. The suspension folders rest on the frames of the shelf side by side, maximising the use of space. Tabs or title strips are placed on the **side** of each suspension folder which indicate the name or number of the file.

Rotary filing system   *Total lateral filing system*

Lateral Filing	
ADVANTAGES	**DISADVANTAGES**
1. Less storage space is required for filing cabinets which are open or which have a sliding shooter as no space is required to open out drawers.	1. Difficult to read file titles and especially files which are placed at a height.
2. Open cabinets or ones with a sliding shooter arrangement can also be built higher as there is no danger of them toppling over. The size of cabinets with drawers must be limited.	2. Difficult to access files stored at a height and lower down.
3. More files can be seen at the same time.	3. With an open shelf arrangement, less protection is given to the files and the files will become dusty.
4. More than one person can access the files at the same time.	4. With an open shelf arrangement it is difficult to implement security as filing cabinet cannot be locked.

Horizontal storage arrangement

In a horizontal storage arrangement, files are stored flat, **one on top of the other**. This method is suitable for small volume temporary storage (ie, in/out trays) or to store large documents unfolded, such as plans and drawings.

Horizontal Filing	
ADVANTAGES	DISADVANTAGES
1. Simple equipment. 2. Cheap. 3. Can hold large documents flat. 4. Suitable for temporary storage or large documents.	1. Difficult and time-consuming to locate specific files. 2. Can become unmanageable. 3. Files are subject to wear and tear. Corners of documents become 'dog-eared'. 4. Can be difficult to replace file in the correct position.

COMBINATION OF STORAGE ARRANGEMENTS

Filing cabinets can be purchased which accommodate all three types of storage arrangements, ie, vertical, lateral and horizontal. These filing cabinets are suitable for a small office which requires a versatile arrangement, ie, to store books, lever arch files, box files, large documents unfolded and suspension folders, etc.

Micro-filing System

A micro-filing system stores files in **film** format (like negatives of a photograph). It reduces the space required to store files as many pages can be stored on a single film. The word 'microform' is the generic term used to describe the format of the film produced, ie, a film strip or a microfiche.

Microfilm is supplied on rolls and cut to the correct length in the development or printing process.

There are different sizes of film available:

a) 16mm suitable for A4 size documents
b) 35mm suitable for A3 size documents (used to archive newspapers)
c) 105mm (used to produce **microfiche,** a 4" x 6" sheet of film about the size of a postcard)

The choice depends on the size of paper being photographed and the format in which you wish to store the film, ie, in film strips or on microfiche sheets. The size of film used also determines the clarity of the image produced relative to the paper size being photographed.

USES OF MICROFORM

1. To archive data and newspapers (ie, transferring data to long-term storage).
2. To publish and distribute data economically through the postal system to a wide number of users for reference purposes, for example, a list of spare parts for a range of cars, sent to all garages. When the information needs updating, a new microform is sent.
3. The banks use microform to store used cheques.
4. To provide an index of a library catalogue.

PRODUCING MICROFORM

Microform can be produced in two ways:

1. Traditional method of photography

   A microform camera is used to photograph original documents. The camera is built into a unit which holds the documents to be photographed the correct distance away from the lens of the camera. The documents can be fed automatically to the camera like a photocopier.

2. Directly from a computer

   The process of printing files onto film instead of paper is known as computer output microform or COM. A special printer known as a **microform printer** and software are required.

A microform duplicator is used to make copies of the microfilm. Microform is duplicated for distribution purposes.

READING MICROFORM

Microform cannot be read by the naked eye. A microform reader is used which displays the image in an enlarged format on the screen. A search facility allows the required information to be brought into view.

Some readers have an in-built printer which allows the image to be viewed on screen and printed on paper if required.

Microform reader/printer

STORING MICROFORM

Microform should be stored like any valuable film to prevent deterioration. Extremes of temperature or humidity should be avoided as well as direct exposure to sunlight. The equipment available on the market includes:

Microfiche index box. Similar to a card index box (see indexing equipment below) but consists of plastic jackets to hold the microfiche. Each jacket has a tab for indexing.

Microfiche visible panel index. A ring binder which consists of panels in which to insert the microfiche. The top line of each microfiche is displayed showing the details of the microfiche.

Microfilm jacket-strip index. A ring binder which consists of transparent jackets in which to insert a strip of film.

Various microfiche storage systems

ADVANTAGES OF MICROFORM

1. Large volumes of information can be reduced to a film, therefore, less storage space is required for files.
2. Duplicates can be made of the microform enabling different departments to have access to the information.
3. Large volumes of information can be sent by post reducing distribution costs.
4. Information can be reproduced on paper if required.
5. Microform is more durable than paper, so the lifespan of the document is increased.
6. It is easier to find information as the film is indexed which allows the reader to search.

DISADVANTAGES OF MICROFORM

1. The information can only be read by a microform reader.
2. Staff may have to wait to access the reader.
3. The film may be unreadable due to poor originals, or poor handling and storage.
4. The equipment is expensive and is only cost-effective where large quantities of information needs to be archived or distributed on a regular basis.
5. Microfilm cannot be updated directly; a new microform must be produced.

Computerised Filing System

Computerised filing can be implemented in many ways, varying from the simplest to the more complex:

1. Individuals keep their files on a computer for their own use.
2. Decentralised filing, ie, a department's files are kept on a central computer within the department. This allows individuals within that department to access the **department's files** from their own computers.

3. Centralised filing, ie, the organisation's files are kept on a central computer for the whole organisation. This allows individuals within the organisation to access the **organisation's files** from their own computer.

4. An organisation's files are available to the outside world. For example, a computer or software company may provide full technical support to its customers via pages on its Internet site (see Chapter 10).

To allow files to be shared among many users, a network of computers must be set up. Files which are shared by individuals are stored on the 'file server' and can be accessed by individuals sitting at their own computer.

Special software is used to allow many different authorised users to access the same file at the same time, but only one user can update the file at any given time. As the files are stored in one location, there will be no duplication of files. A password controls entry to the system and access rights can be set to control what individual users can access within the system.

EXAMPLE OF HOW FILES ARE STORED ON A COMPUTER

Consider a filing system for an auctioneering firm. A sub-set of the work involved in an auctioneering firm is the sale of houses. This part of the filing system could be organised as follows:

A folder-like structure is built using the operating system software, for example, Windows 95. A **folder** is an area for holding files, and folders may be divided into sub-folders.

In the example shown, the main folder, **sales,** is subdivided into sub-folders for the different areas where the auctioneering firm has houses for sale. These are: Dublin City, North Dublin, Other Areas, and South Dublin (the software arranges the directories in alphabetical order).

An auctioneering firm may also categorise the houses within each area according to a price range. Therefore, each area (folder) has further sub-folders to categorise the houses according to their price range. The categories of price ranges are: £50k to £1m, over £1m and Under £50k. Again, these have been arranged in alphabetical order.

Within each price range, the houses may be categorised according to their condition. For example, excellent, good and repairs.

Using this filing system, the required file(s) can be located easily. For example, if information was requested on houses for sale in the Dublin City area which were under £50,000 and in excellent condition, the user of the system would go to the folder called Dublin City. Here they would select the folder named under £50k and in this folder they would select the sub-folder called excellent.

The excellent folder contains the relevant files for the information requested, ie, a list of houses in North Dublin that are in the price range of under £50,000 and are in excellent condition. The required files can then be opened.

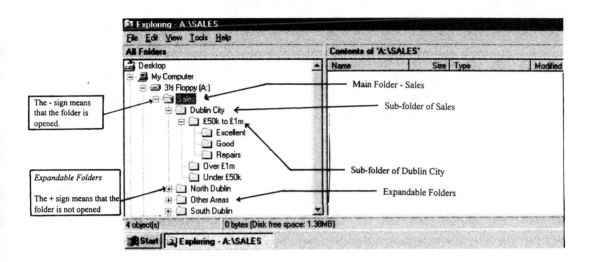

Layout of folders on a disk

The plus sign (+) beside each folder means that the folder is not opened. They are called expandable folders. If it was opened, you would see a breakdown similar to the one for the folder Dublin City.

EQUIPMENT USED

The media on which files are stored on a computer can be classified into:

a) Magnetic disks

b) Magnetic tapes

c) Optical disk storage, ie CD-WORM and CD-R (see Chapter 7)

DISK STORAGE UNITS

Disks should be labelled appropriately and stored in boxes or heavy duty folders to protect them. The types of storage units available are:

Lockable disk boxes: Disk boxes are available in various sizes and capable of holding up to 120 disks. The disks are placed upright in the box and can be separated by movable dividers. Colour-coded labels can be placed on the dividers.

Disk pick box. The box consists of slots in which to insert the disks. The box may be stored in a lateral or vertical position, depending on space available.

Step cube box. A variation of the disk pick box. The inside of the box can be pulled out to display the disks in a step-by-step fashion.

Disk binder. A ring binder which consists of plastic covers in which to insert the disks.

Step cube box

ADVANTAGES OF COMPUTERISED FILING (CENTRALISED)

1. Files exist in one place and can be viewed by many people at the same time.
2. Vast amounts of floor space are saved. (It does not entirely eliminate the need for a manual filing system.)
3. Strict control procedures can be implemented using software. Certain users can be locked out of the system by means of passwords and a user's rights within the system can be curtailed by restricting their level of access.
4. No duplicate files exist, which means that all files are current.
5. It is easy to transfer non-active files from the hard disk to either magnetic tape, CD WORMs or CD-Rs.
6. Retention and deletion procedures can be enforced, as a systems administrator will be in charge of the file server.

DISADVANTAGES OF COMPUTERISED FILING (CENTRALISED)

1. If the network breaks down, users will not be able to access the files. However, this problem can be overcome by having a second file server which is constantly making copies of the files.
2. There may be delays in accessing files if the system is heavily used.
3. The files are unavailable to users when the system is being backed up. Therefore, the backing-up of the system should take place outside normal working hours. Alternatively, a second file server can be set up to automatically take back-ups.
4. If the system is not properly managed, unauthorised users may gain access.
5. Information may be deleted if procedures are not enforced.

Evaluation of Filing Systems

The main filing systems that are likely to feature in all offices are the manual and computerised systems. Microform equipment is expensive and is only cost-effective where large quantities of information need to be archived or distributed on a regular basis. Microform now faces competition with the advent of optical disks, ie, CD-WORMs and CD-Rs.

Today, computer-generated data earmarked for long-term storage can be stored on optical disks. With optical disks, information can be retrieved in seconds in comparison to microform. With microform, when a person needs to view a document, the person goes to the appropriate folder or index box, retrieves the film or fiche, inserts it into a reader and a search is made for the appropriate document. With a computer network and optical disk storage, the person calls up the needed information from their own computer sitting at their own desk.

Comparison of Filing Systems			
Features	**Manual**	**Computerised**	**Microform**
Cost	Cheapest	Expensive	Expensive, and cost-effective only where large volumes of data need to be archived
Space required	Depends on volume of information	Minimal - just the size of the system	Minimal – just the size of the system
Medium used to store files	Paper	Disks	Film
Ease of use	Can be difficult to locate information	Software is used to locate information	Software is used to locate information
Speed of access	Slow	Very fast	Fast
Back-up of data	Not feasible to back-up system due to volume	System is backed-up to tape, disk, CD WORM or CD-R	Film can be duplicated

Categorising and Classifying Information

Information is held about several aspects of a businesses life: staff, stock, customers, suppliers, legal documents, financial position, maintenance, etc. Therefore, when deciding how to organise information, we need to consider both the categories of information involved and how to classify the information within each category. This applies to all types of filing systems: manual, microform and computerised.

Categories of Information

The organisation must decide on the broad categories under which to file its information. For example, customers could be one broad category, legal documents could be another.

When the information has been categorised, the next decision is how to file the information within **each** category. For example, using the customer category, do we file customers alphabetically by surname or do we allocate each customer a number and file the customers in numerical order?

The question we are asking here is, what **method of classification** do we use to store the information within our filing system?

Methods of Classification

The method of classification means the **arrangement** of the information within the filing system. Information can be arranged in:

a) alphabetical order

b) numerical order

c) chronological order

d) subject order

e) geographical order

The arrangement of files under each method of classification is the same whether the filing system is manual, microform or computerised. What is different is the speed and mode of operation. The rules discussed are based on a manual system.

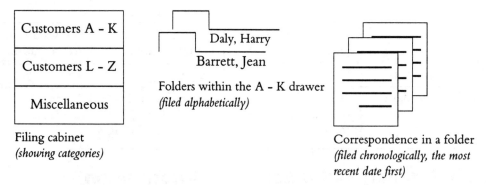

Filing cabinet
(showing categories)

Folders within the A - K drawer
(filed alphabetically)

Correspondence in a folder
(filed chronologically, the most recent date first)

Categorising and Classifying Information
Information organised into categories (customer and miscellaneous). Within the customer category, the classification method used is alphabetical. With each customer file, the information is stored chronologically.

ALPHABETICAL CLASSIFICATION

The alphabetical filing system is a widely used method for filing correspondence. The files are arranged in alphabetical order of category. If the category is customers, the files will be arranged alphabetically by surname.

Alphabetical filing systems are also known as **direct filing systems** as there is no need to look up an index to find the customer's name. A person can go directly to the filing cabinet, and locate the file which will be stored at the correct alphabetical position. It is therefore easily understood.

LOCATING FILES IN AN ALPHABETICAL SYSTEM

The filing cabinet will have labels on the drawer to indicate the contents, eg, Customers A – F, etc.

Inside the drawers, **guide cards** are inserted to divide the alphabet, which makes locating a group of files easier.

After each guide card are the files for customers whose surnames begin with the letter on the guide card.

Each file is labelled with the customer's name and filed alphabetically by surname. For example, in the diagram below, we have customers Leech, Doyle & Co and Mr Harry Louth filed alphabetically after the guide card 'L'.

There may also be a file for **miscellaneous information** which is used for storing infrequent correspondence. For example, there could be other customers whose surname begins with 'L' but with whom the volume of correspondence is minor and infrequent. A separate file will not be opened for each of these customers. They are place in a file called **miscellaneous 'L'**. If the correspondence increases for any of the miscellaneous 'L' customers, a new file is opened for that customer and the details transferred from the miscellaneous file to the new file.

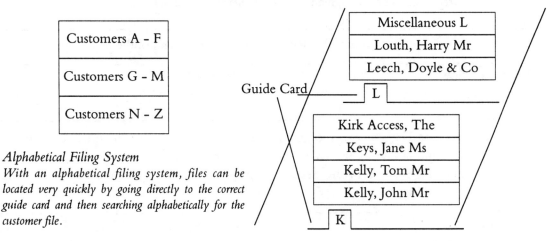

Alphabetical Filing System
With an alphabetical filing system, files can be located very quickly by going directly to the correct guide card and then searching alphabetically for the customer file.

RULES FOR ALPHABETICAL FILING

1. The surname is placed before the first name and if the surnames are the same, the first name decides the position. Titles are placed after the first name, eg:

Before Filing	After Filing
Prof John Keyes	Brady, Alice (Ms)
Ms Jane Keyes	Keyes, Jane (Ms)
Ms Alice Brady	Keyes, John (Prof)
Mrs Lucy Power	Power, Lucy (Mrs)

2. If no first name is given, the surname comes first. Nothing comes before something, eg:

Before Filing	After Filing
Mr John Smith	Smith
Fr J Smith	Smith, J (Fr)
Smith	Smith, John (Mr)

3. If the business name has a personal name, the surname is written first, followed by the first name and the remainder of the name, eg:

Before Filing	After Filing
Sharon Smith & Co	Black, Peter & Co
Peter Black & Co	Smith, Sharon & Co

4. If a business has several names, the first name is taken as the surname and filed accordingly, eg:

Before Filing	After Filing
Messrs Hegarty, Gallagher & Coghlan	Hegarty, Gallagher & Coghlan, Messrs

5. When 'The' is the first word of the name, it is placed at the end of the name, eg:

Before Filing	After Filing
The Open University	Open University, The

6. Prefixes such as De, La, etc, are included as part of the name and filed accordingly. However, names beginning with Mac, Mc, M' are treated as if they were all spelt Mac and names beginning St and Saint are treated as if they were all fully spelt. However, you keep the original spelling, eg:

Before Filing	After Filing
Gerry Devries	De Panter
De Panter	De Vries, Ciaran
Jane De Vries	Devries, Gerry
Ciaran De Vries	De Vries, Jane
La Stampa Restaurant	Last, Thomas
Thomas Last	La Stampa Restaurant
Patricia McSparran	McCarthy, John
Gerald MacDonagh & Sons	MacDonagh, Gerald & Sons
Ciara MacSweeney	McSparran, Patricia
John McCarthy	MacSweeney, Ciara
St Brendan's College	Safe, Ted (Mr)
Michael Sain	Sain, Michael
Saint Michael's Church	St Brendan's College
Mr Ted Safe	Saint Michael's Church
Ms Mary Sweeney	Sweeney, Mary (Ms)

7. The apostrophe is ignored. The word is treated as one, but the original spelling is kept, eg:

Before Filing	After Filing
Brian D'arcy	Darcy, Brendan
Brendan Darcy	D'arcy, Brian
ORM Sales Agents	O'Riordan's Pharmacy
O'Riordan's Pharmacy	Orlagh Park House
Orlagh Park House	ORM Sales Agents

8. Treat numbers as if they were spelt out in words but keep the original name, eg:

Before Filing	After Filing
400 Supercal Co	500 ABC Ltd (**really five-zero-zero and filed under 'F'**)
500 ABC Ltd	
60 Calls Ltd	400 Supercal Co (filed under 'F')
700 Cab Call Lt	700 Cab Call Ltd (filed under 'S')
	60 Calls Ltd (filed under 'S')

9. Departments are filed by keyword of department, eg:

Before Filing	After Filing
Department of Foreign Affairs	Business Studies, Department
Department of Social Welfare	Foreign Affairs, Department of
Business Studies Department	Social Welfare, Department of

10. Treat **known** abbreviated names as being spelt out in full and file them under their full name (see also cross-reference), eg:

Before Filing	After Filing
VHI	Educational Building Society
ESB	Electricity Supply Board
EBS	Voluntary Health Insurance Board

11. Leave **made-up** abbreviations in their abbreviated form, but file the same abbreviations in a group according to the word that follows the abbreviated name.

Before Filing	After Filing
ABC Computer Training Ltd	ABBA Taxis
ABC Services	Abbey Leisure
Abbey Leisure	ABC Computer Training Ltd
ABBA Taxis	ABC Services
Abco Interior Design	Abco Interior Design

Numerical Classification

The files are arranged in numerical order and a new file is simply given the next consecutive number. A **separate alphabetical indexing** system will be kept to link the file to a number. This is known as **cross-referencing**.

Numerical filing is therefore an **indirect system** (unlike the alphabetical system which is a direct filing system), as you cannot go directly to the filing cabinet and locate the file. For example, if you do not know a customer's number, you would have to: (a) look up an alphabetical index of customers' surnames, (b) read the number associated with that customer and (c) go to the filing cabinet and search numerically to locate the file.

To manage the system, the index must be kept up to date, therefore when a new file is opened an entry must also be made in the appropriate place in the index.

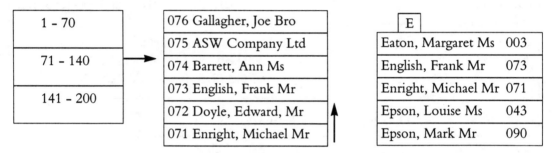

(how files are arranged in the filing cabinet)   (alphabetical index card)

Numerical Filing System
To locate a file in a numerical system, an alphabetical index of customers' names is first referenced for the file number. The file is then located by going to the filing cabinet and searching numerically for the correct customer file.

Other Numerical Systems

There are other numerical systems used for more complex filing. These include:

ALPHANUMERICAL SYSTEM

An alphanumerical system allocates a letter and a number to a document. For example, a document relating to a firm called Office Supplies could be filed under O/3. The letter 'O' refers to the file called Office Supplies, and the number is the position of the document within the file. An alphabetical index of the firms would be maintained.

DEWEY DECIMAL SYSTEM

The Dewey decimal system is used for filing books in a library. It consists of three pairs of digits. The first pair refers to the subject, the middle pair refers to the topic within that subject, and the last pair refers to the particular book.

For example, the following numbers could be allocated to subjects:

Business Studies 10

Accounting 20

Law 30

Each subject is then broken down into topics and each topic is also allocated a number. For example, the subject Law 30 could be divided into:

Business Law 30.01

Company Law 30.02

Land Law 30.03

The books within each topic will then be numbered. For example, using the topics Business Law and Company Law, you could have the following books:

30.01.01 *Business Law in Ireland*

30.01.02 *Business Law Simplified*

30.01.03 *A Guide to Business Law*

30.02.01 *Companies Act 1963*

Using this system, the books can be placed on the shelf in numerical order, but all related topics would be together. If the library purchased another business law book, it would get the number 30.01.04 and would be placed on the shelf beside the other business law books.

Therefore when a new book has to be added to the system it can be placed with the correct subject and topic, simply by giving it the next number within the subject and topic classification. An alphabetic index is also maintained listing the books in alphabetical order of subject.

The decimal system could also be used in business. For example, in a college the following system could be used:

FULL TIME COURSES	20		
Secretarial		20.01	
Certificate in Secretarial Studies			20.01.01
Diploma in Secretarial Studies			20.01.02
Business Studies		20.02	
PART TIME COURSES	30		
Computers		30.01	
Spreadsheets			30.01.01
Database			30.01.02
Word Processing			30.01.03
EXAMINATION RESULTS	40		
Certificate in Business Studies		40.01	
Sept 1994			40.01.01
Sept 1995			40.01.02
Sept 1996			40.01.03

TERMINAL DIGIT SYSTEM

This is a numerical system which consists of three pairs of digits read from right to left. The last pair refers to a drawer, the middle pair refers to the position of the file within that drawer, and the first pair refers to a document within that file. For example, the number 20.02.04 refers to drawer 4, file number 2, document number 20 within that file. Every document will be numbered and placed in the correct position within the filing cabinet. An alphabetical index has to be maintained.

Numerical v Alphabetical

The advantages of a numerical classification over an alphabetical classification are:

♦ The filing system can be easily expanded. A new file is simply given the next number in the system and located as the last file in the system.

♦ Saves space as you don't have to leave room between each letter of the alphabet as with an alphabetical system.

♦ Avoids the trouble of reshuffling the system to insert a new file as the new file is positioned behind all the other files in the system. For example, with an alphabetical system, if the first drawer is full, files will have to be moved from the first drawer to the second drawer so that the new files can be added to the first drawer to maintain the alphabetical sequence.

♦ The business can use the file number as a **reference** in all correspondence. When a reply is received this reference will be quoted, allowing the correspondence to be traced to the file immediately without having to look up an index. This simplifies the numerical filing system.

♦ Related topics can be filed together, for example, books in a library using the Dewey system.

Other Classifications

CHRONOLOGICAL

Chronological means by date order. Documents are filed according to the date, the most recent date first. Chronological filing is not generally used as a core system, but it is the typical method of filing within files.

It is only used as a core classification method where the date would have meaning; for example, in a school when files are archived (put away permanently) it is appropriate to file by academic year. You could have an 'examination results' file for 1995/96 and the results within that file sorted in alphabetical order by classes or subjects.

SUBJECT

There are certain categories of information where subject filing is appropriate. For example, in relation to insurance for a business, it may be more appropriate to have a file labelled insurance rather than filing under the individual insurance broker's name. In this way, all information concerning insurance will be in the same place rather than split between the individual brokers.

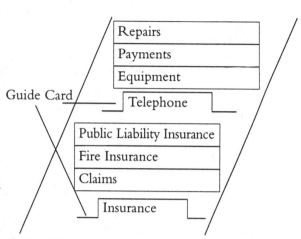

Guide Card

The subject insurance may be sub-divided into categories like fire insurance, public liability insurance, etc, where the volume of data in relation to each type of insurance justifies it. The subjects are filed in alphabetical order. Where subjects are sub-divided into topics, the topics are also filed alphabetically within the subject.

Subject Filing
The files are organised according to subject topic. Within each subject topic files are stored alphabetically.

Other examples where subject filing is appropriate are expenses, training, products, repairs, etc. Subject filing is used by students; their lever arch file is divided into sections such as typing, office procedures, bookkeeping and communications.

GEOGRAPHICAL

Geographical classification is suitable for businesses involved in a high level of sales, mail order, imports, exports, etc. The organisation divides its business into regions. A company involved in sales in Ireland would divide the filing system up into counties; the sales force in each county would then be filed in either alphabetical or numerical order.

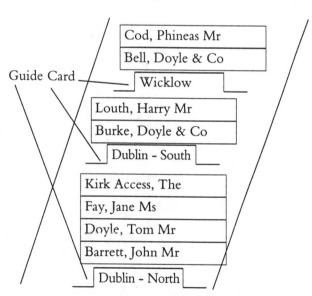

Guide Card

An index is required to link a person to a county. The index stores the names in alphabetical order and states under which county

Geographical Filing
To locate a file in a geographical system, an alphabetical index of customers is first referenced for the geographical region. The file is then located by going directly (alphabetically) to the correct region and searching alphabetically for the correct customer file.

that person is filed. It is therefore an indirect system like the numerical system.

Comparison of Various Classification Systems			
Classification	**Advantages**	**Disadvantages**	**Uses**
Alphabetical	• Easy to understand and operate • Information can be retrieved directly without looking up an index • Miscellaneous files can be set up	• The system is not easily expanded; considerable reshuffling of files may be necessary • Where surnames are the same, there is a danger of mis-filing a document	• Generally where another system is not preferable • Suppliers, clients, personal records
Numerical	• System is easily expanded • No need to pre-allocate space in the filing cabinet • The file number can be used as a reference • The index provides useful information in its own right	• An indirect system – an index must be consulted • Files could be mis-filed if the number was read incorrectly • Can be complicated	• Large filing systems • For business documentation, ie, orders, invoices, etc • By banks • Petty cash vouchers, receipts
Other numerical system	• Each document can be given a unique number • Efficient in large filing systems • Unlimited expansion • High level of accuracy is possible • The Dewey system is particularly suitable for libraries	• Intricate to learn and operate • Requires indexing	• Large filing systems, spread over different locations (terminal) • To file related topics together (Dewey) • Libraries (Dewey system) • For more precision (alphanumerical)
Chronological	• The most recent correspondence is first in the file • Simple to accomplish	• For some applications, it can be difficult over time to locate specific documents, ie, you may forget the time period when a particular transaction occurred • Not a common core filing system	• Documents within files are stored in date order • For temporary storage before filing • Dates on which reminders must be sent to clients, eg, insurance renewal reminders

Comparison of Various Classification Systems continued			
Classification	**Advantages**	**Disadvantages**	**Uses**
Chronological contd.			• Dates on which service is to be discontinued, eg, in expiry dates for overdrafts • Minutes of meetings • Bank statements • Newspaper archives
Subject	• Similar to the alphabetical system – direct • Related information is filed together	• The system is not easily expanded; reshuffling of files may be necessary • Subject areas may overlap, therefore cross-referencing is essential	• To keep related topics together • Expense items • Maintenance contracts • Student folders • Educational institutions
Geographical	• A convenient way of sub-dividing customers or sales representatives • Colour coding can be used to speed up location of files	• A cross-reference is required • A good knowledge of the geographical region is required	• Sales offices & mail order companies • Businesses that deal in import and/or exports • Service area reps

CHOICE OF CLASSIFICATION

The method chosen depends on many factors including:

◆ the type of information (eg, customers, products)

◆ the volume of information (implications for how easily the system can be expanded)

◆ the frequency of use (time factor in locating information, ie, direct versus indirect system)

◆ whether related information is to be filed together (ie, all details relating to a certain region (geographical) or all expenses for a business (subject) or all related books (Dewey system)

Cross-referencing

A cross-reference is used:

1. **to locate information in a numerical or geographical filing system.** In a numerical system an indexing system is used to list the files in alphabetical order quoting the file number beside each file name. When a user requests a file, and the file number is unknown, the alphabetical index is looked up to get the file number. A similar procedure operates for a geographical system, ie, you look up an alphabetical index for the customer to locate the region.

2. **where a file could be filed under two names.** For example, confusion sometimes arises as to where to locate a file. A file on VHI could be filed under VHI or Voluntary Health Insurance Board. There are rules for filing but sometimes an organisation adapts the rules to suit its particular needs. To avoid confusion it may set up two files for that particular organisation; one filed under VHI and the other filed under Voluntary Health Insurance Board. All the information would be stored in one file, say the Voluntary Health Insurance Board file and the other file, the VHI file, would be empty with a reference saying 'see Voluntary Health Insurance Board'.

   A cross-reference card is set up and placed in the alternative location (in this case in the VHI file) so that staff are directed to the correct location.

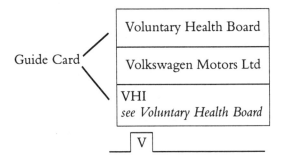

Cross-reference card

3. **to refer a person to a related file.** When a firm changes its name, a cross-reference card would be placed in the old file directing users to the new file. The old file would be closed and the date noted. A card would also be placed in the new file so that users can reference past data.

4. **where files are related or linked.** For example, where do we file documents relating to the maintenance of an item of equipment? Is it in the file of the person who services the equipment (service provider's file) or in the equipment file? The answer to this question may seem simple enough, but what if the service provider also services other equipment and the equipment is serviced by more than one person? Here we need separate files for each item of equipment and for each of the service providers. The service

provider's file would contain correspondence and the equipment files would contain a service history. A cross-reference card is placed with each service provider's file, linking that person to all the equipment s/he services. A cross-reference card is also placed with each equipment file linking those files to the service provider's file. This problem can also be overcome by putting a copy of the linked information in the appropriate files. For example, if Mr 'X' services the photocopier, then the details can be placed in both the Mr 'X' file and the photocopier file. Where the information is duplicated, a cross-reference is not necessary. However, this is not recommended, as the files become bulky. There is also the danger of the information being omitted from one file, leading to inaccurate records.

Colour-coding System

Where the filing system is used to store different categories of information a colour-coding system is used. The files are subdivided into their categories, and different coloured filing tabs or folders are used for each category. This prevents someone placing a document in the correct 'name' file but in the wrong file.

For example, if the filing system contains customers, suppliers and employees, blue coloured tabs may be used for customers, red for suppliers and yellow for employees. The files will be arranged in alphabetical order of category, customers followed by employees then suppliers. The files within each category will also be arranged in alphabetical order.

Colour-coding systems could also be used in a subject or geographical system; for example, in a geographical system counties could be colour-divided into north and south.

INDEXING

An index is a guide that states where information is located in the filing system. It is used with the numerical and geographical filing systems to locate particular files. For example, in a numerical filing system, the files will be filed by number, say customer number, but if someone asked for the file by the customer's name, it would be very difficult to locate the file. Here an index is required to locate the customer. The index is arranged in alphabetical order by customer name. The index is searched to find the number that is associated with the customer's name.

An index will also contain some other information, which may be enough to eliminate the need for further reference. For instance, in the previous example, if the request was for a customer's phone number, the index would provide this information and thus eliminate the need to reference the customer's file.

An index should be kept up to date: every time a file is added to the filing system an entry should be made in the index.

Indexes can also be maintained on computer using an electronic diary (or personal information manager – PIM). The computer screen is organised like a card index and the operator can insert data such as customer name, address and telephone (see Chapter 3). Some database packages also provide templates (a standard layout) for indexing.

INDEXING EQUIPMENT

Various types of indexing equipment are used to record information: page index, card index and strip index.

The choice of indexing system will depend on:

- how much information needs to be recorded (strip versus card)
- space required for the system (visible card index versus vertical card index)
- maintenance of the system, ie, the removal of information or the addition of information
- how frequently the information will be accessed (system needs to be close at hand)

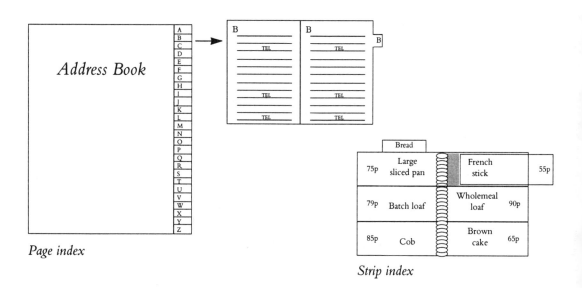

Page index

Strip index

PAGE INDEX

A page index is a book or loose-leaf binder which contains one or more pages for each letter of the alphabet. These are used to store small amounts of information which are accessed frequently, ie, price list, telephone numbers, etc.

CARD INDEX

This indexing system consists of cards, usually A6 or A7 in size. The cards are divided by guide cards labelled A to Z. A separate card is used for each file item and the cards are arranged in alphabetical order. Coloured cards are available for classification purposes. The types of card indexes available are:

Vertical card index. The cards are stored upright in a filing box one behind the other. With this system it is easy to add or remove cards as required, as the alphabetical order will not be affected. However, if the cards are referenced frequently, the cards will become dog-eared.

Vertical card index

Visible card index. The cards overlap each other but the first line of each card is visible. The essential details are recorded on the first line to enable the card to be located. The cards are stored in a visible card filing cabinet which consists of trays to hold the cards. For smaller systems a visible card index folder can be used.

Rotary card index. The cards overlap each other but are separated by guide cards. The wheel is turned to get the required card section.

STRIP INDEX

This indexing system consists of strips of cards which are inserted into plastic frames of a folder. The pages of the folder are arranged alphabetically. These systems are available in folder format or free-standing desk units. They are used for simple data which can be held on one or two lines, eg, telephone numbers, product prices, etc.

SIGNALLING USING INDEXES

Indexing systems allow you to highlight or 'signal' particular items of information. This is achieved by using an alterable colour-coding method, where a coloured tag is placed onto the edge of a card or page. For example, a red tag may signal an overdue account.

How to File

Whether you have dealt with the correspondence received, or intend to deal with it at a later date, it should be filed. The method involved varies slightly depending on whether the filing system is centralised or not.

1. If a centralised system is used, you would indicate on the document that it is ready for filing and place the document in a filing tray. What you write on the document could be the reference number, name, subject, etc of the file into which the document is to be inserted. This enables the filing clerk to file the document in the appropriate place.

2. Sort the documents into batches and arrange the documents in each batch into chronological order. A concertina folder could be used to aid sorting.

3. The documents are inserted in the appropriate file on top of the previous correspondence. In this way the most recent documents are placed first.

4. If no file exists for the document, then a new file is opened. In a centralised filing system, this will involve getting authorisation to open a new file in order to prevent duplication of files and the misplacing of documents.

5. Opening a file means getting the appropriate folder and writing up the identification tag with the correct classification using the colour-coding system if applicable. It may also be necessary to add the new file to an index, particularly if the numerical system is used. A cross-reference may also be necessary if the new file is linked to an existing file. Write the cross-reference on the new file, the related files and the index if used. The folder is inserted in the correct position of the filing cabinet.

6. Where a file cannot hold any more documents a continuation file is necessary. The original file is closed and labelled with a date. The continuation file is placed behind it. However, if the file which is full is not in current use, it should be removed from the current filing system and placed in long-term storage (see retention of files below).

7. Filing should be carried out on a regular basis to avoid pile-ups and disorganisation.

How to Retrieve a File

When a file is borrowed, a record must be kept of the date the file was borrowed, the file name/number, the borrower, and the borrower's department. These details are entered in a book in chronological order or on an 'outcard' which is inserted in place of the file borrowed. Therefore when a file is requested but it is not there, the details recorded in the book or on the outcard will indicate where the file is.

However, recording the details of files borrowed in a book may mean that the whole book has to be searched to discover where the file is. This problem is overcome by placing an outcard in the filing system in place of the file which is removed.

OUTCARD

An outcard will have headings similar to the card shown opposite. When a file is borrowed, the date, file name/number, initials of person who borrowed the file and their department is recorded. The outcard is inserted in place of the file borrowed and remains in the filing system until the file is returned. When the file is returned, the date of return is recorded on the outcard and the outcard is removed from the system. The card can be used again when another file is removed.

Outcard					
Date Taken	**File Identification**	**By**	**Dept**	**Date Returned**	
7/9/95	File B009	JH	Marketing		

An outcard

In a large filing system a combination of a book and an outcard may be used. For example, to keep track of which files are out, the book will be checked; or when a file is requested, you know immediately who has the file by the details recorded on the outcard.

If the file will be accessed by only a few people, then **coloured outcards** can be used. A colour is assigned to each person, and when the file is removed, the appropriate coloured outcard is inserted. This saves the time involved in writing up the outcard.

If the filing system is small, an outcard with the file name or number can be placed with each file. When the file is removed from the system, only the date and the initials of the person removing the file need to be recorded.

FILE-PASSING SLIP

If more than one person needs to use a file, a file may be passed from person to person without being returned to the filing department. However, in order to keep track of where the file is, a 'file-passing slip' is filled in, detailing the file name, who passed the file, the new holder of the file and the date. The file-passing slip is returned to the filing clerk, so that the outcard can be updated.

Confidential Files

Strict procedures will be laid down for confidential files. These include details such as a list of authorised people who can access the file, what files cannot be copied or removed from the filing department.

Retention of Files

Documentation relating to the business may be used on a regular basis for a particular period of time and then may only be referenced on an occasional basis. The current filing system should not be clogged with information which is not accessed on a regular basis.

Retention periods vary for documentation; for example, some documents must be kept forever, such as documents relating to the set-up of the business and the financial accounts. Other documents only need to be kept for a stated period (usually 6 years); these include bank statements, VAT records, details relating to business transactions such as invoices, credit notes, etc. Other documents like correspondence, minutes of meetings, memoranda, etc are kept at the organisation's discretion.

The question then arises as to what to do with the files which are not currently accessed.

The answer to this question is either:

a) Transfer the documentation to long-term storage known as 'archives'.

or

b) Destroy the documentation.

Which option you take depends on the organisation's retention policy. Where a centralised filing system is used, the organisation will devise a retention policy which gives clear details as to how long certain files should be stored. The files will be classified as:

Active files which are files in current use and generally span one year. These files are stored in the current filing system using either the manual system or a computerised system.

Semi-active files which are files no longer needed on a daily basis but which may be referenced on an irregular basis. These files are stored separately from the current filing system, ie, in a separate filing cabinet or on a separate area of the disk.

Non-active files which are files which are not referred to but must be kept until their retention period expires. These files are taken from the semi-active files and either stored elsewhere or microfilmed for long-term storage. With a manual system, when the information has been transferred to another medium, the paper-based information can be destroyed. Confidential information should be put through an automatic 'shredder'. Information held on disk is transferred to microfilm, tape, CD-WORM or CD-R.

Dead files which are non-active files where the retention period has expired. Dead files are destroyed. If a manual system is used to keep files, the file is shredded using a 'shredder' which reduces the information to strips of paper. If a computerised system is used, the files are deleted from the disk.

Nowadays, information which is of interest to the organisation even though it is dead is kept. This is possible because of advances in technology which allow huge amounts of information to be stored in reduced format, ie, microfilm, CD-WORM and CD-R.

Documentation should be reviewed on a regular basis and a decision made to keep it in active storage, transfer it to semi-active storage or non-active storage or destroy it. If you are responsible for your own filing system then the best rule to follow is, 'If you think you may need it, keep it'. Doing a major spring clean of the filing cabinet or your disk may create problems later. The decision to throw away documents should be taken with great care.

DOCUMENT SHREDDER

Shredder

This is a machine which shreds paper into illegible tiny strips. It is used to dispose of unwanted documents in a secure way. Some machines offer a wide range of cutting widths to accommodate the office's security requirements. The cross-cut facility shreds paper into the tiniest of particles.

Models are available in different sizes ranging from deskside units to high volume document shredders capable of handling cardboard. Great care should be taken when using a shredder: you should not bend over the shredder, as loose clothing, eg, a tie, could put you in danger!

The output from the shredder can be used as packing material or recycled.

Follow-up System

A follow-up system (also known as a 'bring-forward' system or 'tickler' system) is an essential part of any filing process. It is used to remind you of correspondence that needs to be attended to on a certain day. It allows you to file away information until required, and yet reminds you of the information before the appropriate date. It ensures that things are not neglected or forgotten about.

Correspondence arrives into the business in many forms, ie, fax, post, e-mail, telephone, etc but it may not be necessary or possible to act upon this correspondence immediately. For example, correspondence inviting a business to a forthcoming exhibition may arrive months in advance.

We need to be able to file away this information until required, yet we want to be reminded of events closer to the time, so that we can retrieve the appropriate documentation. If we kept all the information on our desk until it was dealt with, there would be no room to work.

A follow-up system can be implemented in many ways:

◆ A note is put into a diary indicating when the file is required again.

◆ A 'date file' is set up. This may take the form of a **concertina folder** with a pocket of the folder used for each day of the month and one pocket for the coming month. A note is placed in the appropriate pocket detailing the name of the file to be retrieved. The appropriate pocket for each day is checked and acts as a reminder to retrieve the appropriate file. This system may be used by an individual.

◆ When documents are sent to a centralised filing department, a pre-printed 'follow-up slip' is completed and attached to the document. The filing clerk detaches the 'follow-up slip' and places it in the appropriate pocket of the 'follow-up system' and the documents are filed away.

◆ The 'follow-up system' used in a centralised department is more elaborate: it contains a pocket for each of the months of the year and a pocket for each of the days of one month. When the month begins, the details for the month are placed into the daily pockets. The slips for each day are checked by the filing clerk. The files are then sent to the appropriate person with the 'follow-up slip' attached to the file. Details of the file sent are recorded on an outcard and placed in the filing system.

◆ If files are stored on a computer, then the user can signal when the file is required again by placing an entry in a diary or more appropriately an electronic diary.

Essential Elements of a Filing System

1. It should be up to date and contain all the information that users might want.
2. It should be easy to follow and simple to operate, allowing the user to find particular information quickly, ie, the selected classification system should suit the needs of the business.
3. If an index to the filing system is used it should be kept up to date.
4. Appropriate security measures should be in place to protect the confidentiality of the information. Files should be kept under lock and key and if valuable they should be stored in a fireproof cabinet, safe or at another location.
5. A clear cross-reference system should be in place to enable related files to be located.
6. Procedures should be in place for borrowing files, for example, an outcard system stating the location of the file and a follow-up system to chase up files kept beyond the return date.
7. A policy should be devised in relation to the retention of files, ie, transfer of non-active files, file shredding etc.
8. The appropriate filing equipment should be used, ie, manual or electronic. The system should be easy to expand.
9. The system should be efficient in terms of storage space and cost.
10. A 'follow-up system' should be in place.

The Data Protection Act (1988)

All businesses maintain files with details of their customers, suppliers, employees, etc. For example, information recorded in relation to employees will include absences, accidents at work, disciplinary details, etc. Files may also contain sensitive information such as race, political beliefs, sexual orientation, health details and family circumstances of an individual. It is important that personal information is protected and is not disclosed against the individual's wishes.

The Data Protection Act 1988 was passed to deal with **privacy issues** arising from the increasing amount of information kept on computer about individuals. It regulates the collection, processing, storage, use and disclosure of information about individuals held on computers. This Act **does not** refer to data that is stored on manual files.

The Data Protection Act

a) places responsibilities on data controllers when dealing with personal data;

b) gives rights to the data subjects;

c) created the position of a Data Protection Commissioner.

The Data Controller

The data controller is the body or person that either alone or with others controls the contents and use of personal data held on a computer, for example, financial institutions, insurance companies, direct marketing companies and public sector bodies. All data controllers must register with the Data Protection Commissioner.

THE DUTIES OF THE DATA CONTROLLER

The duties of the data controller may be summarised in the following rules. Failure to comply with these rules is a breach of the Data Protection Act.

1. **The data should be obtained lawfully.** Individuals must be aware of who is collecting the data, where it will be stored (ie, on computer), what the data will be used for and who the data will be disclosed to.

2. **The data should not be used or disclosed for unspecified or unlawful purposes.** An example of an unspecified purpose is where information is used in ways not intended by the individual. For example, a form may state the various purposes in which the data collected on it will be used. If this data is then used for another purpose there is a breach of the law.

   The individuals should have the option of saying if they wish to allow the business to use the information for other purposes, for example, mail orders companies should ask their customers if they wish to be placed on other mailing lists. An example of unlawful purpose would be where the information is used as blackmail. There are some exceptions to the specific rule, eg, where disclosure of information is required by law.

3. **Data must be kept safe and secure.** The business should take appropriate measures to ensure that data cannot be accessed, altered or destroyed either accidentally or intentionally, without authority. Such measures may include:
   ◆ Restricting access to authorised staff by using computer passwords and codes.
   ◆ Restricting access to confidential information on a need-to-know basis.
   ◆ Keeping computer screens hidden from onlookers.
   ◆ Operating a back-up procedure in case of computer failure.
   ◆ Shredding waste paper and printouts immediately after use.

4. **Data must be accurate and as up to date as possible.** The business should ensure that procedures are in place to achieve high levels of data accuracy. This

is especially important at the data collection and data input stages. The normal collection procedure involves the data subject completing a form. The form should be designed to eliminate ambiguity and to extract definite information. The computer facility should be designed to ensure high levels of accuracy at input stage. For example, if inputting an individual's age of 50 the operator keys in 500, the computer should not accept this. The data should be checked by a third party when it is input to the computer. Procedures should be put in place to ensure the data is updated on a regular basis.

5. **Data must be adequate, relevant and not excessive.** The business must make every effort to ensure that complete data is obtained as incomplete data may give a false picture of the individual and may cast aspersions on the character of the data subject. The business should only maintain data relevant to the purposes for which it was collected.

6. **Data should not be stored longer than is necessary.** As it is relatively cheap to store data on computer files, personal information may be retained for longer than is necessary. For example, a customer leaves the business and goes to a competitor. The personal information regarding the customer may no longer be relevant to the original business and should be deleted. Retention periods should be devised for storing and deleting data.

    The business should assign the task of 'purging' (deleting) the data files to individuals to ensure the files are deleted when they are no longer required.

7. **Right of access.** A copy of the personal data must be given to the individual on request. A small fee is charged. The individual must request the copy in writing and give the information necessary to allow the business to identify the individual before complying with the request.

    The business must respond to the request within 40 days. However, the business may be instructed by the Government to withhold personal information from the data subject if a tax or criminal investigation is pending. In some circumstances, information may be withheld if it is likely to cause serious harm to the individual, ie, informing the individual of health matters.

DISCLOSURE OF PERSONAL DATA

The Act allows disclosure of personal data by the business to the Chief Superintendent, the Minister or at the Commissioner's request where such information will be used:

a) To aid in the conviction of an individual
b) To investigate money owed to the State
c) To prevent injury to others
d) To prevent serious loss or damage to another's property
e) Where disclosure is with the consent of the individual concerned

DISCLOSURE OF DATA WITHOUT AUTHORITY

If an individual breaks into a computer system without authority and passes on personal data to another, s/he is guilty of an offence against the Act. The penalty may be a fine of up to £10,000 on summary conviction or £50,000 on conviction on indictment.

RIGHTS OF THE DATA SUBJECT

The data subject is the individual about whom information is stored on a computer. The Act gives individuals the right to:

a) request a copy of the data kept on computerised files from the data controller. This request may not always be granted.

b) rectify any incorrect information.

c) erase information from the file.

THE DATA PROTECTION COMMISSIONER

The duties of the Data Protection Commissioner are as follows:

a) to enforce the Data Protection Act

b) to investigate complaints

c) to maintain a register of all data controllers

d) to promote awareness of the obligations and rights of protecting data

e) to develop codes of practice for various information-sensitive industries, eg, insurance companies and banks

Summary

Information is the lifeblood of the organisation and proper procedures must be in place to safeguard it. This involves setting up a filing system to store the information. The filing systems available are: (a) manual, (b) microform and (c) computerised systems. The choice depends on volume of information, type and size of information to be stored, frequency of access to the information, how the information enters the business, how the information is to be used, security of the system and the cost involved. In practice, the most common types are manual and computerised.

The manual system involves storing files in folders and/or filing cabinets. A colour-coding system may be used to distinguish between different categories of information. It may be the cheapest system to implement but may require huge amounts of space. Strict procedures need to be laid down regarding the removal of files from filing cabinets. A diary or an outcard is used to trace files removed. Information that cannot be dealt with immediately should be filed temporarily in a follow-up system.

A microform system uses film rather than paper to store data and is mainly used to archive data. A microform reader is used to view the information in an enlarged format which may be printed if required using a microform printer. This system is now facing competition from optical disks.

A computerised system involves saving files on disk. A directory/folder structure should be set up to manage the files stored. New advances in disk technology such as the optical disks (CD-WORMs and CD-Rs) make it possible to store huge amounts of information using a computerised system.

Regardless of the system chosen, the location of the filing system must be considered. The choices available are centralised, decentralised and individual filing.

The files within the filing system are stored using various classification methods such as alphabetical, numerical, chronological, subject and geographical. The choice depends on the needs of the business. Where the classification method is an **indirect system**, an index is essential for locating information. For example, in a numerical system the index is arranged in alphabetical order so that it can be searched for the number associated with the file. A cross-reference is essential in any filing system. This involves linking information in one file to information in another file.

The essential features of a filing system are that it should be up to date, easy to use, secure and include cross-referencing where appropriate. A policy should be devised in relation to document retention and strict procedures should be in place for removing files.

The Data Protection Act 1988 regulates the collection, processing, storing, use and disclosure of information about individuals held on a computer.

Questions

Multiple Choice Questions

1. Which of the following is not in the correct sequence?
   a) MacEntyre, John
   b) McElroy, Kathleen
   c) McElvaney, Paddy
   d) MacElwain, David
   e) MacEvoy, Mike

2. An example of a direct filing system is one which is:
   a) geographical
   b) numerical
   c) alphabetical
   d) chronological
   e) indexing

3. A method of filing which is easily expanded by placing new files at the back of existing files is:
   a) geographical
   b) alphabetical
   c) subject
   d) numerical
   e) chronological

4. When documents are filed in chronological order they are arranged by:
   a) reference number
   b) code number
   c) date order
   d) logical order
   e) numerical order

5. The classification method which allocates letters and a number to a file is called a:
   a) numerical system
   b) terminal digit system
   c) alphanumerical system
   d) Dewey decimal system
   e) chronological system

6. The *Golden Pages* is an example of which pair of classification systems?
   a) subject and alphabetical
   b) subject and numerical
   c) alphabetical and numerical
   d) alphabetical and geographical
   e) subject and geographical

7. To distinguish between different categories of information, you use:
   a) a guide card
   b) a colour-coding system
   c) a signalling system
   d) an indexing system
   e) an alphabetical system

8. If the use of an separate suspension folder is not justified because of the small amount of correspondence, the type of file used is:
   a) a ring binder
   b) a box file
   c) a miscellaneous file
   d) an index
   e) a concertina folder

9. A folder which consists of a succession of pockets which open out is called:
   a) a manila folder
   b) a suspension folder
   c) a directory folder
   d) a concertina folder
   e) a lever arch folder

10. The name given to the storage arrangement where files are stored one behind the other is:
    a) vertical storage
    b) lateral storage
    c) computerised storage
    d) flat storage
    e) horizontal storage

11. An index is used to:
    a) remove files from the filing system.
    b) cross-reference files.
    c) follow up on files removed.
    d) separate alphabetical sections in a filing cabinet.
    e) separate subjects in a lever arch folder.

12. A signalling system can be used with:
    a) an indexing system
    b) a guide card
    c) a colour-coding system
    d) an outcard
    e) a file-passing slip

13. In filing, to show that a business has changed its name you use:
    a) an outcard
    b) the follow-up system
    c) a cross-reference card
    d) a file-passing slip
    e) a guide card

14. A file-passing slip is used:
    a) when a file is removed from the filing system.
    b) when a file which is removed is passed to another individual.
    c) to get authority to remove a file.
    d) to indicate that the file is to be filed again.
    e) to book a file.

15. Microform is used to store:
    a) files in reduced format on a magnetic disk
    b) files in reduced format on a CD-R
    c) files in reduced format on a CD-WORM
    d) files in condensed format on paper
    e) files in reduced format on film

16. An efficient filing system is implemented on a computer by:
    a) saving the files to an appropriate magnetic disk
    b) saving the files to an appropriate magnetic tape
    c) saving the files to an appropriate folder structure
    d) saving the files to an appropriate CD-R
    e) saving the files to an appropriate CD-WORM

17. A follow-up system is used to:
    a) keep a record of files removed from the system
    b) check which files are out
    c) give a reminder when a file is needed again
    d) chase up files which have not been returned
    e) add a new file to the system

18. Under the Data Protection Act 1988, which of the following is **not** an obligation on a business?
    a) to obtain and store information fairly
    b) to use the information for specific and lawful purposes
    c) to process and distribute the information
    d) to keep the information up to date
    e) to delete information when it is no longer relevant

19. The data subject is:
    a) the person who controls the collection of data
    b) the person who inputs the data into the computer
    c) the person to whom the data refers
    d) the person with whom the business must register
    e) the person who enforces the Data Protection Act

20. It is important to file documents correctly so that:
    a) the office looks clean and tidy
    b) documents are kept safely on record
    c) only you know where the documents are
    d) the public can find them easily
    e) whoever needs the documents can find them   (NCVA 1994)

21. Place the following in alphabetical order:
    a) 3 Star Cinema
    b) Thomas McDonnell & Co Ltd
    c) Timothy MacDonnell
    d) Peter Paul Jones
    e) P.P. Jones   (NCVA 1994)

22. Put the following files in alphabetical order:
    a) The L'Orient Nights Video
    b) Thai Oriental Cafe
    c) Things Terrific Ltd
    d) The Great Escape Computer Company
    e) Theme Textiles   (NCVA 1996)

23. A firm box with a spring clip used to store documents and keep them secure is called:
    a) a multipart file
    b) an expanding file
    c) a lever arch file
    d) a twinlock crystal file
    e) an index box   (NCVA 1996)

24. Which of the following offers the **most economical space saving** for records management in an office?
    a) floppy disk
    b) hard disk
    c) optical disk
    d) microfilming
    e) vertical filing   (NCVA 1996)

Short Answer Questions

1. List the advantages and disadvantages of centralised filing.
2. List the five main methods of classification used in filing. State a suitable use for each method.
3. List five rules for alphabetical filing. Give an example to show each rule.
4. Distinguish between a direct and an indirect filing system.
5. Distinguish between the alphanumerical system and the Dewey decimal system.
6. Place the following in alphabetical order for filing:
   Peter Smith
   Mr J Smithers
   The Smythe Engineering Co

Smithie and Brown Enterprises Ltd
Henry Smythers

7. Place the following in alphabetical order for filing:
   The Gainsborough Hotel
   Green & Patterson
   Department of Education & Science
   St George's House
   Saint Vincent's

8. Place the following in alphabetical order for filing:
   Patterson and Brown
   The Newport Arms Hotel
   Department of the Environment
   Mr John O'Sullivan
   5-Star Services

9. Place the following in alphabetical order for filing:
   Fred B Walsh
   Walsh Family Foods Ltd
   The Highway Lounge
   Gerry McGovern
   Hugh McGovern
   Tom MacGovern
   Oasis Design Ltd
   O B Marine Ltd
   Frank O'Brien
   Star Society
   The Three Bears Ltd
   In 1 Cleaning Services

10. Place the following in alphabetical order for filing:
    Dr Tom Healy
    John Healy & Associates Ltd
    Ms Marie Collins
    Collins
    Arthur Gibney & Partners
    The Kerry Company Ltd
    William Farrell Ltd
    Saint Clare's Nursery
    St Theresa's Swimming Pool
    Colm De Buitlear
    John Deasy
    One Hour Photo

11. Place the following in alphabetical order for filing:

    Dr J P O'Sullivan
    Department of Education
    The Business Studies Department
    Conor O'Meara (Auctioneer) Ltd
    Prof William O'Meara
    Finlay's Lounge
    Fr F Carthy
    The Two Sisters
    2's Company (Artists)
    David Twohig
    1-Hour Repairs
    One-to-One Swap Shop

12. State four reasons for using a cross-reference in filing.

13. When would a colour-coding system be used?

14. List four factors you would take into account when deciding on equipment to purchase for a manual filing system.

15. List four types of files/folders used in a manual system. State why each may be purchased.

16. List and explain the three main storage arrangements for a manual filing system.

17. What are the advantages and disadvantages of the main storage arrangements for a manual filing system?

18. What kind of material would be best filed horizontally?

19. When would you use an index system?

20. Distinguish between a card index and a visual card index.

21. What is a strip index? Give an example where a strip index would be used.

22. State five important rules for filing when a new file does not have to be opened.

23. State the procedure to be followed when a new suspension file is to be opened.

24. Explain the procedure to be followed when a file is requested from a filing cabinet.

25. What are the advantages of an outcard?

26. When and how is a file-passing slip used?

27. What is microform? State four uses for it.

28. Briefly describe how information stored on microform is viewed.

29. What are the advantages and disadvantages of microform?

30. List and briefly describe two ways in which microform is produced.

31. What is the difference between a fiche and a film in microform?

32. How should microform be stored?

33. State four ways in which a computerised filing system can be implemented.

34. List four storage media for files stored on a computer and give a suitable use for each.

35. What are the advantages and disadvantages of a computerised filing system?
36. List four types of equipment for storing disks.
37. List the four ways files are classified under a retention policy. State the main difference between them.
38. What is a document shredder? Why would it be used?
39. Briefly describe how a follow-up system is used.
40. What are the essential elements of a filing system?
41. State four reasons why an efficient filing system is so important.
42. What are the essential elements of a good filing system?
43. What obligations are imposed on a business that keeps personal data relating to individuals on computers?
44. What rights are given to individuals under the Data Protection Act where information is stored about them on a computer?
45. List four systems for filing and storing paper documents in an office.

(NCVA 1996)

46. List four factors you should consider if asked to design a filing system for an office.   (NCVA 1996)
47. List four advantages of storing information on microfilm.   (NCVA 1994)

10. Telecommunications

After studying this chapter you should be able to:

◆ Describe the various types of voice communication systems: PABX, cordless telephones, mobile telephones, their features and advantages
◆ Describe the services available from Telecom Éireann
◆ Describe the various types of voice messaging communication systems: answering machine, voice mail, their features and advantages
◆ Describe the various types of data networking communication systems: fax machine, computer-based fax machine, e-mail, EDI, radio paging, their features and advantages.
◆ Know how to send and deal with messages received from the various types of communication equipment.
◆ Describe the various types of video/voice communication systems: dedicated video conferencing studios, desktop units, their features and advantages
◆ Describe the various types of external databases: viewdata, teletext, their features and advantages

It is recommended that you read the section on networks in Chapter 7. This will provide the knowledge to fully understand the configurations necessary for electronic communication.

Introduction

Every country has a national telephone network which consists of a number of automatic **switching telephone exchanges** connected together. The telephone network is known as a PSTN (public switched telephone network).

All telephones are connected to their local telephone exchange. When a local telephone call is made, the local exchange makes the connection. If the call is a long-distance call, the local telephone exchange automatically switches the call to the appropriate exchange so that a connection can be made.

The telephone system was originally designed to carry voice communication. New technology has made it possible for the telephone system to send data and voice messages combined with video.

Telephone Systems

The telephone is perhaps the most important means of communication. A business will operate a variety of telephone systems such as: a switchboard (PABX), digital cordless telephones and mobile telephones.

Private Automatic Branch Exchange (PABX)

The PABX (known as a switchboard) makes it possible for a telephone to be on everybody's desk without having all the telephones permanently connected to the public telephone network. The PABX is connected to the public telephone network by a number of exchange lines which depend on the PABX model.

The individual telephones are known as telephone extensions; as they are not directly connected to the public telephone network, calls from one telephone extension to another are free.

The PABX allows a number of incoming calls to be received at the same time and permits telephone extensions to make outgoing calls if a line is free. Extension users make external calls by dialling a single digit code or pressing a line number that is free.

FEATURES OF A PABX

All the features and facilities of the switchboard are under software control and can be easily customised. Switchboards vary in their degree of sophistication, but will include some or all of the following features.

Hold and transfer. Calls are received through the switchboard and need to be routed to the appropriate telephone extension. The receptionist puts an incoming caller on hold and dials the appropriate telephone extension number to transfer the call.

The person at the telephone extension can also put the incoming caller on hold or can transfer the incoming call directly to another extension. For example, assume the switchboard has transferred a call to the Sales Department. If the query is about a delayed order, the Sales Department can put the incoming caller on hold, dial the Production Department to check progress and then return to the caller. Alternatively, the call can be transferred directly to the Production Department.

Music on hold. Music is played to callers while they are on hold.

LCD (liquid crystal display). A panel on the telephone which displays the duration of the call, the number called or a number retrieved from memory. This is useful for checking the accuracy of the telephone number dialled.

Call reason display. Coloured lights are displayed to indicate whether the calls are internal or external, transferred, picked up or forwarded.

Hands free operation. Also known as 'full duplex operation'. The user can dial a number without lifting the handset and carry on a conversation via a built-in microphone and loudspeaker. A useful feature if information needs to be checked while on the telephone or if more than one person needs to hear the conversation.

Memory recall. Also known as 'last number redial'. By pressing a special key a user can redial the **most recently** used number without having to manually dial the number again. A useful feature when the number dialled is engaged.

Single key dialling. Also known as 'speed dialling'. The PABX can be programmed to recall and dial frequently used numbers by assigning a code to each telephone number. The assigned code is then dialled rather than the full telephone number. An index is maintained in alphabetical order of surname to locate the codes.

Clear last digit. A function to erase a misdialled digit while entering a telephone number.

Call forwarding. Also known as 'follow me'. This is a diversion facility which diverts all incoming calls to another telephone number (internal or external) under certain conditions. For example, if the receiver is busy the call can be transferred to another appropriate telephone extension. This is known as CFB — 'call forward busy'. If the receiver is not replying, the call can be transferred to another telephone number. This is known as CFNR — 'call forward not replying'. This facility could be used in the evening, when the switchboard operator is off duty.

Call waiting. This facility alerts a person on the telephone to the presence of another incoming call. S/he can then put the other call on hold, deal with the incoming call and return to the first call.

Call barring. Telephone extensions can be prevented from making specific calls such as local, trunk or international calls. This is a useful cost-saving feature as it prevents private calls being made.

Call logging. A metering facility to record the origin of incoming calls and the destination and duration of outgoing calls by extension number. This can be used for cost control or charging purposes.

Call pickup. Allows a telephone extension to answer a call ringing on another telephone extension. This is useful where the person requested is not at their desk and the call can be dealt with by someone else in the office.

Camp on busy. This feature allows automatic redial of an engaged telephone extension. This saves time trying to contact individuals and avoids the pitfall of forgetting to redial.

When an extension number is engaged, the caller enters a code. When the extension becomes free, the caller's telephone will automatically ring. When the caller lifts the receiver, the extension number previously dialled is automatically redialled and the call can be completed. If many individuals are trying to contact the same extension number, the callers are notified in sequence when the extension number becomes free.

Conferencing. A number of telephone extensions and, if required, a number of exchange lines can be connected. This allows more than two people to be involved in a conversation.

Direct dialling in (DDI). A facility which supports the DDI service available from Telecom Éireann. If a caller knows the person's extension number, the caller can dial directly to the user without going through the switchboard, thus reducing the

Detailed switchboard

pressure on the switchboard. The business is allocated DDI numbers for each telephone extension. If the person is unavailable, features such as call forwarding and call pickup are implemented, ensuring that all incoming calls are answered.

Hunting. Allows incoming calls to a listed directory number to be answered by a defined group of lines. Useful where several staff can deal with the query.

Uniform call distribution. Allows incoming calls to a listed directory number to be evenly distributed over a given number of lines. This is useful for distributing calls on a 'helpline'.

Digital Cordless Telephones

Special switchboards can be linked to cordless telephone extensions. This allows calls to be transferred to the required person even though s/he is not at the office.

A **cordless** telephone is a handset with a built-in telephone keypad, allowing calls to be made and received once the user stays within the coverage area of the PABX.

Cordless telephones are particularly useful where employee mobility is important, such as in hospitals, large factories, building sites, garages, airports and large stores.

ADVANTAGE OF CORDLESS TELEPHONES

1. Calls can be transferred to employees no matter where they are in the building.
2. Allows 'real' communication with the caller, in comparison with radio paging.

3. The PABX can implement features to prevent unauthorised use of the telephone, ie, call barring.

4. Ideal for locations where employee mobility is important, for example, hospitals, large stores, airports, etc.

Mobile Telephones

Mobile telephones have become an essential part of business communications. A mobile telephone is a portable telephone powered by a battery and calls can be made and received at any time and place. They differ from cordless telephones in that their range is not limited. However, they are more expensive to use than the ordinary telephone.

The mobile network in Ireland is operated by **Eircell**, a subsidiary of Telecom Éireann. Today there are two mobile telephone technologies in use: cellular analog telephones and Global System Mobile (GSM) which is a digital telephone.

Differences Between Cellular and GSM Mobile Telephones	
Cellular Analog Telephone	**Global System Mobile (GSM) Telephone**
First model of the mobile telephone and still available today.	New and expanding network.
Does not work outside Ireland, therefore, no point in taking it abroad.	Works within and outside Ireland. Telephone calls can be made or received while abroad.
Prefix number is 088.	Prefix number is 087.
Telephone number is specific to each telephone.	Telephone number is contained on a SIM card (subscriber identity module). Allows the same number to be used by people with more than one mobile telephone, eg, a car telephone and a hand-portable, by inserting the SIM card in the appropriate telephone.
Suitable for people whose communication needs are within Ireland.	Suitable for people whose communications needs are in Ireland and abroad.

TYPES OF MOBILE TELEPHONES

Car telephones. These are fitted into vehicles and receive power directly from the vehicle battery. They provide hands-free operation so the handset is not used while driving.

Transportable car telephones. These are similar to the car telephone, but can be detached from the vehicle and used as a portable telephone. They are heavier and bigger than a hand portable mobile.

Hand portable mobiles. These are extremely portable and some are small enough to fit into your pocket. They do not emit as much power as a car telephone, and in weak signal areas the quality of the line will be affected.

The features available on a PABX are generally available with most mobile telephones, such as: single key dialling, last number redial, clear last digit, hold, memory recall, call forwarding, call waiting and call barring.

Other features are:

Security options. A PIN is required to make telephone calls.

Battery warning. Signals when the batteries *Mobile phone* are running low. The battery is recharged using electrical power or the cigarette lighter in a car.

Scratchpad mode. While on a call, a telephone number can be entered in the telephone's scratchpad memory.

Data transmission. Some GSM telephones can be connected to a portable computer or a portable fax machine allowing the user to send and receive faxes and data files while on the move. A personal computer card (PC card) is inserted into the portable computer and linked to the mobile telephone allowing communication to take place.

BENEFITS OF MOBILE TELEPHONES

1. A user can keep in contact and be contacted while on the move.
2. A user can create a mobile office by connecting a portable computer to the GSM telephone, allowing faxes and e-mail messages to be sent and received.
3. Gives freedom of movement to people who require mobility in their jobs and yet need to keep in touch and be contacted by their customers. For example, architects, surveyors, doctors, etc.
4. The 'hand portable' type is small enough to fit into a pocket or handbag.

Services Offered By Telecom Éireann

Operator Services

TELEMESSAGE AND INTERNATIONAL TELEGRAMS

A telemessage can be sent anywhere in Ireland by dialling 196 and dictating the message to the operator. The message is typed and sent in a Telemessage blue envelope and delivered by An Post anywhere in Ireland the next working day. The cost of the service is £1.82 for twelve words.

Messages can also be sent on presentation cards (for new baby, good luck etc) for an additional fee. International telemessages can also be sent.

Telemessage blue envelope

AUDIO CONFERENCE CALLS

Up to ten callers (national or international) can be connected at the one time to share a conversation. An audio conference call is booked by dialling 114. Each connection is charged as a separate call.

DIRECTORY ENQUIRIES

If you do not know a person's telephone number you can contact the operator. The service number dialled depends on whether the number required is national (dial 1190), in Great Britain (dial 1197) or international (dial 1198). Four free directory enquiries are allowed in a two-month billing period.

No fee is charged for calls made from public payphones or mobile telephones. Exemptions are also given to those who have a physical or medical difficulty in using a directory.

ALARM CLOCK CALLS

An alarm clock call can be booked with the operator by dialling 10. The charge for each call booked is 91p. At the appropriate time, the telephone will ring and a recorded message will tell you the time. Customers with modern digital telephones can program their own alarm clock calls.

ADVICE OF DURATION AND CHARGE (ADC)

This service informs the caller of the cost and duration of a call. Dial 10 and request an ADC call stating both the telephone number to be dialled and your telephone number. When the call is finished, the operator calls back giving details of the cost. This service could be used when making a call from someone else's private telephone or for charging employees who make personal calls.

The cost of the service is 36p and the call is charged at the operator rate which is slightly more expensive than dialling the call direct.

REVERSE CHARGE CALLS

This service allows you to make a local, national or international call and charge the call to the **called number**. A useful service if you need to telephone home or the office and you do not have change or a callcard.

The caller dials 10 and requests a reverse charge call, stating both the telephone number to be dialled and his/her own telephone number and name. The operator dials the number to seek permission: if the charge is accepted, the person being called pays for both the telephone call (charged at the operator rate) and the service, which is charged at 61p.

PERSONAL CALLS

This service allows a caller to book a call to a specified person. If the person requested is not available or an acceptable substitute cannot be contacted, there is no charge for the call; only the service fee is payable.

SPEAKING CLOCK

Dial 1191 to listen to a speaking clock which gives the time in the 24-hour format at 10-second intervals. The call is charged at the local rate.

Travel Services

Telecom offers two cashless call services: Chargecard and Ireland Direct.

CHARGECARD

A Chargecard is used to make telephone calls to and from any telephone worldwide; the cost of the telephone calls are charged to your Irish telephone bill, itemised free of charge.

Chargecard

To use the Chargecard within Ireland, the caller dials a FreeFone number; when abroad, the caller dials the Ireland Direct access number. In both cases the caller is requested to key in the card number, a security number and the telephone number required.

IRELAND DIRECT (INTERNATIONAL REVERSE CHARGE CALLS)

This service allows a caller to be connected directly to a Telecom Éireann operator while making a call from abroad. There is a service charge per call. The caller dials the appropriate Ireland Direct access number from the country s/he is in (Telecom Éireann provides a mini table). The caller can request reverse charges or can bill the call to his/her Chargecard. The advantages are: you speak to an Irish operator and there is no need for coins.

Telemarketing Services

Telemarketing means using the telephone to generate sales. Telecom Éireann provides a range of services to a business to generate sales in a cost-effective manner.

FREEFONE – 1800

The FreeFone number starts with 1800 and calls are free of charge from anywhere in the country. The cost of the call is paid by the business. The business can choose its own distinctive FreeFone 1800 number.

CALLSAVE – 1850

The CallSave number starts with 1850 and calls are charged at a special rate (12p) regardless of the duration of the call from anywhere in the country. The balance of the telephone charge is paid by the business.

LOCALL – 1890

The LoCall number starts with 1890 and calls are charged at the local rate from anywhere in the country, the balance being paid by the business.

Premium Services

This service allocates numbers in the range of 1530 to 1580 to businesses, allowing them to provide an information service to the public, 24 hours a day, 7 days a week.

The type of information available includes news and weather, sports commentaries and results, competitions, flight information, horoscopes, advice, vote lines and entertainment.

The charge for the call is based on the number dialled as displayed below.

Number Dialled	Rate per minute
1530	£0.26
1540	£0.46
1550	£0.58
1560	£0.75
1570	£1.00
1580	£1.50

Other Services

CALLCARD

The Callcard allows you to make cashless local, national and international calls from any public payphone in Ireland.

The card is inserted into a public cardphone and the units on the card are displayed on the LCD. When the connection is made the units are reduced accordingly. The used cards have now become collectors' items. Callcards are purchased from local shops and businesses can purchase callcards at a discount direct from Telecom Éireann.

There are a certain number of free units on the Callcard, depending on the number of units purchased, thus calls will be slightly cheaper than calls made using coins.

Units	Price	Saving	Units Free
10	£2.00	–	–
20	£3.50	£0.50	2
50	£8.00	£2.00	10
100	£16.00	£4.00	20

VOICE MAIL

Telecom Éireann offers a voice mail service to telephone users (see computer-based voice mail below). A subscriber does not need a computer; the only hardware required is a telephone and Telecom Éireann sets up the mailboxes for subscribers at the telephone exchange.

If the telephone is not answered the caller will be switched to the telephone exchange where a pre-recorded message is played inviting the caller to leave a message. The pre-recorded message can be Telecom's own standard message or the owner of the telephone can personalise the message.

The messages are retrieved from any telephone by dialling your telephone number and entering your PIN. The cost of the service is £1.66 per month.

Voice Messaging Systems

A voice messaging system is an automatic answering and recording facility. It is an essential business tool today, allowing communication to take place even though there is no-one in the office. Voice messaging systems include: the answering machine, computer-based voice mail and voice response which gives standard information.

The Answering Machine

This is a recording machine attached to the telephone or built into modern telephones. It allows telephone messages to be received even when there is no-one available to answer the telephone. It operates as follows:

1. When an incoming call is received, the telephone automatically switches over to the answering machine after a certain number of rings.
2. The machine plays a recorded message inviting the caller to leave a message after the beeps.
3. The messages are recorded on a tape and can be played back when the person returns to the office.

FEATURES

Some or all the following features may be present on modern answering machines.

Message counter. An LCD which displays how many messages are recorded.

Automatic cut-off. A facility to limit the length of each message. The caller should be informed in the recorded message of the duration.

Call screening. A facility to listen to calls as they are received. Useful for taking urgent calls.

Recorder. A facility which allows a telephone conversation to be recorded.

Remote access. A facility which enables the owner to call the answering machine. The owner dials his/her telephone number, enters a PIN, and presses certain keys to listen to the messages received, record a new message or erase the messages.

RECORDING AN OUTGOING MESSAGE

1. Write down your message in advance, keeping it short.
2. Record the message in a quiet area; speak slowly and articulate each word.
3. The message should do the following:
   - Greet the caller and state the name of the business.
   - Apologise that there is nobody available to take the call.
   - Ask the caller to leave their name, number and message after the 'beep'.
   - If there is an automatic cut-off facility, inform the caller of the length of time s/he has to record the message.
4. Play back the message, to ensure that it is audible and clear. If not, delete it and repeat the process.

EXAMPLE 1 – MESSAGE RECORDED

You have reached the office of Tom & Gerry, Solicitors. We apologise that there is no-one available at present to take your call. Please leave your name, number and message after the beep and we will contact you as soon as possible.

EXAMPLE 2 – MESSAGE RECORDED

Hello, High Flyer's Ltd. We regret that our office is closed. Opening hours are 9.00 am to 1.00 pm. weekdays. Please leave your name, number and message after the beep.

In the above message, the opening hours of the business are stated. This is not usually required, but as the opening hours are not standard, it does provide the caller with information. Hello is used as the greeting, as it is suitable for all times of the day.

LEAVING A MESSAGE

1. Do not hang up. Listen carefully to the instructions.
2. Speak slowly and clearly.
3. Give your name and business name, date and time of call.
4. State who the message is for.
5. If the message is short, state your message and telephone number.
6. Do not leave a message if it is long and complex, or confidential; just ask to be called back at a specific telephone number.
7. Spell out any words or figures that may be confusing. For example, the number 15 could sound like 50, and some foreign names are difficult to comprehend on tape.

EXAMPLE 1 – LEAVING A MESSAGE

Good morning, this is Michael Carty from Shape-Up. Message is for Harry Smith, Sales Department. Please add two more boxes of All-Green Shampoo to my order. If you need further details, contact me at 234987 up to 6.00 pm. Thank you.

Here the caller leaves a message. This is very efficient as the receiver can act on the information and may not need to contact the caller again, saving time and money.

EXAMPLE 2 – LEAVING A MESSAGE

Good afternoon, this is Bro. Joe. Message is for Nora Shannon, Public Relations. Please call me at your earliest convenience.

In the above message, the caller's full name, business name and number were not given. This is acceptable if the receiver knows the caller very well. The caller does not state a message, maybe because it is too complex, private, or the receiver knows the topic from an earlier conversation.

DEALING WITH RECORDED MESSAGES

It is generally the case that an answering machine will be located in the general office. Incoming messages should be played back and the following details transcribed onto a telephone message pad:

- ◆ the caller's name, business and telephone number
- ◆ the date, and time of call
- ◆ the name of the person to receive the message
- ◆ the details of the message
- ◆ the name of the person who transcribed the message

The messages should be given to the appropriate person as soon as possible. This can be achieved in a number of ways:

- ◆ Telephoning the appropriate person and relaying the message.
- ◆ Placing the messages in the person's 'pigeonhole' (internal mailbox).
- ◆ A junior in the office distributes the messages.

If the message is 'urgent', it should be relayed immediately.

Computer-based Voice Mail

Voice mail is a computer-based telephone answering facility. Voice mail can be installed on a personal computer (PC) or a PABX or you can subscribe to the service available from Telecom Éireann.

PC-BASED VOICE MAIL

A modem with voice capabilities is installed in the computer and connected to the telephone line. Using software, individuals are given their own personal answering machine called a 'mailbox' which is an area of the hard disk used to record messages.

If the telephone is not answered within a certain number of rings, the software answers the telephone and plays a pre-recorded message explaining to the caller that they should press specific keys on their telephone according to the service required, for example, 'Press 1 for the Sales Department'. The software records the message in the specified mailbox together with the time and duration of the call. Messages can be retrieved on site or from a remote location. This system is suitable for home use or a small business as only one PC and one telephone line is required.

PABX-BASED VOICE MAIL

This is similar to the PC-based voice mail except that it deals with a network of computers. The network has a 'mail server' which is a central computer with a voice modem installed.

The incoming call is answered by the switchboard operator, who transfers the call to the appropriate telephone extension number. If there is no reply, a pre-recorded message is played by the 'mail server' inviting the caller to leave a message or to press a specific key to return to the switchboard.

If the PABX has DDI, a caller who knows the extension number can dial directly without having to go through the switchboard. Again, if there is no reply, a message can be left on their voice mail.

To retrieve messages, the recipient must log on to the mail server. This can be done on site or remotely using the telephone system.

FACILITIES AVAILABLE ON BOTH PC-BASED AND PABX SYSTEMS

Hands-free operation. If a microphone and speakers are attached to the computer, the user does not need to use the telephone handset, giving hands-free operation. This facility is excellent for people who need to take notes while on the telephone.

Telephone dialler. A telephone is displayed on the screen and the number is dialled by clicking the appropriate numbers on the telephone dialler.

Telephone book. Names and telephone numbers are entered into the telephone book. A number is dialled by selecting the person from a drop-down list and pressing Dial.

Log. A record is kept of every contact attempt.

Reminder. A schedule can be set up to remind you to follow up on a call. A message will pop up at the relevant time.

Forwarding. A facility to automatically call your 'pager' which displays a code indicating that a voice-mail message has been received (See Radio Paging below).

ADVANTAGES OF VOICE MESSAGING SYSTEMS

1. Messages can be received even when there is no-one in the office.
2. Customers can communicate with the business outside of business hours.
3. Messages can be picked up remotely.
4. Forward contact numbers can be left.
5. Calls can be screened. The receiver can cut in on urgent calls.
6. With voice mail, a message can be forwarded to someone else on the network.

DISADVANTAGES OF VOICE MESSAGING SYSTEMS

1. They are impersonal; some people do not like talking to machines.
2. The person leaving a message sometimes forgets to state their name and telephone number making the message useless.

Voice Response

A business can use voice response to store certain messages at each mailbox so that information can be given to callers without anybody answering the telephone. Telephone numbers are assigned to each mailbox.

Voice response is used to give general information to the public, ie, transport timetables (nicknamed 'the talking timetable'), cinema times, etc. For example, a caller requesting information on trains to Tralee dials the appropriate number and the relevant details are played from the disk on the computer. This service could also be set up with dedicated telephone lines answered by an ordinary answering machine.

Data Networking Communication

A data networking system allows written communication to be sent over the telephone line. It is therefore much faster than the ordinary postal system and like the voice messaging system it allows communication to take place even when there is no-one in the office. It is an essential business tool today. The systems available are the fax, e-mail, electronic data interchange (EDI) and radio paging.

The Fax Machine

The fax or facsimile machine is a convenient and fast way in which to transmit exact copies of documents locally, nationally or internationally. The machine transmits the **image** of the page; it makes no attempt to understand the data on the page, thus printed text, written text, pictures and other images can all be sent by fax with ease.

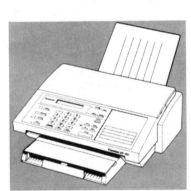

The simplified view of a fax machine is that of two photocopiers connected by a telephone line. The sending fax is where you insert the original and the receiving fax is where the copy is made.

Both coloured and black and white faxes can be transmitted, but a fax can only be received in black and white. Often a fax machine includes a telephone handset and functions as a telephone and basic photocopier (ie, a 3-in-1 machine: a fax, telephone, and photocopier).

Fax

The fax machine is connected to the telephone line. The machines at either end of the line do not have to be of the same make. In the case where one machine is of a lower specification than the other, the call proceeds at the speed of the lower of the two specifications.

The fax machine can be connected so that it either:

a) **shares a telephone line with a telephone.** When the telephone line is shared between a fax and a telephone it means that a telephone call cannot be received or made when a fax message is being received or sent and vice versa. Incoming fax messages are switched to the fax machine; this may be done manually by the person who answers the telephone or automatically by sophisticated fax machines which are able to distinguish between voice and fax calls. Sharing a line is suitable where the volume of incoming and outgoing faxes is low.

   or

b) **has its own dedicated telephone line.** This allows the fax machine to answer incoming calls directly, leaving the other telephone line(s) free to receive telephone calls. The fax machine in this case is answered automatically. The dedicated telephone line can also be used to make telephone calls when required.

SENDING FAX MESSAGES

1. Place the original(s) in the input tray. (Some fax machines only accept single sheets.)

2. Enter the fax number. It may be possible to use a 'speed dial' facility to dial frequently used numbers.

   If the message is to be transmitted at a later time, ie, after office hours, the message can be scanned into the fax machine's memory and the time of transmission set.

3. Press the start button. The outgoing fax machine dials the number.

4. When the receiving fax machine answers, the mode and speed of communication between the two fax machines is negotiated. This takes into account the capabilities of both machines, the quality of the telephone line and if any special settings (like fine mode transmission) have been selected for the transmission. The page is then scanned through the transmitting fax machine. If the machine is not capable of coping with multiple pages the pages must be manually fed through the fax machine.

5. At the end of the communication, the outgoing fax machine will print a **transmission report** which gives details of the date and time of the transmission, the receiving fax machine's number, the number of pages sent, and whether the transmission was successful or not. (Transmission report should be attached to fax as a record of the fax sent.)

   If there is an error in the transmitted documents, some fax machines also print out the page in question allowing the sender to re-transmit that page only.

RECEIVING FAX MESSAGES

1. The fax machine must be set to ON.

2. No other action should normally be required. (However, if the fax machine shares the same telephone line as the telephone, and the fax machine does not have the capability to distinguish between voice and fax messages, operator assistance is required. The person answering the telephone switches the line to the fax machine so that the call can proceed.)

3. Ensure sufficient paper is loaded to print incoming messages. This is extremely important if the machine is to be left unattended overnight. Some fax machines read incoming messages into memory if the paper runs out. The messages are then printed from the memory by the operator when the fax machine is reloaded with paper.

4. When the message is transmitted, the receiving fax machine will print a **transmission report**.

5. The fax is distributed to the appropriate person and if the fax is to be distributed to several people, it is photocopied and distributed to the relevant people.

COMPILING A FAX MESSAGE

Many companies prepare their own fax coversheet using the templates available with word processing packages. The salutation and complimentary close are normally omitted; the message will be signed.

If a fax coversheet is not used, the following information should be typed on the business headed notepaper: for the attention of; from; date; number of pages including this page.

SHARPMAN
Fax Message

Computer Books and Software
11 Northgate Street   Tel No: 0902 - 342675
Athlone   Fax: 0902 - 342677
Co Westmeath

Attn: _____   Dept: _____

From: _____   Date: _____

Number of Pages including Coversheet:_____

THE COST OF SENDING A FAX

The fax machine uses the ordinary telephone line, and therefore the charges are the same as for telephone calls of similar duration over similar distances. Fax messages should be sent during off-peak periods where possible.

FEATURES OF THE FAX MACHINE

Features	Functions
Automatic Document Feeder	Documents to be transmitted are stacked on the input tray and transmitted in sequence.
LCD (Liquid Crystal Display)	A screen display that keeps you informed of all on-going fax operations; it displays the fax number dialled and gives messages such as 'dialling', 'sending', etc.
Fax/Tel Auto Change	A function which automatically distinguishes between voice and fax calls when one telephone line is used.
Automatic Redial	The fax machine automatically redials a number if the receiving fax machine is engaged.
Speed Dialling	Frequently used numbers can be stored in memory and dialled automatically with a simple two-digit code ensuring dialling times and mis-dialled numbers are reduced.
Store & Forward	Also known as **batch** or **delayed transmission**. Messages can be stored in memory and a timer is pre-set for transmitting the message at a cheaper rate.
Confidential Reception	The message is stored in the memory of the receiving machine. To print out the message an identification code is keyed in.
Substitute Reception	The message is stored in the memory if there is no paper in the receiving machine to print out the incoming message.
Broadcasting	Allows the same document to be sent to multiple destinations just by scanning it once. A list of recipients is created and everyone on the list gets the document.
Dual Access	Allows faxes to be sent even while another fax is being received or sent. The fax is scanned and stored in memory and sent automatically as soon as the machine is free.
Automatic Contrast Control	The machine automatically detects the brightness or darkness of the image and adjusts the exposure accordingly.

Features	Functions
Fine Mode Transmission	A function to increase the resolution (number of dots per inch) of the image to improve the quality of the output. Used for sending documents with small letters and fine lines.
Automatic Cutter	On machines that use rolls of thermal paper, a cutter will cut each page to size.
Forwarding	The fax machine can be programmed to forward all incoming faxes to another fax machine. Useful when you are away from the office; the documents are sent from memory to the destination fax machine.
Copier Facility	Some fax machines can be used as ordinary office photocopiers.
Error Correction Code	Interference on a telephone line can cause messages to be garbled. Detects and corrects such errors before the message is printed.
Automatic Log	A facility to log all incoming and outgoing faxes.
Fax On Demand	A facility which is used to give standard information to the public, eg, details of advertised articles are placed in the memory of the fax machine. They are retrieved by dialling the fax number and entering the code associated with the particular article.
Fax Polling	A facility which provides a list of faxes available for retrieval at a single request. Unlike the fax-on-demand which allows the caller to request a specific article, each polling request results in the transmission of all documents in the polling list. Used by head offices to pass information to branches. A password prevents unauthorised use.
Answering Machine (TA/FAX)	This facility is also known as a **TAM** (telephone answering mode) **interface**. It is a fax machine with a telephone answering service. The machine automatically switches between the answering mode and the fax mode depending on the nature of the call.

PAPER USED IN FAX MACHINES

Features	
Thermal Paper	**Plain Paper**
• Thin paper which tears easily and is difficult to write on. • Is generally photocopied before filing as the paper curls and fades over time. • The paper turns black when exposed to heat. • Variable size paper, cut to the length of the message received.	• Standard quality paper which is more durable and can be written on. • No need to photocopy received messages. • Easy to file; the paper does not curl like thermal paper. • Standard size – A4. • Easier to recycle.

ADVANTAGES OF THE FAX MACHINE

1. Easy to use and therefore little or no training is necessary.
2. Transmission is fast and as a result, information can be transmitted at a relatively low cost.
3. All types of data can be transmitted: handwritten documents (blue or black ink), text, pictures and diagrams.
4. Facilitates communication worldwide regardless of time zone differences or different business hours.
5. Transmission occurs instantaneously.
6. Maintenance costs for fax machines are low and the machines are extremely reliable.
7. Fax-on-Demand is a new marketing tool enabling a business to provide literature on its products. No postage costs are involved. The recipient pays as s/he dials to receive the information.

New Developments in Faxes

FAX/MODEMS

A modem with a fax capability installed in a computer (or attached) enables the computer to act as a fax machine.

The fax software may incorporate a character recognition system to convert received faxes from a bitmap image to text format and therefore allow the received fax to be edited.

The advantages of a fax capability in a computer are:

a) Less office space is required for equipment.
b) The document can be faxed directly from the computer to another computer or to an ordinary fax machine.
c) The fax can be filed on disk rather than in a filing cabinet.
d) There is no need to print the document in order to fax it.

The disadvantages are:

a) The computer must be left on all the time in order to receive faxes.

b) The information must be stored in the computer in order to be faxed. This problem can be overcome by using a scanner.

TO SEND A MESSAGE USING A FAX/MODEM

1. Select the fax machine as the output device instead of the printer.
2. Enter the fax number on the dialog box and press Dial.

The fax machine at the receiving end (may be another computer with a fax/modem or an ordinary fax machine) acts as the output printer to your computer.

RECEIVING MESSAGES

1. Messages received on a fax/modem computer based system are saved to disk.
2. To edit the fax, character recognition software is used to convert the image to text.
3. The received messages can be circulated as an e-mail message.

LASER PRINTER WITH FAX CAPABILITIES

Laser printers with a fax capability are now available. This dual functionality reduces the space required for office equipment.

The printer is connected to the computer as normal and acts as both a fax machine and a printer. When the printer is busy incoming fax messages are stored in the printer's memory.

The laser printer can fax 'hardcopy' documents or documents directly from the computer. The fax is sent or received in **background mode** which allows you to continue using the computer while a fax is being sent or received.

These new developments have increased the functionality of a network (see Chapter 7). If the 'server' has a fax/modem attached, the users of the network can send and receive faxes through the server while sitting at their own computer. Alternatively a laser printer with a fax capability can be attached to the network.

Electronic Mail (e-mail)

E-mail allows messages to be sent from one computer to another over a network. In addition to sending text messages the user can also attach files that are prepared in other software packages. However the recipient must also have the same software package so that s/he can read the file. E-mail systems can be private or public.

PRIVATE E-MAIL SYSTEMS

Intra-Company Communication

Intra-company means communication within the company. If the organisation has implemented a network, it can operate a private e-mail system which allows the users on the network to communicate with each other without having to leave their desk.

A private e-mail system is set up by installing e-mail software on the server and the computers on the network. 'Mailboxes' are set up on the server's hard disk for each person on the network to hold their 'post'.

Messages are collected in the following way:

1. Individuals log on to the server and enter their password to check their mail. If mail is present, it is sent from the server to their hard disk.

2. Individuals can configure their own software so that they are notified of incoming mail. A recipient could be notified of incoming mail by (a) an audio bleep, or (b) the mouse pointer changing shape or (c) a message being displayed on their screen.

As the system is local, there is no charge involved; it is similar to making internal telephone calls as the system does not use the PSTN. Therefore you can only communicate with people within the company.

Inter-Company Communication

Private e-mail systems can also be set up over a wide area network (WAN). Inter-company means communication **between** companies which allows different branches within a company to exchange information using the PSTN. The service is provided by Eirtrade (a subsidiary of Telecom Éireann) and Post Gem (a subsidiary of An Post). The branches establish a connection with Eirtrade or Post Gem which acts as an electronic mail room. The individuals log on to the system to check if they have mail.

PUBLIC E-MAIL SYSTEMS

Public e-mail systems allow users to send and receive messages at any time of the day or night from any location.

Post Gem and Eirtrade also provide a public e-mail service called E-Mail and Eirmail 400 respectively. Subscribers can communicate with all e-mail users on the Internet.

A public e-mail system is also provided by organisations known as **service providers**. The service providers may also provide access to the Internet. Examples of service providers in Ireland are: Ireland On-Line, Indigo, and ieunet.

E-MAIL ON THE INTERNET

The user must have a modem connected to the computer to access the PSTN. The user pays a monthly subscription fee to the service provider and in return the user is assigned a 'mailbox' on the service provider's computer. A telephone charge is also incurred every time the user accesses the system.

When a user sends an e-mail message, it is sent out on the network. The network looks at the destination address of the e-mail message and forwards it to the correct destination (which is the recipient's service provider's computer). The message is stored in the recipient's 'mailbox' for collection.

To collect mail, you log on to your service provider. If there is mail it will be downloaded to your hard disk. Business users should check their mail regularly.

Messages can be read **off-line**, which means that the recipient is not connected to the service provider, saving money on telephone bills. Replies to e-mail messages are also composed off-line. Multiple messages can be sent at the same time, all for the price of a local telephone call.

DECODING A PUBLIC E-MAIL ADDRESS

a) Every user connected via a service provider has a unique address. The address on Internet messages typically takes the form:

User_Name@service provider.country

where User_Name refers to the address of the person the mail is intended for and the entries after the @ symbol (known as the **domain**) indicate the location of the recipient's service provider's mailbox.

EXAMPLE:

f_carty@iol.ie

This means the recipient's address is f_carty; s/he has a mailbox with Ireland On-Line (iol) which is located in Ireland (ie).

---

b) Decoding an address when the user has their own registered domain

Some organisations have a direct connection to the Internet and therefore do not need to connect to service providers (ie, they are their own service provider). Their address on Internet messages typically takes the form:

User_Name@location.organisation.type.country

location means the location of the computer in the organisation

organisation means the name of the organisation

type means the type of organisation. (.com = commercial company, .edu = educational establishment)

country means where you live

Example
j_hegarty@ccm.SCDL.edu.ie

This means the recipient's name is j_hegarty; s/he has a mailbox at a computer called ccm, which is located in an organisation called SCDL, an educational establishment in Ireland.

ADDRESSING THE MESSAGE

To simplify the addressing of a message, an address book can be set up using the e-mail software package. A person's e-mail address plus their full name can be entered in the address book. When the recipient's name is selected from a scrolling list in the address book, their e-mail address is inserted into the e-mail message.

At present, there is no equivalent of a telephone book to source a person's e-mail address. The simplest way is to telephone and ask for it. However, a sender's e-mail address can be seen on received e-mail messages. This can be copied to your address book for further correspondence.

SENDING AN E-MAIL MESSAGE

1. Load the e-mail package. (In the case of a public e-mail system do not make a connection to your service provider while preparing your message, as there is a telephone charge.)
2. Select the option **Create a New Message** from the menu. You are presented with a blank screen similar to the one shown below.

To:	Enter the recipient's e-mail address or select it from the address book.
From:	Your e-mail address automatically appears here.
Subject:	Enter a heading to indicate the subject of the message.
cc:	cc means carbon copy. Enter the addresses of people who are to receive copies of the message; the recipient will know who received copies.
bcc:	bcc means blind carbon copy. Enter the addresses of people who are to receive copies of the message without the recipient knowing who they are.
Attachments:	Files are attached by going to a menu and selecting the file you want to send.

This is where you type your message.

3. Enter the appropriate details in the top part of the screen and type the message in the blank area provided.
4. When the message is complete, you can send it immediately. If the message is not urgent, you should queue the message. In this way **all** the queued messages can be sent for the price of one local telephone call.

RECEIVING AN E-MAIL MESSAGE

1. Load the e-mail package and select the option **Check Messages**. This option makes the connection to your mailbox and informs you if there are any new messages. These are downloaded from your mailbox to your computer's hard disk. (Alternatively, the e-mail software can be set up so that it automatically logs on to your service provider at pre-defined times to check for new mail.)
2. When messages are received they should be read off-line.
   a) If the message needs to be relayed to others in the office, it can be forwarded directly from your computer to the recipients if you have a private e-mail system or else the messages can be printed out, photocopied and distributed.
   b) If the message is to be distributed to people outside your organisation, it can be forwarded using the public e-mail system. If your recipients don't have e-mail it can be faxed directly if you have a fax/modem facility on your computer or network. Alternatively, it can be printed and sent by fax or 'snail mail' (nickname for postal system).
   c) If the message is important it can be stored on the hard disk for a specified period of time, otherwise it can be 'binned' (nickname for deleting a file) by clicking on the 'trash can' icon.

ADVANTAGES OF E-MAIL

1. It is the fastest and the most inexpensive way to communicate.
2. Messages can be sent at any time to **anywhere** in the world for the price of a local telephone call.
3. Files can be attached to e-mail messages.
4. All queued messages are sent for the price of one local telephone call.
5. The broadcasting facility enables one message to be sent to a number of recipients. No mail-merge facility is involved and all messages are sent for the price of one local call.
6. Messages can be prepared and read off-line, saving on telephone bills.

DISADVANTAGES OF E-MAIL

1. You must know a person's e-mail address in order to send them messages.
2. Very large files don't travel well over e-mail.
3. Files attached to e-mail messages may have to be decoded by the recipient if the recipient does not use the same e-mail package.
4. Businesses now receive a lot of junk e-mail.

Electronic Data Interchange (EDI)

This service, offered by Post Gem and Eirtrade, is based on an international standard for the transfer of EDI documents (structured business documents) between computer systems.

EDI, also known as electronic commerce, is the computer-to-computer exchange between **different** organisations of structured business documents, such as purchase orders and invoices, using agreed standards and formats.

Organisations that have EDI can conduct their business electronically. For example, an organisation can send a purchase order from its computer to another organisation that also has the EDI facility. The purchase order will arrive in the computer of the receiving organisation. This eliminates the need to manually enter the purchase order into the computer system.

EDI is also used between businesses and banks when paying for goods and services. For example, a business sends a special standard form from its computer system to the bank's computer system authorising the bank to debit its account (reduce it) and credit the account of the supplier named on the form. Details of the payment will appear on the supplier's next bank statement.

ADVANTAGES OF EDI

1. Increased productivity within an organisation as it eliminates re-keying of data. With EDI, the information is sent directly from one computer to another.
2. No stationery, printing or posting costs.
3. Reduced administration costs as the cost of manually handling business transactions is eliminated.
4. Increased efficiency through faster order acknowledgement and fewer errors.
5. Time zones are irrelevant.

Radio Paging

The radio paging network is provided in Ireland by Eirpage, a subsidiary of Telecom Éireann. A radio pager is a small lightweight device which employees carry with them when they need to be contacted when away from the office. The message is generally a 'bleeper' sound which 'tells' the holder to contact the office. Different models are available with more sophisticated features, such as displaying the number to contact, a coded message or a text message.

Radio paging is a **one-way message system** which means that the holder of the pager can only receive a message; s/he cannot communicate with the caller.

PAGERS

Tone-only pager. This radio pager only provides a bleep. The bleep indicates to the owner that they must contact the office. Models are available with different types of bleeps, so that the person knows from the sound of the bleep whether to contact the office, home, or another contact point.

This is achieved through the pager having more than one telephone number. The owner of the pager gives one telephone number to the office, so when this number is dialled a certain kind of bleep will sound.

Numeric pager. This radio pager bleeps and also displays a telephone number to ring (which is stored in memory for later retrieval) or displays codes which are used to give a message. For example, if you were unsure whether a meeting was going to take place, you could arrange a code with your caller, eg, '660', to mean 'the meeting is cancelled'.

Display pager. This is the most versatile pager: it bleeps but can also display a numeric or text message. Messages can be up to 240 characters long and the pager can store up to 40 messages.

The cost of the service for the above pagers is: (a) the cost of the unit itself, (b) a connection fee, and (c) a monthly service charge irrespective of how many messages you receive. Therefore, the more use you make of the system, the cheaper each call will be.

Minicall pager. This is a relatively new type of paging system. There is no connection fee or on-going monthly charges. The person contacting the Minicall holder pays for the call at the premium 1550 rate. When a caller dials the Minicall number, s/he is answered by voice mail. The caller is invited to leave a message of up to 80 characters which is then transmitted to the Minicall pager within minutes. Alternatively, the caller can enter a coded message.

Swatch the Beep. A Minicall built into a watch.

All of the above types of pagers may have added features such as a **visual signal** or a **vibrapage**. Each of these features allows the user to turn off the bleeper during meetings, etc; the radio pager gives a visual signal or a gentle vibration to alert the user.

EXTRA SERVICES AVAILABLE FROM EIRPAGE

ToneExtra. This is a telephone answering service. The owner of a pager can divert calls into this service. The owner records their personalised message and every time a message is received the pager will bleep. Messages are retrieved using the telephone.

ADVANTAGES OF RADIO PAGING

1. Simple messages can be transmitted.
2. Nationwide service allowing the user to be contacted anywhere in Ireland.
3. Portable and easy to carry.
4. The pager can be set up to bleep when a message has been left on a voice mail answering machine.
5. A cheaper method of locating individuals than a mobile telephone.

DISADVANTAGES OF RADIO PAGING

1. The system is one-way; messages can only be received.
2. The user must find a telephone if s/he needs to reply to the message.

Video-conferencing

Video-conferencing is a system which allow parties not only to converse but also to see each other on a television or computer screen. Therefore it allows meetings to take place between participants in different locations without the participants having to get together physically.

Video-conferencing Systems

DEDICATED VIDEO-CONFERENCING STUDIOS

These are studios set up with the appropriate equipment, ie, microphones, cameras and monitors which are available for renting. For example, if a business outside Ireland wants to set up a video-conferencing meeting with someone in Ireland, it would rent the studio closest to it. The participants would travel to the studio and conduct the meeting there.

Dedicated video-conferencing saves the time and cost involved in getting participants to travel to one place. However, it does have the inconvenience of having to book the conferencing suite and having to travel to use it. Telecom Éireann has public studios in Cork, Limerick and Dublin.

DESKTOP UNITS

A computer can be upgraded to incorporate a video-conferencing facility. This involves purchasing a small camera which sits on top of the monitor, a microphone, loudspeaker and video-conferencing software. A popular desktop system in Ireland today is 'Proshare' developed by Intel Corp.

This allows the person sitting at the computer to display a small window image of themselves and communicate with another user. Files can be displayed and transferred or the participants can sketch diagrams, etc using a 'shared whiteboard' available with the video-conferencing software. The advantage of this system is that a conference can be set up without having to leave your desk.

In order to run this system, an organisation needs a faster telephone line, known as an ISDN line. ISDN (Integrated System Digital Network) allows information and pictures to be sent faster with better quality output than the ordinary PSTN.

ADVANTAGES OF VIDEO-CONFERENCING

1. It allows meetings to take place face to face without the participants having to be in the same place.
2. It saves on travelling time and cost.
3. It enables people with conflicting schedules to 'meet'.
4. Problems can be solved quickly by sharing live data with participants.
5. It can bring expertise into the company or classroom. For example, guest speakers can be asked to provide their lecture through video-conferencing.

6. Can be used to interview potential employees or foreign students for courses.
7. Used in distance learning courses.

Desktop video-conferencing system

Accessing Information Stored in External Databases

Videotex

Videotex is the internationally agreed term given to computers which provide information to users who access a central database via a remote computer equipped with a modem. Videotex is divided into two areas: Viewdata and Teletext.

VIEWDATA

This is a **two-way** communication system, ie, users can send information to, or retrieve information from, the central database. The information is provided by the government, public bodies and private companies who pay the Viewdata operator for having a page of data included in the central database.

It has considerable application in business as it can be used:

- To find information on almost any area of interest: banking, education, finance, insurance, telecommunications, business equipment, car hire, services, computers, employment agencies, travel, office services, agriculture, entertainment (eg, cinema shows, plays, golf, swimming, etc). Having found the information, a user can initiate communication; this means that when a user has found an appropriate hotel in a particular area, they can make a booking. Further information can be requested by e-mail.
- To advertise a firm's products.
- To set up on-line shopping centres. The shop displays a catalogue of goods and prices. The goods are ordered by completing an order form displayed on the screen and asking for details of the purchaser's credit card. The goods are sent by post to the purchaser.

Prestel

This is the UK's public viewdata system operated by British Telecom. Prestel was set up in 1979 and was the UK's first on-line information network. Since then, the service has been continually updated and expanded to provide up-to-the-minute business and financial information.

Prestel offers different levels of access to its services, allowing users to select the most appropriate one for their needs.

Its **Starter Pack** gives 2 hours' free usage each month, the excess being charged at an hourly rate. An e-mail address is also provided.

The **Added Value Pack** provides unlimited free usage and an unlimited number of e-mail addresses, so each member of a department can have their own address.

Other services offered by Prestel include: **Closed User Group**, a service which links specific users privately. The travel industry, for example, uses a Viewdata system connecting tour operators with travel agents, which enables the travel agent to check on availability and book flight seats and accommodation at the time of enquiry (subject to confirmation and deposit); **E-mail**, an electronic mail system; **Outside links**, a facility to link through Prestel to other central databases such as CompuServe and also to the Internet.

HOW PRESTEL WORKS

1. The user enters the Prestel database and provides an identity number and password. Once they are connected, telephone costs are incurred by the minute for the duration of the on-line connection.
2. The information on Prestel is organised in 'pages'; a page is a screen of information. Each page is given a unique number which is used to locate it and display it on the user's screen.
3. The user starts at an initial menu which lists the sections by topic. When they select a particular topic they are offered further sub-divisions of that topic. Alternatively, the user can search for information by keywords, or go directly to a particular page if the page number is known.
4. When the information required is found, it can be saved to disk or printed out. This saves money as the information can then be read off-line.
5. Some pages require an additional fee to access them. This is paid by entering your credit card number on the screen provided.

MINITEL

Minitel is a public viewdata system available in Ireland. It is based on the French Minitel system but it has not been a huge success in Ireland. A user can access the system by purchasing a Minitel set or installing Minitel software on a computer. It operates in a similar way to Prestel and some of the services offered are:

Banking and finance. A user can access their accounts, check balances, transfer funds, pay bills and do a cheque enquiry. They can also view details of the stock market and foreign exchange rates.

Travel. Details are given of flight schedules and seat availability on both domestic and international airlines worldwide.

News/weather. Irish and international news and a 24-hour weather forecast.

Credit reporting. Information on Irish companies including their registered office, capital structure, directors and judgements against the companies.

Directories. Electronic directories for the telephone, fax, telex and the Golden Pages.

Marketing and research. The KOMPASS directory which provides information on the products, services and management of companies in Ireland. Other services include articles from business magazines and the official economic and social statistics.

MemoMail. This is Minitel's e-mail service and provides a directory of all MemoMail users.

The Internet

The Internet is a worldwide network of computers. It is made up of many independent networks which are linked together through the telephone system.

There is no single connection that can be pointed to as the 'Internet'. Every computer on the Internet is connected indirectly to every other computer on the Internet. (Think of it in terms of the telephone: your telephone is linked to your local telephone exchange. Your local telephone exchange is linked to other telephone exchanges. This allows you to telephone another person even though you are not directly connected to that person. You are indirectly connected as your local telephone exchange will do the switching for you.)

Access to the Internet is usually through a service provider who sets up the connection. However, large companies may have sophisticated equipment allowing them to set up their own connection to the Internet.

There are several factors to be considered in selecting a service provider. These include:

Cost. All service providers charge a monthly subscription for using their services and some service providers also charge for the time you spend accessing the Internet (known as 'surfing the net').

Locality. Ensure the service provider is in your local telephone area, otherwise the telephone charge to access the Internet will be a trunk call.

Speed. What speed of modem does the service provider allow as a maximum? This affects the rate at which the information is transferred to your computer which has implications for your telephone bill.

Access. What Internet access does the service provider offer: full, e-mail only, or none? (Some service providers only offer their own information.)

Names. Does the service provider give commercial users their own domain names? For example, after the @ symbol you can have your own company name rather than the name of the service provider, eg, j_kelly@RTE.ie rather than j_kelly@iol.ie.

Support. What level of technical support is available?

Home page. Does the service provider allow subscribers to post their own 'home page' free? A 'home page' is information that subscribers can put on the Internet. This is generally free to non-business users.

Parts of the Internet

Some of the areas of interest on the Internet are:

THE WORLD WIDE WEB (WWW)

The World Wide Web consists of data files stored on computers connected to the Internet all over the world. The files are written by anybody connected to the Internet using the Hypertext Markup Language (HTML) format. Hypertext is text in which certain words or groups of words are marked by an underscore as a link to another page. If the user selects the link the software issues a request over the Internet to transmit that page.

A wide variety of topics is covered on the Internet. A user can access information by typing in an address or by doing a search using the **search engines** such as Gopher or Alta Vista, to mention just two. Information is available on business, investments, computers, education, government, health, arts and entertainment.

NEWSGROUPS

A newsgroup is like an interactive noticeboard and deals with a particular topic. There are various newsgroups on the Internet dealing with topics such as business, computers, general news, recreational interests, science, etc.

Subscribers to a newsgroup will write messages on topics of interest to the newsgroup. However, unlike e-mail, the message is sent to every member of the group. It is ideal for exchanging views with people who have an interest in the subject being discussed.

E-MAIL. (SEE ABOVE.)

The Internet and Businesses

A business can use:
- the WWW to give general information to the public, advertise or sell its products/services. The information is up to date, allowing a business to keep abreast of the latest developments.
- e-mail to communicate with the public and employees located in different branches.
- newsgroups to discuss areas of interest and exchange views on a particular topic.

Teletext

Teletext is the information channel available from the TV broadcasting stations. Teletext broadcasts pages of information and entertainment to television sets equipped with a teletext decoder or computers fitted with a teletext decoder. Teletext is a free service, financed by advertising.

The teletext services provided by the main broadcasting stations are:

Aertel, provided by RTE

Ceefax, provided by the BBC

Teletext, provided by ITV

Oracle, provided by HTV

All services provide information in the following areas: news, sport, business, weather, finance, travel, shopping and TV and radio guide. The Aertel service is now also available on the Internet allowing faster access to the information which may be printed out if required.

HOW DOES TELETEXT WORK?

The information on the Teletext system is provided by information providers, advertisers, and the station's own in-house team of journalists.

Viewers access the Teletext service by pressing the text button on their TV remote control. They are presented with an opening screen which displays the most frequently used services and an index to all the other services.

Teletext consists of pages of information, known as source pages. The source pages are numbered, and the viewer enters a source page number using the remote control. Each page has a three-digit number. The source page may consist of a single page or several pages arranged in a carousel.

The single page remains static on the screen until another page is selected or the user leaves the system. Multiple pages are arranged in a carousel, which changes from page to page in a continuous cycle. The user can stay on a particular page by pressing the HOLD button on the remote control.

Summary

The world of communications is developing at an enormous rate with the sophisticated developments of telecommunication technology. Telephone lines, originally developed to carry voice communications, can now cater for two-way data and video transmissions, ie, video conferencing. Telecommunications incorporates the telephone system.

The telephone system has advanced enormously with sophisticated PABX (switchboards) which automate and monitor the routing of calls. Modern switchboards have facilities for call forwarding (to divert incoming calls to another telephone), call waiting (to indicate the presence of another incoming call), call pickup (to allow a call to be answered from another telephone extension), camp on busy (to automatically redial an engaged telephone), DDI (to dial direct to an extension number), uniform call distribution (to distribute incoming calls). Switchboards are available to operate with cordless telephones which are ideal for locations where employee mobility is important, eg, hospitals. If employees need to move from base, the mobile telephone ensures they can be contacted no matter where they are.

Voice message systems such as the answering machine, voice mail (PC or PABX), and voice response are essential business tools today, allowing communication to take place even though there is no-one in the office.

Telecom Éireann offers a vast range of services to its customers such as audio conferencing, directory enquiries, ADC and reverse charge calls, voice mail and telemessage service. The chargecard and the Ireland Direct service facilitate travel, and the telemarketing services (freefone, callsave, locall) facilitate businesses in generating sales.

Telecommunications also allows data to be sent over the telephone line with data networking systems, offering a vast range of tools to choose from : fax, e-mail, EDI and paging. The fax machine has been around for some time, but more sophisticated facilities are now offered such as: store and forward, confidential reception, substitute reception, broadcasting, dual access, forwarding, fax-on-demand and fax polling. The computer can now receive and send fax messages if a fax/modem is installed, and with the modem an e-mail service can be availed of, if the business subscribes to a service provider. EDI, which will reduce the amount of paper flowing between businesses and eliminate the re-keying of data, is gradually being introduced into this country.

To facilitate 'real' communication, video-conferencing units are available. Depending on the business's requirements a dedicated video-conferencing studio may be rented or the business may invest in a desktop unit.

Businesses can conduct national and international meetings without leaving the office through video-conferencing. The members of the meeting can see and hear each other, even though they are in different geographical locations. This facility may save a business huge amounts of time and money but the necessary equipment is expensive – a business may have to rent out a dedicated video-conferencing room for 'international meetings'.

Newspapers, magazines, television and radio are no longer our only sources of current information; information can be retrieved from external databases via viewdata (Prestel, Minitel and the Internet) and teletext services such as 'Aertel' available from RTE.

Questions

Multiple Choice Questions

1. A diversion facility which diverts all incoming calls to another telephone number is called:
   a) call waiting
   b) Follow Me
   c) call logging
   d) call pickup
   e) hunting

2. A facility which allows a caller to dial direct to a telephone extension is called:
   a) uniform call distribution
   b) voice mail
   c) voice response
   d) DDI
   e) call forwarding

3. An internal mobile system to allow callers to receive and make calls is:
   a) voice mail
   b) cordless telephones
   c) mobile telephones
   d) pager
   e) telephone extension

4. A SIM card is used to:
   a) charge telephone calls to your own telephone account
   b) charge telephone calls to your credit card account
   c) make calls from a GSM telephone
   d) call Ireland from abroad
   e) make calls from a cellular telephone

5. The quickest way to send a photocopy of a page to America is:
   a) e-mail
   b) fax machine
   c) Internet
   d) computer fax/modem
   e) network

6. The feature of a fax machine which allows you to send the same document to several destinations is called:
   a) forwarding
   b) dual access
   c) batch transmission
   d) store and forward
   e) broadcasting

7. Fax polling means:
   a) to forward incoming faxes to another fax machine
   b) to send the same document to multiple destinations
   c) to receive a specific article from a fax machine
   d) to receive all the articles in the list from a fax machine
   e) to send a fax while another is being received

8. A subsidiary of Telecom Éireann which provides an e-mail service is called:
   a) Eirtrade
   b) Eirpage
   c) ieunet
   d) Eircell
   e) EirMail

9. Which of the following is an appropriate address for sending an e-mail using a service provider?
   a) User_Name@country@service provider
   b) User_Name@country.service provider
   c) User_Name@service provider@country
   d) User_Name.service provider@country
   e) User_Name@service provider.country

10. Which of the following is an appropriate address for sending an e-mail to a user who has their own registered domain?
    a) User_Name@location.organisation.type.country
    b) User_Name@location.type.organisation.country
    c) User_Name.location@organisation.type.country
    d) User_Name@organisation.type.location.country
    e) User_Name@location@organisation.type.country

11. The electronic system by which structured documents are sent from one computer to another is called:
    a) e-mail
    b) video-conferencing
    c) EDI
    d) viewdata
    e) videotex

12. The difference between teletext and viewdata is:
    a) The information for teletext is provided by service providers.
    b) Teletext is a one-way communication system.
    c) Teletext uses telegraph lines.
    d) Teletext uses telephone lines.
    e) Teletext is not up to date.

13. Which of the following is not a teletext system?
    a) Oracle
    b) Ceefax
    c) Prestel
    d) Aertel
    e) Teletext

14. Which of the following is a search engine used to find information on the Internet?
    a) WWW
    b) UseNet
    c) HTML
    d) Gopher
    e) Home Page

15. To charge telephone calls from any telephone to your own telephone account you would use:
    a) a callcard
    b) a SIM card
    c) a chargecard
    d) a reverse charge
    e) a personal call

16. A telemarketing service where calls are charged at a fixed rate regardless of duration and distance is called:
    a) CallSave – 1850
    b) FreeFone – 1800
    c) LoCall – 1890
    d) Premium Service – 1530
    e) Cellular Service – 087

17. A service where a message can be given to the operator to be delivered by An Post is called:
    a) MicroPost
    b) MemoMail
    c) Telemessage
    d) Ireland Direct
    e) Coast Radio Station Service

18. The service you would request to find out the cost and duration of a call is:
    a) an ADC call
    b) directory enquiries
    c) reverse charge call
    d) speaking clock
    e) Premium Service

19. If a detailed message with diagrams is to be sent overseas the most speedy and efficient method is:
    a) telephone
    b) electronic mail
    c) facsimile
    d) telex
    e) express mail   (NCVA 1994)

20. Which of the following methods is most suitable for making contact with a doctor while s/he is doing his/her rounds in a hospital?
    a) tannoy (loudspeaker)
    b) telex
    c) mobile telephone
    d) radio pager
    e) electronic diary   (NCVA 1994)

21. Which of the following systems would be used to relay internal messages most efficiently?
    a) facsimile
    b) telephone answering machine
    c) electronic mail
    d) memorandum
    e) notice board   (NCVA 1994)

22. Which one of the following services allows you to send a congratulations message on a presentation card to a friend of your boss who has recently been promoted?
    a) Telephone Plus
    b) chargecard service
    c) Telemessage
    d) premium rate service
    e) FreeFone 1800/1850 service   (NCVA 1996)

Short Answer Questions

1. Explain what the following features on a switchboard are:
   a) single key dialling
   b) call forwarding
   c) call waiting
   d) direct dialling in

2. Explain what the following features on a switchboard are:
   a) call pickup
   b) camp on busy

    c) uniform call distribution

    d) hunting

3. List four advantages of a cordless telephone.

4. List four differences between a cellular mobile telephone and a GSM mobile telephone.

5. List and briefly describe the three types of mobile telephones available.

6. Give four benefits of a mobile telephone.

7. Describe four features of an answering machine.

8. List four steps to follow when recording an outgoing message for an answering machine.

9. State the information that you should give when leaving a message on an answering machine.

10. How would you deal with messages left on an answering machine?

11. Distinguish between an answering machine and voice mail.

12. Describe the voice mail service offered by Telecom Éireann.

13. List four advantages of voice messaging systems.

14. What is voice response?

15. What information should be included on a fax coversheet?

16. State how you would send a prepared fax message.

17. Explain what the following features on a fax machine are:

    a) fax/tel auto change

    b) store and forward

    c) substitute reception

    d) broadcasting

18. Explain what the following features on a fax machine are:

    a) dual access

    b) forwarding

    c) fax on demand

    d) fax polling

19. List four disadvantages of thermal fax paper.

20. Give four benefits of a fax machine.

21. Distinguish between a fax/modem and a laser printer with a fax capability.

22. What is e-mail?

33. Distinguish between a private e-mail system and a public e-mail system.

24. What is the address structure for sending an e-mail message to a subscriber of a service provider?

25. How would you send an e-mail message?

26. List four advantages of e-mail.

27. List four advantages of EDI.

28. Distinguish between a numeric pager and a Minicall.

29. State four benefits of radio paging.

30. State four benefits of video-conferencing.
31. What is videotex?
32. Distinguish between viewdata and teletext.
33. What is Prestel? List four services provided.
34. What is Minitel? List four services provided.
35. What is the Internet? Briefly describe three parts of the Internet.
36. How would a business use the Internet?
37. Describe the following services offered by Telecom Éireann:
    a) Telemessage
    b) Audio Conferencing Calls
    c) Directory Enquiries
    d) Alarm Clock Call
38. Describe the following services offered by Telecom Éireann:
    a) ADC
    b) Reverse Charge Call
    c) Personal Call
    d) Speaking Clock
39. Describe two ways to make a cashless call from abroad.
40. Differentiate between the following:
    a) Premium Service
    b) FreeFone
    c) CallSave
    d) LoCall
41. Give four benefits of having a mobile telephone. (NCVA 1994)
42. List four characteristics of a computerised switchboard (CABX).(NCVA 1994)
43. Describe the principal systems in use for receiving messages overnight in an office. (NCVA 1995)
44. List four telecommunications systems available to businesses for contacting people. (NCVA 1995)
45. List four monitoring features available in modern computerised PBXs. (NCVA 1995)
46. List four features on a modern computerised switchboard which monitor calls made by extension users. (NCVA 1996)

Appendix: Blank Documents for Business Transactions

Materials Requisition		No_____
From _____		
To: _____		
Qty	**Details**	
Signature		Date

Materials requisition form

Purchase Requisition		Ref No _____	
Department			
Supplier's name (if known) _____			
Address _____			
Qty	**Details**	**Cat No**	**Unit Price**
Signature		Date	

Purchase requisition form

Order No.

VAT No: 284 3455 89

Tel No:
Fax: Date:
Quotation No:

Please supply the following:

Qty	Description	Cat No	Unit Price	Total Price

Terms of Sale

Order form

Delivery Note No:

VAT No: 284 3455 89

Tel No:
Fax: Date:
Quotation No:

Qty	Description	Cat No	

Delivery:

Received by:

Delivery note

Goods Received Note No:

Supplier:
Date Received:
Delivery/Advice Note No:

Order No	Description	Qty Received

Received by:	Date:	Entered in stock by:	Date:

Inspected by: Date:

Shortages:
Damage recorded:

Goods received note

Invoice No:

Tel No:
Fax:
Delivery Note No:
Order No:

Qty	Description	Cat No	Unit Price £	Total Cost £

VAT No:
Date:

Invoice

Credit Note No:

Tel No:
Fax:
Invoice No:
Order No:

VAT No:
Date:

Qty	Description	Cat No	Unit Price £	Total Cost £

Credit note

Debit Note No:

Tel No: VAT No:
Fax: Date:
Invoice No:
Order No:

Ref	Description	Amount £

Debit note

Statement

Tel No: VAT No:
Fax: Date:

Date	Ref No	Details	Debits	Credits	Balance

Statement